D0281062

Interactionism

ONE WEEK LOAN

Sheffield Hallam University
Learning and Information Services
Withdrawn From Stock

BSA *New Horizons in Sociology*

The British Sociological Association is publishing a series of books to review the state of the discipline at the beginning of the millenium. *New Horizons in Sociology* also seeks to locate the contribution of British scholarship to the wider development of sociology. Sociology is taught in all the major institutions of higher education in the United Kingdom as well as throughout North America and the Europe of the former western bloc. Sociology is now establishing itself in the former eastern bloc. But it was only in the second half of the twentieth century that sociology moved from the fringes of UK academic life into the mainstream. British sociology has also provided a home for movements that have renewed and challenged the discipline; the revival of academic Marxism, the renaissance in feminist theory, the rise of cultural studies, for example. Some of these developments have become sub-disciplines whilst yet others have challenged the very basis of the sociological enterprise. Each has left their mark. Now therefore is a good time both to take stock and to scan the horizon, looking back and looking forward.

Recent volumes include:

Nationalism and Social Theory
Gerard Delanty and Patrick O'Mahoney

Feminism
Sara Delamont

Interactionism

An Essay in Sociological Amnesia

Paul Atkinson and William Housley

⑤SAGE Publications
London • Thousand Oaks • New Delhi

© 2003 Paul Atkinson and William Housley

First published 2003

All rights reserved. No part of this publication may be reproduced, stored in a retrieval system, transmitted or utilized in any form or by any means, electronic, mechanical, photo-copying, recording or otherwise, without permission in writing from the Publishers.

SAGE Publications Ltd
6 Bonhill Street
London EC2A 4PU

SAGE Publications Inc
2455 Teller Road
Thousand Oaks, California 91320

SAGE Publications India Pvt Ltd
B-42 Panchsheel Enclave
Post Box 4109
New Delhi 110 017

British Library Cataloguing in Publication data

A catalogue record for this book is available from the British Library

ISBN 0 7619 6269 7
ISBN 0 7619 6270 0 (Pb)

Library of Congress Control Number Available

Printed and bound in Great Britain by TJ International Ltd, Padstow, Cornwall

contents

acknowledgements

We are grateful to Sara Delamont for her enthusiasm and support in the preparation of this book, and for her unfailing ability to identify examples and references. William thanks Janice Limmar, Bill Housley and Sara Liviero for their kindness and unstinting support.

introduction

Our book has three aims. First, we shall provide a general outline of interactionist sociology; second, we shall locate interactionism within the context of British sociology; and finally, we shall also reflect upon the relative neglect of interactionism today as an example of the collective amnesia that afflicts contemporary sociology. The intertwining of these three themes is not an easy argument to bring off. It is compounded by the nature of our subject matter itself: the topic of 'interactionism' is a potentially diffuse one and is susceptible to various characterizations of varying degrees of inclusiveness. Moreover – as we shall discuss in much greater detail as this book unfolds – interactionist sociology is not a distinctively British tradition within the discipline at large. Interactionist sociology, sometimes defined more narrowly as symbolic interactionism, was born in American sociology and has developed primarily within that national context. It has a history that goes back to the early decades of the twentieth century, and it continues to be of relevance today. It has inspired and informed a great deal of empirical sociological research over that time, and it has also provided a distinctive array of concepts for the understanding of social action, social order and social identities. Furthermore, the history and the historiography of interactionism are themselves disputed terrain – reflecting in part the different definitions and boundaries that have been imposed on the field. In the course of this book, therefore, we shall be treading carefully, trying to reconcile the different analyses and interpretations that present themselves.

Over the years, a number of British sociologists have conducted research and have contributed to more general theoretical and methodological ideas under the auspices of interactionism. However, there has never really developed a coherent school of British interactionism. Interactionist work has influenced many developments in empirical research. It has also – indirectly but powerfully – exerted a considerable influence on the development of methodological work. But a simple review of interactionism from a British perspective would not be especially illuminating. We have, however, resisted the possible temptation to undertake a review of developments in American interactionism, and then simply to pick up specific instances of British work that reflects them. At first blush, in other words, the inclusion of a book on interactionism in a series on distinctively British contributions to sociological scholarship can look perverse. There are, of course, distinguished individuals in the United Kingdom who have made distinctive contributions to the development of interactionist thought. They are relatively few in number, and as we have just acknowledged, they hardly constitute a school or a movement in their own right. It would be wrong, however, just to dismiss interactionism for that reason. Our aim here is not just to chronicle the specific uses of interactionist ideas, or the individual commentators on interactionist theory who happen to have been British rather than American.

In this book we explore the influence of interactionism, as a North American-inspired sociological tradition, in terms of its reception and development within the United Kingdom. However, it must also be noted that interactionism has also had an impact upon wider European sociological thought. Tomasi (1998) has edited a collection on the Chicago School including chapters from scholars working in France, Italy, Poland and Germany. A useful review of this edited collection has been provided by Fine (2000). Hans Joas is, of course, an acknowledged expert on the thought of George Herbert Mead (Joas, 1985); Horst Helle has also made a major contribution to the interpretation of symbolic interactionism in Germany (e.g. Helle and Eisenstadt, 1985). In France Isabelle Baszanger has conducted empirical research in the tradition of Anselm Strauss and Chicago interactionism (Baszanger, 1998). In addition to these open acknowledgements of the influence of the Chicago School, later influences must also include the work of Erving Goffman and its impact upon discourse analysis as practised and developed within the wider European context (see Titscher et al., 2000). The widespread publication and translation of *Ethnography: Principles and Practice* (Hammersley and Atkinson, 1983, 1995) and the proliferation and development of qualitative methods have also provided a conduit through which certain interactionist ideas have exerted a European influence.

We believe that there is a more interesting story to be told here. This makes our book intentionally different from just a literature review of interactionism over the past century or so. We have approached our task in part as an exercise in the sociology of knowledge. It is an exercise, therefore, in the reception, use and neglect of a body of thought as it translates from one national disciplinary culture to another. We shall argue that there has been a recurrent pattern to the assimilation of interactionist thought in British sociology.

The general argument will develop in the chapters that follow. Here we shall foreshadow it briefly. British sociology has been marked by eclecticism. Few sociologists have followed purist agendas adhering to any one school of thought. It is arguably the strength of British social thought that its practitioners have drawn on diverse sources of inspiration. Certainly there have been relatively few who have been single-mindedly 'interactionist'. Interactionist sociology has normally been incorporated into a broader set of sociological interests. There is a distinctively British eclecticism that escapes the intra-disciplinary boundaries of American or European schools of thought. Certainly there have been few British sociologists who have identified themselves exclusively as 'symbolic interactionists', even though many more have engaged with interactionist ideas and have used the ideas in the course of their substantive research or their methodological reflections.

The visibility of symbolic interactionism in British textbooks of sociology has varied. Some texts all but ignore the interactionist tradition, reflecting the kind of theoretical amnesia with which we deal in this book. In past years, interactionism was sometimes treated as a loyal opposition to functionalism, while its contribution to programmes of empirical research was under-represented. Recent textbooks have tended to move away from organizing principles in terms of schools or traditions, in favour of thematic domains such as globalization, structure and agency. Interactionist contributions to such conceptual domains have been underplayed. Undergraduate textbooks that have sought to characterize postmodern ideas as well as classical sociological ideas have also repeated this process of amnesia despite detailed interactionist commentary upon agency, action and the performance. However, symbolic interactionism has been represented as a living tradition within some texts and part of the established canon. An example can be found in Cuff et al.'s famous undergraduate text *Perspectives in Sociology*. This long-standing and successful textbook has, to this day, continued to provide a detailed and accurate account of interactionist thinking. This in part can be explained by the local concerns of the authors and the reception and influence of this tradition at the department of sociology at Manchester University during the 1970s and 1980s. With the honourable exception of that and a few others, textbooks that have included interactionism have represented it almost exclusively as a theoretical school, rather than as a research tradition. It is also noticeable that Erving Goffman is no longer part of the taken-for-granted canon of sociological authors discussed in introductory textbooks. Standard accounts of British sociology have not always reflected the amount of interactionist-inspired research and programmes of inquiry that have been undertaken within British sociology departments. In some respects this book aims to recover this activity within the context of the UK and the reception and development of key interactionist ideas that continue to sustain an often unacknowledged relevance.

ix

For that reason we begin our argument with the apparent paradox that 'we were never interactionists'. Towards the end of the book we argue that 'we are all interactionists now'. The first exaggeration, then, reflects the argument that interactionism *per se* has not flourished as a strand in British sociological thought, although its more general influence has been apparent in various ways. We are all interactionists now, on the other hand, in the sense that many of the key *ideas* of interactionism have become part of the contemporary mainstream of sociological thought. They are not, however, explicitly recognized as interactionist ideas. Currently fashionable approaches to sociology display, we argue, a kind of collective amnesia. The actual and potential contributions of interactionism are often lost to view. So many ideas that are viewed as novel appear so because earlier contributions – interactionism among them – are not acknowledged explicitly.

Between those two polar extremes, we explore some of the actual contributions of interactionist thought in British sociology. These chapters are not intended to be comprehensive in their coverage. Rather, we have selected a small number of key ideas and applications through which we can document the reception and use of interactionist work in British sociology. This reflects our more general approach, treating our general topic as a study in the reception, use and neglect of the interactionist tradition. Here for instance, we document sociological approaches to the categorization and typification of social actors drawing on studies of deviance and institutional settings. We also discuss the very significant contribution of interactionist thought to the study of socialization, in educational and occupational settings. We also explore the place of interactionist thought in research on work and organizations. Throughout, we seek to avoid narrowly sectarian preoccupations: we are not primarily interested in whether the ideas were interpreted and applied according to a canon of pure interactionist theory. We are, as we have suggested already, more interested in *how* the ideas were used or not used, rather than writing a definitive account of interactionism itself.

One of the obvious domains in which interactionism has had an impact is in the development of methodology. So-called qualitative methods in sociology were characteristic of interactionist work. They were codified and disseminated more widely in the methodological texts and anthologies deriving from interactionist research. Their advocacy and use have now spread well beyond the confines of interactionism, indeed well beyond sociology's boundaries. In the process, they have become somewhat detached from their intellectual roots. Here is a prime case of that sense in which 'we are all interactionists now', without being aware of the origins of influential ideas. This is also a key area in which British sociologists have contributed to the general process of development and dissemination.

Clearly, we do not expect all our readers to be equally conversant with interactionism's key figures and key ideas. Consequently, we include an introductory overview of interactionism: we concentrate on the development of interactionism within American sociology, and inevitably on its association with the Chicago School of sociology. This is not a comprehensive intellectual history. It is not a detailed exposition of the key figures and their relationships to one another. It is inescapably an over-simplification. Detailed histories take different perspectives, and readers will be referred to those works for more detailed historical guidance. Our intention is merely to provide an initial orientation to some of the key issues. We emphasize in doing so that 'interactionism' has always been a broad approach to sociology, having several strands in its origins and developments. Even the more narrowly defined 'symbolic interactionism' is a broad church. Moreover, interactionism has never been static. Its ideas and their applications have changed over the course of most of the last century. It continues to develop. We therefore need to sketch out interactionism's tradition in order to provide a backdrop to the intersection of American interactionism and British sociology. This latter aspect is emphasized when we also address the various historical constructions of interactionism and Chicago School sociology. British authors have made significant contributions to the disputed terrain of the history of these strands of American sociology. As we shall see, there is no single vision of the past. The past has projected onto it different perspectives and predilections. The contrasting accounts of the past reflect different intellectual interests and commitments. Ironically, there has been a disproportionate British contribution to historical commentary over the past two decades. There is a clear danger of devoting more collective effort to historical reflection than to active sociological research. Such a development would be inimical to the abiding spirit of interactionist sociology, which has always found its fullest expression in a practical engagement with the social world.

Indeed, we find the legacy and the continued inspiration of interactionist sociology through empirical research and through the collective commitment to research of a distinctive kind. Consequently we devote the central chapters of this book to an exploration of interactionism's contribution to methodological development (arguably its strongest influence on contemporary social science) and major themes in substantive research. In discussing the role of interactionism in empirical sociological domains, it would be easy to deal with at least the main ones serially. We could have discussed, say, interactionism in medical sociology, then crime and deviance studies, then educational research, and so on. We have not done so. Instead, we have tried to synthesize work across a number of different fields of sociological inquiry in order to explore over-arching themes. They have been chosen to display what we regard as some of interactionism's core interests and aspects of its intellectual legacy. We review and explore sociological work on the production and distribution of social identities. We do so through two chapters. The first is concerned with the construction of *social types*. This is a recurrent theme in interactionist sociology – empirically and theoretically. It reflects the specific development of labelling theory out of interactionism, especially in the context of deviance studies, but it goes well beyond that specific application. The social construction of social categories and moral types is a recurrent motif in interactionism – and in interpretative sociology more generally – and has been since interactionists and other Chicago sociologists started to grapple with the distinctive organizational and cultural consequences of urban modernity in the early decades of the twentieth century. Social processes of labelling, the marking of status passages, the categorization of clients and consumers – these are all fundamental social processes through which identities are fashioned and shaped.

The second of our analytic domains is closely related. It concerns the relationships between social actors and social organization. It follows directly from the initial discussion of the ideas, themes, issues and social processes surrounding types and typification. It explores how social actors come to be who and what they are, through processes of socialization. Interactionism has identified the *moral career* as one of the key concepts through which the personal and the institutional are brought into analytic synthesis. This is not just a matter of so-called 'micro-sociology' or of the sociology of the person. It reflects on one of the most abiding and central topics of sociological thought - the mutual constitution of social actors and social institutions. The moral career captures this dialectic between social identities and social organization. This issue has been approached from a range of different sociological perspectives. It is one of the strengths of the interactionist tradition that it has never lost sight of its centrality. Moreover – and herein lies a particular strength – it has approached it as a series of empirical topics and not just as an abstracted theoretical principle.

If the empirical programme of interactionism is one of its lasting contributions, then its own methodological programme is its most pervasive influence. Interactionism is by no means the only source of inspiration and exemplar for qualitative sociological work. But qualitative methodologies owe a great deal to the interactionists. As the popularity of qualitative research has spread through sociology and other social and cultural disciplines, the methods themselves have become more diffuse and varied. The epistemological justifications for such research have become increasingly diverse, and in recent years they have been caught up in the claims and counter-claims concerning postmodernism in the social sciences. Nevertheless, much is still owed to the interactionist inspiration. Even where the intellectual debt is not explicitly recognized, there are powerful influences. Consequently we devote a further chapter to the methodological commitments of interactionism and their contemporary influence. Simultaneously, we highlight the contribution of British methodologists and the significance of qualitative methods for British sociology. Both have been of considerable importance.

The overall rationale for this book is neither a wholesale endorsement of interactionist sociology, not is it intended to be an unremitting criticism of it. For the most part we are interested in documenting the trajectory of its reception and use as a body of knowledge, especially in the translation from one intellectual context to another. We do, however, have a somewhat polemical point to make as well. We have referred already to a collective amnesia on the part of many fellow sociologists. There are important concepts and methodological principles that derive directly or indirectly from interactionism's legacy. These are in turn part of a broader stream of interpretative sociology that has included at various times phenomenological, linguistic and other theoretical strands. Many of the key ideas in that tradition have become especially relevant to contemporary ideas in sociology and related cultural disciplines. But the actual and potential contribution of interactionism seems to be overlooked. The sociological amnesia we have already referred to means that contemporary sociological work seems unnecessarily shallow – lacking an awareness of historical depth and equally deficient in terms of the value of existing ideas. What passes for novelty too often rests on a shared ignorance of origins and antecedents. In itself, of course, this does not matter too greatly. After all, it makes rather little difference whether or not one considers an idea to be a new one or the re-emergence of previous ones. On the other hand, it does make a difference if contemporary social thought is so lacking in historical awareness that it mistakenly thinks that there is something special and even unique about the contemporary social world and its understanding as a consequence of its collective ignorance. It is fashionable to claim, for instance, that there are special features of the social world at the end of the twentieth century and the start of the twenty-first that are particular – whether the epoch is referred to as 'late' or 'post' modernity. Equally, it is fashionable to claim new forms of social inquiry and epistemology that are especially current – also sometimes going under 'post' rubrics – such as 'postpositivism'. The history of interactionism suggests something rather different, however. It suggests that 'modernity' in the earlier decades of

xiii

the last century looked – sociologically speaking – remarkably like late or postmodernity viewed nearly a century later. Equally, many of the ideas that are invoked today do not reflect radical disjunctures and ruptures with earlier concepts and methods. Rather, they reflect more strongly a remarkable continuity of thought and research practice in the interactionist tradition and – more generally – within the broad stream of interpretative sociology of which interactionism is a resilient strand. It is for this reason that we end our book with the assertion that 'we are all interactionists now'. Clearly, this is not meant to be taken literally. We do not think that there has been a mass conversion experience among sociologists, in the United Kingdom or elsewhere, to the effect that we are all adherents of symbolic interactionism or of George Herbert Mead. That is clearly not the case. On the other hand, we contend that many of the ideas that are currently prominent in sociological theory and that feature prominently in its research agendas are congruent with the interactionist programme. Indeed, much of contemporary thought recapitulates the ideas of former eras, while its authors seem unaware of the fact. What passes for novelty is often a reflection of amnesia rather than of genuine invention.

We are all interactionist now in the sense that contemporary preoccupations with identity, with the mutual constitution of agents and organizations, and with the interpretative exploration of social worlds all repeat the motifs of interactionist sociology. Likewise, contemporary interests in language and discourse – the 'linguistic turn' – direct attention to phenomena of long-standing interest to interactionists, of symbolic systems and the constitutive powers of language. Our argument here, then, is not for the wholesale incorporation of all of interactionist sociology into contemporary social thought. More modestly, however, it is a plea for the repair of the collective amnesia that leads to the periodic rediscovery of the wheel and the unjustified neglect of the sociological past. The sense of the new has been given particular impetus, and claims for novelty accelerated, by the claims for 'postmodernism'. This entails two things simultaneously. First, there is the claim that social conditions are qualitatively different, so that a condition of postmodernity can be identified in the social formations and cultural forms of the late twentieth century and the beginning of the twenty-first. Second, there is the parallel claim for postmodernism as a distinctive style of thought, characterized by fluid meanings, shifting identities, a rejection of the grand narratives of historicism and social determinism, a preoccupation with the local. We argue that far from being confined to the most recent period, these preoccupations recapitulate those of earlier periods of social thought – not least those in which urban ethnography and interactionist sociology were born.

In tracing out these arguments and their implications for current sociology, therefore, we draw attention to a general failing of social thought: the unjustified neglect of a sociological tradition. In doing so we cover an argument that is very similar to that of David Maines (2001). Maines has – from the perspective of an American sociologist within the interactionist tradition – drawn attention to the relative neglect of interactionism in more mainstream American, British and European social theory. The convergence between Maines and our work is striking. We had completed the outline of this book, had set out its argument and had substantially drafted its contents when Maines' own book became available. His approach and ours are complementary; they are not in competition. We shall incorporate his arguments with ours at appropriate points in this book. For now we outline briefly how Maines has stated his case.

Maines argues that 'the entire field of sociology ..., without seeming to be aware of it, has been moving in the direction of symbolic interactionism' (ibid.: 2). He argues that many recent developments in sociology have overlooked previous interactionist inspirations while incorporating their key ideas, so that 'on the one hand, sociologists expressing these interactionist ideas are doing so authentically and in the name of good sociology, but on the other hand they seem almost totally unaware that the ideas they are promoting are in fact interactionist ones' (ibid.: 11).

Consequently, Maines argues, one can now identify two streams of interactionist thought. On the one hand there is an acknowledged use of interactionist ideas, both by avowed interactionists who actively promote the ideas and by others who selectively – but overtly – use the ideas as part of a more eclectic approach. On the other, Maines suggests that there is 'a kind of invisible interactionism' (ibid.: 16) that can be identified in various domains of contemporary sociological theory and empirical inquiry. Key interactionist ideas, such as agency, situation and meaning are given wide currency, Maines suggests, by authors who pay little or no explicit attention to the interactionist legacy.

In a formulation that we sympathize with, Maines invokes Pitrim Sorokin's observations on the 'fads and foibles' of sociology (Sorokin, 1956) to suggest that there is a condition of collective amnesia among contemporary sociologists, leading to the appearance of novelty in sociological ideas when the reality is more akin to the recapitulation of previous sociological thought. Paradoxically, Maines suggests, we are therefore witnessing 'a fairly mindless fractured drift toward increasingly good sociology' (2001: 27). Like Maines, we see this book as an essay in the collective amnesia of current sociology. Like him, we believe that a broadly interactionist inspiration is detectable in many strands of contemporary sociology. Our exaggerated claim that 'we are all interactionists now' is intended to capture that tendency. Like Maines too, we believe that the general tenets of interactionism should not be relegated to the margins of the discipline, and certainly deserve a more honourable position that that ascribed to it by Mullins (1973) – a 'loyal opposition'. In some ways our treatment differs from that of Maines, however. Crucially, of course, we view the field from outside the United States. We are ourselves 'outsiders', in that neither of us has ever been a member of the 'core set' that defines symbolic interactionism institutionally and intellectually. We are not intent on reclaiming a somewhat narrowly defined American 'symbolic interactionism' and elevating it to a renewed position of legitimacy within the sociological pantheon. From our distinctive position as sympathetic outsiders, and with our specific brief to pay attention to the contributions of British sociologists, we construct a slightly different argument. We believe that we should recognize a broad tradition within American sociology, that combines interactionism *per se* with a more general interest in the personal and social consequences of modern metropolitan life. That is far from being captured by the narrow rubric of symbolic interactionism (a label that sits uncomfortably with many of the tradition's main practitioners and inspirational figures anyway). That tradition has provided a broad inspiration for theoretical, methodological and empirical sociology on a wide front. It has had a considerable, if sometimes diffuse, impact on British sociology. Paradoxically, as its influence has spread, the overt intellectual debts to 'interactionism' have become diluted. They are increasingly embedded in a broadly interpretative, humanistic sociology that places considerable emphasis on social action, language and social identities. It pays increasing attention to the embodied character of social life. It employs an ever wider array of qualitative strategies for social research, and it is reflexively aware of its own conventions of representation. We do not need to reaffirm 'symbolic interactionism' in the strict sense in order to appreciate some of the origins and inspirations for these contemporary interests.

Indeed, in reviewing and re-assessing the legacy of 'interactionism', it may ultimately be most fruitful to depart from the rhetorical strategy of our American counterparts. Rather than reviving symbolic interactionism, therefore, we need to look backward and forward, in order to take a yet wider perspective. There never was a single school of interactionism or symbolic interactionism. There always was a variety of conceptual, methodological and empirical commitments, derived from a number of different inspirations. If we acknowledge that, then there is no insurmountable problem in tracing continuities as well as changes, and in recognizing the contemporary relevance of those and related ideas.

In tracing through this argument and some of its ramifications, we are not going to attempt a comprehensive review of all the possible applications of interactionist thought in British sociology. Equally, we have not reviewed all the strands and developments in American interactionism and then tried to plot them against British work on a one-to-one basis. Rather, we have been selective, drawing on particular authors and substantive research fields in order to illustrate some more general arguments. Believing that the enduring legacy of interactionism is to be found in the programmes of empirical research, we therefore draw attention to the British uses of interactionist thought within the sociologies of medicine, education, deviance and work. We also provide some discussion of empirical enquiry into cultures that pervades much of this form of work.

We also – for the same reason – focus attention on the interactionists' influence on the methodological developments of recent decades. We argue that interactionism's most pervasive, if relatively invisible, impact has been on the general conduct of sociology. British sociological research has undergone several sea changes in recent years. Within living memory, major sociological research was often assumed to be grounded in applied social statistics or demography – the sample survey, the secondary analysis of data from official sources – deployed in the interests of social class and social mobility measures, the correlation of demographic characteristics with the distribution of social problems and relative deprivation. Field research had its particular niches – in community studies, for instance – but was not widely perceived to be the method of choice. Indeed, the differences in method defined – for their respective practitioners – the symbolic boundaries between sociology and social anthropology. The change has been remarkable. Contemporary sociological research in Britain is characterized by a very widespread use of qualitative research approaches, while statistically-based research is in relative decline. (This has led to periodic moral panics in which agencies like the Economic and Social Research Council have tried to safeguard quantitative research and research skills through deliberate interventions in postgraduate research training and research funding initiatives: why they should do so rather than administering the social sciences as defined by its practitioners in the academy is somewhat beyond the scope of this book.) The picture in the United Kingdom is – for that reason – rather different from that prevailing in the United States. While qualitative research methods have certainly flourished in the American social sciences, there remain many quarters in which quantitative work is accorded greater prominence and status. There remain key sociological journals, for instance, that are dominated by large-scale quantitative research approaches.

In a similar vein, sociological work in the United Kingdom has become increasingly coloured by the so-called cultural turn. Whereas social structure, social institutions and social change were the defining preoccupations of previous generations of British sociologists, recent and contemporary generations have been increasingly attentive to the phenomena of culture. While some authors would like to claim a completely autonomous realm for 'cultural studies', in practice, sociology, media studies, literary studies, human geography and other cognate disciplines have found shared interests in cultural forms, their production, circulation and consumption. One need only inspect, for instance, the prominence of sociological work deriving from the 'Theory Culture and Society' group and their associated publications to find a clear symptom of this shift. While it would be idle to suggest that the origins of cultural sociology are to be found in interactionism, the fusions of qualitative research and cultural subject matter make contemporary sociology a much more fertile soil for the reception of interactionist and other interpretative ideas, even when they are part of a relatively understated tradition.

one
interactionism in perspective

This book is not a general survey of interactionism in the history of sociological thought. Nevertheless, an overview is necessary, if only to put the rest of our discussion into context. This is especially desirable, given that our brief concerns a specifically British perspective, and interactionism is not in itself an indigenous British perspective. On the contrary, its roots and its development are to be found within the intellectual traditions of American social science. Born of a particular constellation of social, institutional and personal influences in the early years of the twentieth century, it has continued to inspire a developing programme of empirical social research into the early years of the twenty-first. It is useful to gain a broad sense of its central concerns, not least because we shall go on to argue that they continue to have considerable relevance for current sociology. Rather than providing a detailed historical account (which in itself demands monograph-length treatment, and can be found in different versions already), we therefore try to convey a general flavour of its key ideas, its influential personnel, and some of the main continuities in its ideas. Equally, we are not interested in sectarian disputes as to who 'really counts' as an interactionist, or in theological disputes over the true messages. We are certainly not interested in trying to demarcate an orthodoxy, nor to establish tight boundaries. Rather, here and throughout this book we are treating 'interactionism' as a broad approach to sociology. It is, in any event, a sociological perspective that has had multiple origins and inspirations. It derives from the work of different founders, and has benefited from a number of strands of thought.

Inevitably, the story of interactionism in America is bound up with the story of sociology at the University of Chicago. Between the two world wars, that department was the site where interactionist sociology developed. After the Second World War, the same department saw a vigorous flowering of interactionist sociology. The Chicago influence was then dispersed much more widely, as there was something of a diaspora to other parts of the United States. The University of Chicago Department of Sociology was also a significant site in the development of research styles that would later be called 'field work' and later still 'ethnography'. Chicago became associated, therefore, with field research in urban and institutional settings. Now, it is not our major task to outline and unpick those various strands of influence, and others have done the painstaking work already. However, in order to avoid misunderstanding, and to forestall being criticized for making claims we are not in fact making, it may be useful to summarize the general positions as follows:

- Interactionism is a broad perspective in sociology that traces its origins to some of the sociologists working at the University of Chicago in the inter-war years.
- By no means all the sociologists at the University of Chicago in that period are equally associated with the origins and inspirations of interactionism.
- Interactionism is broader than symbolic interactionism, which is explicitly linked to Mead's social psychology, which is also a part of the University of Chicago's intellectual history.
- Symbolic interactionism is a particular codification that does not capture all of the empirical work.
- The development of interactionism is associated with the development of qualitative field research in Chicago. But by no means all Chicago sociology was based on qualitative fieldwork, and not all of the urban fieldwork was 'interactionist'.

In other words, this is far from being an account of the Chicago School itself (even if it makes sense to think of a Chicago School anyway). One has to think more flexibly than that, recognizing that institutional setting, theoretical ideas, empirical research and methodological commitments have rarely been coterminous. Rather, we are dealing with a series of elective affinities between sociologists and ideas, between practical research and epistemological glosses, between general theoretical trends and the work of individual sociologists.

It is especially difficult to produce a simple summary of interactionist thought and its institutional contexts. Contrary to some textbook over-simplifications, interactionism – whether or not defined as 'symbolic interactionism' – is by no means characterized by a single, consistent line of development. Rather, we must look to a number of different strands of theory and empirical research, which sometimes come together, and at other times trace parallel paths. Some sense of this rather 'messy' intellectual development may be gained from a variety of historical reviews. Consider, for instance, the authoritative essay by Berenice Fisher and Anselm Strauss (1978a). They point out that the referents of 'interactionism' and 'symbolic interactionism' are varied: interactionism, symbolic interactionism, the Chicago School – these

2

terms seem to be used if not interchangeably, then at least imprecisely to cover a variety of related authors and topics. For some commentators, it is the contribution of Herbert Blumer that is central; for others, the work of the generation of Howard Becker. The role of George Herbert Mead is also accorded different significance by different commentators. Erving Goffman (e.g. Goffman, 1959, 1961, 1963) is sometimes included within the canon, and sometimes not. To complicate the issue further, by no means all the sociologists themselves associated with the interactionist tradition endorse the term 'symbolic interactionism', and distance themselves from unduly narrow definitions of a distinct specialism within sociology.

Fisher and Strauss (1978a, 1978b) resolve this, in part at any rate, by suggesting that there are at least two main traditions of interactionism, grounded in different intellectual traditions, and not always being in close conjunction. Interactionism is, they suggest, a 'dual tradition' (1978a: 458). On the one hand, there is a sociological tradition, associated with the University of Chicago School, that is rooted in the work of W.I. Thomas and Robert Park. On the other, there is the tradition that stems from George Herbert Mead (1932, 1934, 1938) that was codified by Herbert Blumer (1962, 1969). There are points of contact, and some individual scholars have been influenced by both traditions. Others have worked much more in one or another. Yet others, Fisher and Strauss suggest, probably cannot tell the difference, having been socialized into a generalized 'interactionist' perspective (see also Strauss, 1994).

The Park–Thomas tradition was particularly associated with the developing programme of empirical sociological research that developed in the University of Chicago's Department of Sociology. That department was special in several ways. It was part of a major new university, located within a city that was itself undergoing rapid social and economic transformations. Chicago changed with extraordinary speed in the closing decades of the nineteenth century. In the years following the great fire of Chicago, the city expanded physically and in terms of its population. It became a major centre for industry and commerce. It was a magnet for in-migration. Migrants came from the post-bellum southern States, and from Europe. The city's ethnic mix became highly diverse. It became spatially differentiated. Successive generations of migrants established areas such as 'little Italy' or 'little Poland'. The physical structure of the city and its spatial relations were also dramatic. Chicago was one of the first cities in which the distinctive modern high-rise style of the downtown district was established. Office blocks, department stores and other features of the modern metropolitan scene were built in the rapidly developing area of Chicago in the area that came to be known as 'the Loop'.

For the sociologists of Chicago, the city around them provided inspiration and subject matter. Under the inspiration of Park, Thomas and others, the sociologists explored what they called the 'natural areas' of the city – its distinctive neighbourhoods. They explored the extreme differences between the poorest and the wealthiest neighbourhoods. The city provided them with what they themselves referred to as a 'natural laboratory'. It furnished the opportunity to study the effects of social change and migration. The contrasts between the 'old world' of the Europeans' origins and the 'new world' of the American metropolis were exciting opportunities for the sociologists. It allowed them, for instance, to study the social processes of disruption and renewal as new populations became detached from the cultures of their origins, and underwent their adaptations to the modern social contexts of Chicago (Thomas et al., 1921).

The programme was a thoroughly empirical one. It gave rise to one of the most famous of all American studies – the multi-volume study of the Polish peasant by Thomas and Znaniecki (1918–20). It also fostered detailed investigations of various neighbourhoods and locales within the changing city – such as Zorbaugh's *The Gold Coast and the Slum* (1929), Cressey's study of the taxi dance hall (1932), or Thrasher's study of territorial gangs (1927). The influence of Park and Thomas was profound in the development of interactionist research in general. Chicago sociologists were committed to the development of research methods and empirical inquiries of a wide variety of types. Subsequent accounts of the Chicago School can all too easily stress just one side of its development – often emphasizing the first flowering of urban ethnography in American sociology, while paying too little attention to the spatial and quantitative techniques that were also promoted within the department. It is, however, the strong Chicago commitment to the investigation of the local manifestation of societal processes of change that gives the subsequent history of interactionism some of its characteristic approaches. In that sense, therefore, the collective commitment to an ethnographic engagement with the urban milieu is a persistent legacy of Chicago. It owed much to Park's own biography and intellectual development, reflecting as it did his experience as a journalist and his personal exploration of the urban scene.

It owed a great deal too to the distinctive conceptualization of the city. The Park–Thomas inspiration involved seeing the city as a distinctive social form in its own right, with its own dynamics and evolutionary movement. The city included in it a new 'frontier', where the old world met the new, in the 'zone of transition', where waves of new in-migrants first settled, while longer-established groups migrated out of the inner-city zones towards the suburbs. The idea of the frontier is significant in American thought, and the identification of this urban frontier was a powerful one. So too was Park's metaphor of marginality. The 'marginal man' was the personal counterpart of the frontier (Wacker, 1995). Marginality was intrinsic to the social conditions of an emergent urban modernity. Wirth's conceptualization of 'urbanism' as a way of life encapsulated several of the themes of the Park–Thomas strand of Chicago thought. The city was conceptualized not merely as a physical space, but as the site of a distinctive form of social life. It was marked by its density and its fragmentation; it provided multiple stimuli; it was a site in which anonymous strangers were engaged in multiple fleeting encounters (see Wirth, 1938).

Evolutionary change was thus being played out in the rapidly changing urban environment of the city of Chicago. Intensive local studies captured the general social processes at work. This was not, however, a programme merely of social observation. The Park–Thomas tradition was conceived as the exercise of engaged social science, geared to the understanding and promotion of social reform. Like other social scientists before them and like their contemporaries, the Chicago sociologists were exercised by the broad themes of evolutionary social change, its social, institutional and personal consequences. In the early decades of the twentieth century American intellectuals – including the sociologists – were grappling with the development of a modern industrial nation-state, to be forged out of diverse groups of new immigrants. Social disorganization, the weakening of primary social groups, and the rise of individualism all posed potential threats to orderly social change. The role of the engaged intellectual was to find ways of rational intervention in these social processes. The Chicago School approach to sociology was itself a part of the Progressive era in the United States. One version of the history of the department and its intellectual commitments emphasizes the role of the sociologists as engaged public intellectuals, involved in public affairs. They were indeed firmly committed not only to research but also to public discourse concerning crime, race relations, and other 'social problems'.

Park and Thomas both believed in the inherent value of social organization and association. This is a recurrent preoccupation within American sociology, quite irrespective of the interactionist tendency. The existence and persistence of social institutions, they held, provided the basis for orderly social change. They sought a middle way between social determinism and pure individualism. They believed in the power of a well-informed public opinion. Park's own work – substantially influenced by the work of Georg Simmel – distinguished between the 'public' and the 'crowd'. The public permits the exercise of individual will, and is susceptible to rational intervention; the crowd subsumes the individual will within its collective identity. The goal of the public intellectual, then, was to promote rational social change through

5

the promotion of a well-informed public and through the promotion of social organization (Matthews, 1977).

The Park–Thomas strand of thought was significant in the development of interactionist sociology. It stressed the centrality of social change. In doing so, the sociology of Chicago reflected the times: the manifest turmoil of the end of the nineteenth century and the early decades of the twentieth. The transformations of an urban and industrial society, increasingly characterized by ethnic and cultural diversity, provided the backdrop and the subject matter of the sociological programme. The sociologists saw themselves, and acted as, public intellectuals, actively engaged in shaping social transformations, and involved in the creation of a well-informed public.

The second major strand in the formation of interactionist thought derived from the social philosophy and social psychology of George Herbert Mead (1932, 1934, 1938). Mead was also a University of Chicago figure. But it would be wrong to assume that there were direct lines of influence between Meadian philosophy and Chicago sociology from the outset. Mead developed a view of social change that was congruent with that of the sociologists. He believed that social change was a form of general evolutionary movement, but with a crucial difference from the processes of natural evolution. The crucial difference, he believed, lay in the distinctive human characteristic of language and its consequences. While all organisms can receive and transmit signals and stimuli, human language is unique. Mead referred to the general form of communication as 'gesture' and language as 'significant symbols' – a special evolutionary development of gesture. Animal gesture is essentially a matter of stimulus and response. The gesture or signal cannot be separated from its immediate behavioural contexts or consequences. On the other hand, human language allows the speaker to stimulate another in a way that is different from how he or she is stimulated. In other words, the animal may feel fear and convey fear to other species members. The human speaker does not have to feel fear in order to convey fear to others, or to warn others of danger, or to talk about danger, or to discuss the hypothetical or future possibility of danger, or to describe the feeling of fear or danger in the past, or on the part of some third party. Language thus transcends the concrete limitations of stimulus–response reactions. Language allows for the creation of culture, in that human social actors can exchange experiences, cumulate experiences and share meanings.

The human actor can also act reflexively on herself or himself. Language permits a particular kind of dialogue. In addition to the dialogue between actors, so there is the possibility of a sort of internal dialogue. The actor can treat herself or himself as a kind of 'other'. Consequently, the human actor has a dual character. On the one hand, there is the origin of action – what Mead referred to as the 'I'. On the other, there is the object of self-awareness – what Mead referred to as the 'Me'. The I and the Me are aspects or moments of the Self: they are not separate entities. They refer to tensions in the self and its dual nature: the impulsive and creative impulse versus the socialized internalization of social mores. This general capacity therefore permits the human actor to take the role of the other – in being able imaginatively to grasp how another actor is stimulated. One can, therefore, monitor and adapt one's conduct in the light of others' perceived perceptions and judgements. The process of socialization also means that actors internalize not merely the judgements of concrete, specific others; they also develop a sense of the 'generalized other', so that they come into a fully socialized awareness of the social milieu in which they are placed.

The capacity of language gives rise to the possibility of culture. It also transforms the evolutionary process. It removes social change from the domain of natural processes and renders it susceptible to human direction. Social transformation is therefore susceptible to rational intervention. To that extent, then, Meadian philosophy was congruent with the progressivist ideals of the Chicago sociologists. They shared a commitment to rational intervention in social processes and problems, although Mead himself never formulated or engaged in a programme of social reform or sociologically informed expertise. Mead's contribution to interactionist thought lies primarily in his thoroughly social view of the self, and his formulation of the triad of mind, self and society. In Mead's treatment, these three terms do not stand for three separate entities. Rather, they are all three parts of the same general phenomenon: the self and the mind are both equally social processes.

Mead did not formulate a systematic sociology. His work was not directly influential in the earliest days of empirical social research in Chicago. It is, however, true that versions of social psychology were part of the developing school of sociological thought. The sociologists at Chicago were increasingly exposed to social psychology from Mead himself and others such as Faris. Indeed, interactionism in general is one of the few among earlier movements in sociology to have treated social psychology seriously. (The Frankfurt School's inspirations in Freud and Marx is an obvious exception.) Cooley's notion of the 'looking glass self' was an influential statement of the significance of self-consciousness in the development of the social self and the management of human conduct. Cooley suggested that others acted as a metaphorical mirror, reflecting back their perceptions and judgements, and in turn giving rise to feelings of pride or shame – depending on how those perceptions accorded or diverged from one's self-perceptions. Cooley and Mead thus stressed the dialogic nature of conduct and the self as an emergent phenomenon arising out of such transactions (Cooley,

7

1902). Conduct is monitored by the self and by others. There is therefore – in principle at least – the possibility for conduct to become mutually aligned. This is not just a cosy picture of mutual gratification and accommodation, however. The mutual gaze of social actors and their simultaneous acts of perception and judgement can clearly be threatening and potentially damaging.

Authors like Fisher and Strauss (1978a, 1978b) are clearly right to provide a balanced view of the significance of Mead's work as a theoretical basis for the early development of 'interactionism' as a programme of empirical social investigation (Fisher and Strauss, 1979). In the development of Chicago sociology, it was Georg Simmel who provided much of the intellectual impetus. The Chicago textbook of sociology (Park and Burgess, 1921) gave considerable prominence to Simmel. Simmel's own sensitivity to the metropolis as a site of modernity had a close affinity with the emergent sociology of Chicago. The distinctive forms of urbanism were a common theme linking the Chicago School with European concerns with modernity, and Simmel was the key link (Rock, 1979). In some ways, therefore, one should think of the early development of social research in Chicago as a Simmelian rather than as a Mead-inspired programme. The role of Mead in the development of interactionist research is itself contested. On the one hand, Mead is acknowledged as a founding figure in the tradition; on the other, he may be viewed as a symbolic founding hero, invoked but with rather little direct influence.

It is really with the emergence of the so-called second Chicago School that the work of most direct relevance to us emerges (Fine, 1995). The generations that were taught in the Chicago department and then founded departments or groups elsewhere took forward key ideas and a distinctive programme of empirical research in a variety of domains. In the years following the Second World War, varieties of interactionism also became codified and promoted. One of the most important of these exercises was Blumer's codification of 'symbolic interactionism', which explicitly linked the sociological work with Mead, and it is largely through Blumer's formulations that Mead is widely perceived to be a founding influence (Blumer, 1969). Blumer himself inherited both strands of Chicago thought – the social psychology and the Park–Thomas strand. He is always referred to as an inspiring teacher, and his influence was direct as a mentor, as well as more widespread through the book *Symbolic Interactionism*, as well as his methodological writings. In attempting to establish a codified 'symbolic interactionism' he sought to establish a number of fundamental principles.

Blumer insisted that the subject matter of sociology is social action. His positive appeals on behalf of interactionism were thus also part of a critical dialogue with sociologies based on theories of the social system. Individual and group action, Blumer insisted, is meaningful. He thus stressed the 'symbolic' function in emphasizing that human beings act on the basis of their interpretations and understandings. This reflected not only Mead's work on the significant symbol and its relevance for human conduct, but also Thomas's formulation of the 'definition of the situation': suggesting that situations are real insofar as they are defined as real and are real in their consequences (Thomas, 1923). Meanings are themselves created through action – acts of interpretation and definition. Blumer's account of symbolic interactionism places particular stress on the Meadian notion of process. Social order and social meanings are emergent phenomena. Blumer characterizes the social world in terms of unpredictable and contingent processes. In common with other interactionists, Blumer's analysis seeks to reconcile social action and societal constraint, but his overall account veers towards the voluntaristic side of social action. This was a major antidote to the over-socialized view of the social actor that was enshrined in functionalist social theory. Blumer's codification of symbolic interactionism was accompanied by several key methodological principles. Indeed, it was perhaps Blumer's particular contribution to suggest a distinctive affinity between the Meadian strand of social psychology, the Park–Thomas strand of institutional analysis, and the Chicago tradition of research practice.

Blumer himself believed that research methods should above all be faithful to the empirical world under investigation. He promoted a version of naturalism, in that he suggested that there could be research methods that were in themselves 'faithful' to the social phenomena under investigation. In practice, such fidelity would avoid the premature application of conceptual schemes a priori. Indeed, Blumer's methodology is founded on a sceptical attitude towards systematic theory. He advocated the use of 'sensitizing concepts'. Sensitizing concepts are intended to contrast with what Blumer called 'definitive concepts'. The latter are concepts that are precisely delimited or defined in every particular. Sensitizing concepts, on the other hand, are essentially heuristic ideas, or 'directions along which to look'. The idea of the sensitizing concept thus reflects the relative indeterminacy of research ideas, and runs counter to ideas that suggest that productive and valid research can only be conducted if research hypotheses and variables are specified with complete precision. Blumer's version of naturalism implied that the social world escaped such precise specification, that the appearance of definitive concepts would be spurious, and that their invocation would imply some degree of violence towards the phenomena under investigation.

Blumer did much to create symbolic interactionism as a distinctive

9

speciality within American sociology. His own definitional and methodological writings became part of its canon. In his own work more widely, however, he also reflected interactionism's dualism. In his empirical work – which was not as well known or as influential among wider intellectual circles – he continued in the vein of the Park–Thomas tradition. This strand also continued to be prominent in the empirical social research of the other members of the second Chicago School. Everett Hughes, Blanche Geer, Howard Becker, Anselm Strauss, Rue Bucher, Leonard Schatzman, Virginia Olesen and others contributed – often in collaboration – to major empirical research studies (see Fine, 1995). They worked on diverse substantive topics. They brought to bear ideas and research practices that had strong family resemblances between them, and were differentiated from much of what passed for sociological orthodoxy around them in post-war America.

Everett Hughes and his circle contributed a major programme of research and publications on work and occupations. These studies were all concerned with the relationship between individual careers and trajectories and the constraints of social institutions. The title of a representative edited collection – *Institutions and the Person* – helps to encapsulate some of the abiding preoccupations of this work (Becker et al., 1968b). In studying how institutions shape persons and persons shape institutions, the post-war generation of sociologists were in direct line of descent from earlier Chicago School studies. They also placed correspondingly less emphasis on voluntaristic social action than did Blumer's formulation of symbolic interactionism.

Socialization was a key theme in the research on work and organizations. The study of medical students at the University of Kansas medical school was a collaborative piece of team research, and it captured much of the broader programme (Becker et al., 1961). This research project – based mainly on participant observation and interviewing – examined how medical students survived and coped with the heavy demands placed on them by the rigours of medical school. It documented how the students developed collective perspectives on their shared experiences, and how they developed collective responses. The book describes the maintenance of a distinctive culture among the medical students, operating like a resistance movement, finding ways to subvert the demands of a faculty that seemed to expect more work and more knowledge than the students could practically manage. In addition to its intrinsic merits, the work was in direct opposition to contemporary functionalist accounts of similar processes, where professional socialization was much more likely to be described in terms of the assimilation and internalization of the core values of the medical (or any other) profession. It was in keeping with the Chicago response to the functionalist formulation that Hughes and his colleagues rejected the notion of 'professions' as an analytic category. The functionalists found the professions an especially interesting case – allegedly displaying distinctive traits and value systems (such as a service ethic) that differentiated them from other categories within the modern division of labour. Hughes and his colleagues, by contrast, argued that professions were no different in kind from any other occupational group. The suggested that the supposed core traits of professionalism were in fact self-interested claims that were mobilized in collective strategies of occupational closure. Occupational socialization, for Hughes and his colleagues, was a matter of situated learning: more a series of coping strategies and survival tactics than a smooth internalization of knowledge and values. Equally, such coping mechanisms became part of a self-sustaining culture and had practical consequences for the conduct of education and work. Socialization was thus seen as a process of mutual adaptation between the institution (such as the work place) and its members.

These perspectives were applied to a wide variety of occupational and educational settings. They also reflected the more general interest in the transformation of social selves or identities. The notion of the 'career' captured this style of approach. From the career of the marijuana user, to the career of the hospital inmate, the idea brought together the personal and the institutional. The marijuana user, in Becker's account, must learn the appropriate responses to the possible physiological effects of the drug, and learn to find them pleasurable, as well as learning any more practical issues about how to actually use it (Becker, 1953a). The hospital inmate must also, over time, navigate her or his way through the organizational constraints – temporal, spatial and moral – of the hospital environment (Goffman, 1961; Roth, 1963). The career thus has its trajectory, shaped by personal action and institutional constraint. The work on 'status passage' thus reflects this tendency. Socially managed processes of transition from one social position to another reflected the interactionists' preoccupations with changes in social identity over time, and also the intersections between the collective and the individual.

This also helps us have a feel for the interactionists' more general stance towards the analysis of social roles. Here again, the contrast with functionalist analysis is the most helpful approach. Functionalist role theory treated roles as relatively determined positions within the social system. Role incumbency was thus the outcome of the internalization of culturally prescribed behavioural norms. This view of social roles thus led to the 'over-socialized' model of the social actor – the kind of 'cultural dope' that Garfinkel (1967) would write about from another perspective. In contrast, interactionism stressed 'role-making' as much as role-taking The language of social roles was by no means

11

alien to interactionism, but in the hands of the interactionists, it was used to convey a more creative and dynamic interaction between the self and the social milieu. Role incumbency involves a process of creative adaptation to social circumstances, and an active part in shaping the social milieu. There was an emphasis on work among the second Chicago School sociologists, and in an important sense this reflects the more general conviction that the social self and social order were themselves process and product of collaborative work.

Social order was conceived of in terms of negotiation (Strauss, 1978). The general metaphor of a negotiated order affirmed the creative work of social actors and groups. Order is not the property of a social system, but an emergent phenomenon. To that extent, social order is contingent and provisional. Moreover, the process of negotiation is never final. This is an image of the social that emphasizes its potential for constant challenge and renewal. The outcome of negotiated order is further negotiation, not a final settlement. The metaphor of negotiation thus rests inescapably on the imagery of process rather than structure, of emergence rather than systems, and of contingency rather than determinism (see also Strauss, 1993).

The work of Goffman is an interesting and important chapter in post-war interactionist thought. In many ways, Goffman's sociology was *sui generis*. It did not derive from nor did it belong to any specific sociological school or tradition. His proper place and the categorization of his work remain contested. For our purposes, it does not matter hugely whether he was a 'symbolic interactionist', an 'interactionist', more broadly defined, a member of the 'Chicago School', or was unique. His doctorate – though very different from much of his other work – was from the Chicago department (Goffman, 1953). No doubt Goffman assimilated a variety of inspirations, and created his own unique approach. It must, however, be counted among the general family of interactionist work. He has not inspired a following of purely Goffman-inspired research. He himself founded no school. It normally makes more sense to think of research inspired by, influenced by or drawing on his ideas – 'Goffmanesque' – rather than a school of research using his ideas systematically and exclusively 'Goffmanian'. But the development of interactionist sociology and its lively application to multiple sites of empirical research owe a great deal to Goffman. Indeed, for many students and researchers not especially concerned with the niceties of disciplinary history and internal boundaries, Goffman's work is among the key contributions to interactionism. So whether or not he was at the time a part of the second Chicago School, and whether or not he was among the mainstream of interactionism in his lifetime, there is absolutely no doubt as to the significance of Goffman's publications to the broad thrust of interactionist sociology, and its continuing relevance to work of that sort. In substance, at any rate, Goffman's work continued the spirit of much of the early Chicago sociology. His interests in behaviour in public can be read as a continuation of the early preoccupation with modernity and urbanism. Goffman's world, after all, is a world of relative strangers who are thrust together into fleetingly enforced intimacy. The modern world of strangers is one of fleeting encounters and lasting impressions. It is a world of appearances and messages. The gaze of the other can affirm our sense of self as a moral agent. Equally, it can threaten and destroy that sense. Goffman's own sociological gaze recapitulates that of Simmel and the other urban *flâneurs* who surveyed the metropolitan streets and the theatre of modern society (Parsons, 2000; Tester, 1994; Wilson, 2001). Goffman's social actor was Wirth's or Park's urban dweller, the social observer occupying a disengaged marginal position, and the social world itself a terrain of moral danger. Likewise, there was a direct continuity between Goffman's view of the 'total institution' (Goffman, 1961) and its inmates, and the second Chicago School's collective interest in institutions and the person. The inmate of the asylum followed a moral career that brought into conjunction the individual and the institutional. The transformation of the self – such as the processes of role-stripping and mortification of the self in the asylum – was a particular instance of the more general processes of status passage explored by Strauss and his colleagues. Moreover, Anselm Strauss's social psychology of appearances and identities – *Mirrors and Masks* – provides a manifest link with Goffman's general orientation, as well as a more mainstream link with Meadian symbolic interactionism (Strauss, 1959).

13

If the post-war years were marked by a flourishing programme of empirical work, they were also remarkable for the promotion of research methods. Again, the usual caveat is in order. The post-war Department of Sociology at the University of Chicago was not exclusively interactionist, and like the first Chicago School it was not dominated intellectually by qualitative research methods. Those are not the relevant propositions. What is significant and incontrovertible is that Chicago-based and Chicago-inspired interactionist sociology led to a growing awareness of qualitative methods as methodological issues rather than just common-sense practice. The result was a series of methodological writings that helped promote interactionist-inspired qualitative research far beyond interactionists alone, and far beyond the American networks that were its social and intellectual origin. Junker's (1960) monograph on field methods was an early example of the genre. It was based directly on the research practices of the Chicago School, and it gives an especially useful insight into the research work of the Chicago field researchers. His work was the first to translate the oral tradition of research apprenticeship into a published account. In doing so, Junker reproduced extended extracts from documents such as field notes and journals. It was as much an ethnographic account of the Chicagoans' ethnographies as a systematic account of methodological precepts. From that point of view, Junker's book is far more useful as a historical record for today's readers, and from that point of view deserves closer attention that it probably receives today.

In publishing a series of papers on methodological topics, many of which were included in influential anthologies of papers, the interactionists did more than any others to help promote and codify field research in sociology. Indeed, at the time – and for years subsequently – social and cultural anthropologists published very little about the methods of field research: they remained part of a personal oral tradition. The 1960s saw the proliferation of methodological writing, either by Chicagoans or inspired by their work. Howard Becker, Blanche Geer, Anselm Strauss and Leonard Schatzman were among the authors whose methodological observations became part of the interactionist canon, and spread more widely (e.g. Becker, 1958; Geer, 1964; Schatzman and Strauss, 1973).

Of all the methodological contributions of the second Chicago School of interactionists, *The Discovery of Grounded Theory* by Barney Glaser and Anselm Strauss (1967) was one of the most significant. Like most of the other methodological work, its influence in the decades since its publication has spread way beyond the confines of an explicitly interactionist sociology. It has also been widely misinterpreted. It set out to describe a general approach to the heuristics of theory generation. Deriving from American pragmatist epistemology, especially that of Peirce, the book argued for a crucial role for experience and observation in the formulation of concepts and theories. It has remained a key methodological text – though one suspects that it is cited much more frequently than it is read – but is often invoked inappropriately. Glaser and Strauss themselves were not proposing an approach that was restricted exclusively to the analysis of qualitative data. Equally, they were not arguing for a purely inductive approach to data analysis. Sadly, both interpretations have been widely attached to their work. As qualitative research has become increasingly fashionable, and as methodological literatures have burgeoned, Glaser and Strauss have too often been treated as advocating the equivalent of data-dredging in the search for analytic categories. Their work has been used as a justification for an inductive form of qualitative inquiry as a distinct approach to social research. Ironically, therefore, their influence has not always been based on an accurate or sympathetic reading of the original work. The more elementary manual of practical advice for field researchers was provided by Strauss and his colleague Leonard

Schatzman (Schatzman and Strauss, 1973). This was one of the few student-oriented textbooks that could be used to plan and conduct field research, and was also influential in promoting and justifying the conduct of qualitative field research. By the end of the 1960s the literature also included a major textbook by another leading interactionist – Denzin's *The Research Act* (1970). This reviewed and synthesized most of the major methodological commitments of interactionist field research and in successive editions provided one of the most systematic accounts of research strategy in the interactionist tradition. John Lofland (1971) provided an exemplary textbook account of fieldwork in a work that also (subsequently with Lyn Lofland as co-author) went into several editions (Lofland and Lofland, 1984). In other words, the interactionist tradition was especially influential in the development and advocacy of research that was variously (and later) referred to as 'field research', 'ethnography' and 'qualitative research'. The research methods that were practised and recommended were participant observation, interviews, and life-histories. These had been the stock-in-trade of the interactionist tradition since its early days and the development of research methods among the second Chicago School interactionists was focused primarily on these tried-and-trusted approaches to the collection of field and biographical data.

Chicago-style interactionism by no means remained the preserve of the Department of Sociology at the University of Chicago itself. There was a diaspora. Leading figures took the interactionist approach elsewhere. Anselm Strauss, Leonard Schatzman and Virginia Olesen re-created its vigorous empirical research programme and its methodological commitments at the University of California, San Francisco: this was a remarkable site for the development of a sociological research programme, being in the University of California's medical school. From within the School of Nursing, the interactionists and their colleagues developed a major programme of research on medical, nursing and scientific topics. Olesen also united the interactionist tradition with a major commitment to feminist scholarship. Blumer was a major figure at Berkeley. The Loflands developed their empirical and methodological work at the University of California, Davis, where Julius Roth also worked. There was, therefore a strong presence in North California, while Fred Davis and Robert Emerson were among Southern California's interactionists. There remained a mid-Western strength in interactionism. Howard Becker spent many years at Northwestern University, and Denzin is at the University of Illinois. Interactionist work in the United States thus spread through a number of academic departments. The Sociology Department at Brandeis University became a new focus for interactionist sociology. The University of Chicago itself ceased to be a major centre for interactionist work, however.

Interactionism's association with a network of sociologists across the United States was formally institutionalized through the establishment of the Society for the Study of Symbolic Interaction. This provided interactionists with a focus for their shared interests. It gave them the opportunity to claim a distinctive identity and a presence within American sociology. Accounts of its foundation make it clear that, amid the personal bickering that seems to have gone on, there was a collective sentiment. Interactionists found themselves to be a minority, lacking a presence and a voice. They found it hard to persuade editors of mainstream journals and their editorial boards to take seriously their work. For all the apparent success of their work – such as the impact on deviance studies by Becker and others, the growing recognition of the work in other substantive fields such as medicine and education, or the widespread use of Glaser and Strauss's methodological work – the interactionists felt something of an embattled minority. The foundation of the Society also entailed the creation of their own specialist journal – *Symbolic Interaction* – which would provide a more sympathetic outlet and reach a sympathetic readership through the society's membership. Elsewhere, the creation of the journal *Urban Life and Culture* – re-named *Urban Life* and re-named again *Journal of Contemporary Ethnography* – provided an outlet for the distinctively interactionist strand of empirical field research that has remained one of its strengths throughout its history.

16

THE CONTESTED HISTORIES OF INTERACTIONISM AND CHICAGO SOCIOLOGY

As we have already seen, historical commentary on interactionist sociology has been mingled with histories of the Chicago School. While the traditions of symbolic interactionism, urban sociology and Chicago sociology are clearly interlinked, it is important to recognize – as most of the authors do – that they are by no means synonymous. Chicago sociology was by no means confined to the conduct of interactionist work, nor exclusively devoted to the practice or urban ethnography. It has a number of intellectual currents, by no means all of which were rooted in pragmatist social philosophy or interactionist sociology. The strong emphasis on empirical sociological research embraced a variety of quantitative and qualitative research strategies, and there was no single preoccupation with ethnographic or other qualitative approaches.

It is striking that European sociologists – British authors most prominently – have been among the most active of historians of interactionism and Chicago sociology. Before dealing briefly with their contributions, it is worth pausing to speculate as to why the themes have exercised the degree of fascination that they have for British authors. As we suggested in the Introduction, there has never been an interactionist tradition that is indigenously British. Insofar, therefore, that British authors have wished to explore the intellectual, historical and biographical antecedents of their own work, they have naturally turned to the American roots of interactionism. There is, by contrast, little in the British sociological tradition to inspire interactionist thought. One finds nothing in the political arithmetic tradition, nor in the history of policy research to link with interactionist interests. There is, of course, nothing inherently incongruent in British authors writing about ideas from elsewhere. There is nothing especially remarkable in British scholars writing about Parisian or Viennese ideas, and it is equally unremarkable that there should be British scholarship on American traditions. If there is any detectable difference, it lies in the fact that the American traditions are less fashionable than many of the European counterparts. Perhaps, too, it may seem a trifle superfluous to engage in a work of history and commentary relating to American traditions: English language scholarship is, after all, eminently accessible to British scholars and students and does not, on the face of it, require linguistic and intellectual translation into British contexts. Another slight difference from much of the writing about European social theory is the fact that much of the American work under discussion – Chicago School or symbolic interactionist – is strongly based on or linked to empirical work. There is in fact relatively little that is transferable in terms of pure abstract theory. There is, therefore, relatively little scope for the kind of hagiography that marks so much of the secondary literature on European theory. For the same sort of reason, work on the American past of symbolic interactionism and Chicago sociology has displayed a particular interest in research methodology. This clearly reflects two things. First, the sociology itself was rarely divorced from the practical work of exploration and research. Second, and unlike the influence of many other traditions, the research methods of interactionists and some Chicago sociologists have been among the most significant of their legacies.

17

As we stated earlier, there are many different histories of interactionism and of the Chicago Schools of sociology. They include British- and American-authored accounts. It is striking that the historical accounts construct contrasting versions of the past, each stressing different aspects of the sociologies and their lines of development. We pause here to consider those constructed parts, in brief, partly because the various themes can help us to project possible futures for interactionist thought (in the broad sense). We repeat here the basic point that we ourselves are *not* confusing interactionism, Chicago sociology and qualitative methods. But if we are to capture the relevant issues, then we do need to take account of all three of those domains: their areas of overlap and of complementarity are among our major concerns, and are among the themes explored by the various authors. Moreover, it is clear that there is no single entity to which one can easily apply the term 'interactionism', any more than there is a homogeneous 'Chicago School'. Each historical account creates a different past, each provides a historical charter for a particular tradition, and each focuses on a particular mix of topics.

It is striking that there are quite different versions of the history of Chicago. Abbott's (1999) historiography of Chicago sociology is illuminating from this perspective. The brief account that follows was constructed independently of Abbott's, but our treatment and his contain many similarities. They reveal how different versions of the past can be constructed in order to represent and justify subsequent interests. They also help us to see how different futures can be projected for interactionist ideas and cognate commitments. Abbott's own account is one of the most recent books to appear. His primary focus is on the history of the *American Journal of Sociology* and its relation to the Chicago department. By way of background, he reviews the history of the Chicago department, and also reviews some of the historical treatments of the topic. In company with others, he documents the diversity of personal and intellectual styles that were to be found among the leading lights of Chicago sociology. It would be impossible to sustain any simplified view of the Chicago department after reading Abbott. The differences between the major figures and the recurrent strains within the department may be no more pronounced than one would find in any academic department that had a sufficiently long and well-documented history, but they dispel any sense of a single 'Chicago' style with a dominant theoretical or methodological thrust. Indeed, much of the historical literature is at pains to dispel any such belief. British authors have been prominent in promoting that revisionist position.

The history of symbolic interactionism by Meltzer et al. (1975) is a characteristically 'insider' account of the tradition. While the work is by no means blind to some criticisms of symbolic interactionism, the authors trace a conventional internalist account of its development and varieties. They identify the inspiration of the pragmatists – James and Dewey – as well as Cooley and Mead. Because they are themselves engaged in symbolic interactionism, Meltzer et al. pay attention to the internal differentiation of the tradition at the time they were writing. Consequently they distinguish between the Chicago and Iowa schools of interactionism. The former reflected the thought of people like Blumer (and was therefore as much a Californian as a Chicago tendency), and was the humanist or interpretative wing of the tradition. It contrasts clearly with the Iowa school, associated with Manford Kuhn, which was characterized by positivist methodological outlooks, and a more 'scientific' social psychology. Meltzer et al. include Goffman's dramaturgy as a third variety of interactionism. Intriguingly, they also add ethnomethodology as a variant of symbolic interactionism. The latter inclusion reflects a kind of reception of Garfinkel's work, that assimilated it to the broader church of interactionist thought rather than endorsing what appeared to be its more narrowly sectarian approach. This interpretation has not, of course, been endorsed by most ethnomethodologists in the past, who have been at pains to distinguish themselves from all forms of conventional sociology, including interactionism (although many have acknowledged the contribution of Goffman in his pioneering attention to the interaction order). Although the influence of Georg Simmel is acknowledged in passing, the thrust of the argument by Meltzer et al. is to stress the indigenous American roots and subsequent developments of the interactionist tradition.

Faris (1967) provides a broad coverage of the period from the early years of the twentieth century to the mid-1930s. He places particular emphasis on the development of urban sociology, including the ecological work on the spatial organization of the urban environment as well as the research programme on urban behaviour. He also devotes a chapter to Chicago's social psychology, where he stresses the background in the psychology of William James and James Dewey. He then stresses the combined contributions of George Herbert Mead, Charles Horton Cooley (at Michigan) and Ellsworth Faris. While he acknowledges the general significance of social psychology in the development of Chicago sociology, Faris does little to link social behaviourism with the more overtly sociological work he also discusses. Quite rightly he points out that the term 'symbolic interactionism' would not have been heard by Chicago students or faculty members in the period his book covers. He does not, however, suggest that there was a much broader 'interactionist' tradition (by whatever name). Faris rightly insists on the diversity of sociological approaches that were represented and practised in Chicago during the period of his survey. His account tends to juxtapose the various strands, however, rather than suggesting many over-arching themes or commonalities.

In considerable contrast is an account by Carey (1975). Carey deliberately emphasizes aspects of the Chicago School that are too readily overlooked in more 'internalist' sociological histories of Chicago. He concentrates on the role of Chicago sociologists as engaged public intellectuals. Rather than focusing on the theoretical and methodological innovations of the Chicago School, he describes their commitment to public affairs. His main preoccupation is with the urban-sociology groups at Chicago, and he consequently pays relatively little attention

19

to the social psychology, or to the more overtly interactionist strands in the development of Chicago sociology. The treatment places the sociology firmly in its political and economic context. Carey directs attention to the Progressivist movement as the intellectual and political environment within which Chicago sociology was pursued. It was an *applied* sociology: the British reader will be reminded that the United States has never entertained the disciplinary division between sociology and social policy. Sociology has always had a strong 'social problems' focus. For the Chicago sociologists, according to Carey's account, public engagement took two routes – public commissions and community clinics. The former included such bodies as the Chicago Commission on Race Relations. The latter included sociologists' participation in child guidance clinics. There was also a direct engagement with what would now be identified more in terms of social work, notably the Settlement House projects and the Charity Organisation Society. Carey's history thus places Chicago sociology in a context of applied research and an engagement with social problems. It is part of a broader intellectual and political pattern, associated with the rise of the professional and managerial classes, that laid emphasis on the rational management of social processes and problems. The complex social changes that took shape in the city of Chicago in the early years of its new university and in the decades that followed, provided the new Department of Sociology with its natural laboratory. This was not the subject of a detached gaze, however. Carey's history emphasizes the extent to which the Chicago sociologists developed their analyses of urban ecology and its transformations, and their theories of social disorganization, against the background of social reform and social intervention.

Among the British histories of the Chicago School, Smith's is probably closest in tone to Carey's (Smith, 1988). Smith's characterization of Chicago sociology in terms of a 'liberal critique of capitalism' captures the spirit of his analysis. His account is couched in terms of the contrasts and tensions between American capitalism and American democratic liberalism. This, then, is an account that re-asserts the significance in Chicago thought of a well-informed public, an enlightened and scientifically informed intelligentsia, and a reformist ideology. Here again Smith suggests that there is little space for the specifically interactionist tradition. Yet the Park–Thomas tradition *is* central to the reformist ideals of the Chicago School, married to a programme of empirical social inquiry. Consequently, the relevance of 'interactionism' in the broadest sense is rather under-played. Certainly, if we take the sort of broad perspective offered by Strauss and Fisher, among others, in recognizing *two* major strands in interactionist sociology and thus granting some significance to the study of urban behaviour and personal transformation, then the interactionist tradition is by no means divorced from the reformist engagement with the rational management of social change. There is, indeed, a very clear continuity between reformist ideology and the Meadian view of social evolution, susceptible to the reflection and purposeful direction of human social actors. Clearly historical accounts of the kind offered by Strauss and Fisher are not intended to be histories of Chicago sociology itself. They do not therefore seek or need to do justice to the entire range of sociological work undertaken there, although they do more than most to draw together a number of complementary intellectual strands to construct a broad interactionist stream.

Paul Rock's is a British history of symbolic interactionism that looks superficially like a similarly sympathetic account (Rock, 1979). His is also an intellectual history of symbolic interactionism. But it is one that takes a broad perspective and places the development of interactionist thought in an intellectual framework that embraces several major sociological themes. Rock understandably concentrates on theory and methodology in accounting for symbolic interactionism. He reminds us that as an 'understated sociology' interactionism is not susceptible to summary definition, and that it is constituted by a collection of works rather than a single vision: 'Its definition emerges as those works mount up' (ibid.: 23). It is understated, in that it does not rely on major statements of general theory, apart from a small number of basic precepts and perspectives. Most importantly, perhaps, Rock provides a sophisticated and sympathetic review of interactionism's origins and its developments. Notably, he links it with major strands of European – especially German – social thought, and derives its key commitments from a number of engagements with the philosophy of Kant. Specifically, Rock places Simmel at the centre of interactionism's intellectual genealogy. Interactionism is shot through with formalist thinking – some of which is attributable to Simmel's influence directly, some of which is not. As with much of interactionism, however, the intellectual debts to and affinities with Simmel's sociology have often been lost to view. Because of the very character of interactionism itself, Rock argues, it has tended to lose sight of its own past. Its lack of interest in – indeed, its suspicion of – grand systematic theory and its recurrent emphasis on practical sociological research, coupled with its oral transmission in a small number of departments and networks, have often meant a neglect of antecedents. Consequently, Rock argues that it is not always easy to determine precisely the extent and the limits of Simmel's direct influence on interactionist thought in the development of Chicago sociology. A strong influence is not in doubt, however. Park's direct exposure to German formalism is an abiding influence, and Simmel was one of the most cited of sociologists in Chicago. Indeed, as Rock reminds us, Simmel was the most frequently cited and the most anthologized of the sociologists gathered together in the highly influential textbook edited by Park and Burgess (1921), the *Introduction to the Science of Society* (which went into subsequent editions, and enshrined much of the basic approach to sociology of the department itself). Seen from this perspective, interactionism can be seen as an American reception of a distinctively German sociological tradition, rather than an autochthonous American style of social thought. Indeed, it would seem appropriate to stress the convergence of American pragmatism and German formalism in the making of interactionism's distinctive direction.

Rock (1979) suggests that the more immediately American philosophical background of pragmatism, of Dewey, James and Mead, was also a specific set of responses to Hegelian philosophy. The synthesis that was pragmatism gave to interactionism a distinctive view of knowledge. The pragmatist solution to the problem of knowledge stressed its emergent character, dependent on the knowing subject's engagement with the natural world. Ironically, Rock suggests, American pragmatism all too readily became diluted into an anti-intellectualism. Pragmatism's rejection of axiomatic thought and its positive emphasis on the emergent nature of scientific understanding could, reflexively, lead interactionists to neglect their own intellectual genealogy. Rock thus suggests that interactionism has its own in-built memory loss. While histories have promoted it and its institutions have flourished, the actual practice of interactionism has not been promoted in an atmosphere that is conducive to a deep historical self-understanding (see also Rock, 2001).

If formalism and pragmatism are the firm intellectual foundations of interactionism, Rock maintains that the thinking and observing self is its central concept. This in turn gives rise to the centrality of participant observation to the interactionist research enterprise. The interactionist self is itself an emergent phenomenon – a product of language and an outcome of the general processes of social interaction. The self is also a knowing subject. Hence, interactionism must stress participant observation not merely as a method or technique, but as the core mode of knowing as practical engagement with the social work. There is, Rock's treatment establishes, a key homology at the heart of interactionism's model of social processes and its research practices. The social world and the social actors who produce it (and themselves) are grounded in the reflective capacities of the knowing and acting human subject. That same human subject, capable of interacting with others and with herself or himself is also the model social explorer. Social inquiry is itself perfectly homologous with social life itself. In this way, the epistemological roots of interactionism and its methodological precepts are brought into conjunction in the mundane practices of sociological research. In Rock's treatment – which is by no means confined to an uncritical celebration of symbolic interactionism – the tradition is revealed as one with deep roots, consistent themes, a coherent episte-mology, and a distinctive voice in the development of sociological thought. It is simultaneously a distinctively American synthesis, and a response to major strands of European philosophy and sociology. It carries those ideas forward, but often in an implicit manner. It is col-lectively as guilty as its critics of overlooking its past in the celebration of its practical achievements.

Martin Bulmer's British history of the Chicago School places partic-ular emphasis upon the development of research methods and empiri-cal research (Bulmer, 1984). He seeks to redress what he believes to be the imbalance in previous accounts (including Paul Rock's): 'There is far more to Chicago sociology in the 1920s than, for example, the mini-industry of Mead studies would suggest' (ibid.: xiv). Like others writ-ing in the same sort of vein, Bulmer seems to think that authors like Rock cannot tell the difference between the full variety of sociology at the University of Chicago and the interactionist strand within it. (And why the disparaging trivialization of the tag 'mini-industry'?) On the broader front Bulmer is quite right to document how qualitative research developed in the context of field research projects in Chicago, and also that Chicago was a major site for the development of quanti-tative research methods as well. Bulmer repeatedly argues that quanti-tative research at Chicago has been neglected, while qualitative work has been exaggeratedly associated with the pre-war Chicago depart-ment. But it is clear that most commentators are not guilty of the myopia that Bulmer wants to find. A broad perspective on interaction-ism is by no means confined to the study of George Herbert Mead and his immediate influence. Equally, the assertion that there was a distinc-tive tradition that included urban ethnography and interactionist social psychology, which in turn led to further major, empirical, theoretical and methodological work in the post-war years at Chicago does not amount to a claim that there was nothing else. Bulmer's examination of research in Chicago is valuable in its own right, but he sets up straw arguments in asserting his own thesis. There is, perhaps, something interesting to be observed about the shared discourse of methodologies in the social sciences. Qualitative methods remain personalized, in that they remain – despite their widespread use – associated very closely with individual authors, and with their individual research projects. Quantitative methods, on the whole, have been treated in less person-alized and less localized ways. To that extent, it is perhaps less surpris-ing that the specific components of the Chicago tradition might some-times have created the impression that qualitative research was of supreme significance.

Also deriving from the UK, Harvey's careful review is aimed at rectifying some of the perceived distortions of retrospective accounts of Chicago sociology (Harvey, 1987). He identifies five 'myths' and sets about demonstrating their partial (at best) truth. The myths are: (a) that Chicago sociology was primarily liberal and Progressive; (b) that its members were dogmatically committed to qualitative research and hostile to quantitative methods; (c) that the sociology was lacking in strong theory, and had little to offer beyond descriptive accounts; (d) that it was primarily associated with symbolic interactionism and the thought of Mead; and (e) that it was dominant in American sociology until the 1930s. Harvey's is just one of the several revisionist accounts of Chicago sociology to have been written by British sociologists. Jennifer Platt has adopted a similar stance (Platt, 1983, 1996). She too has set about debunking the close association between Chicago sociology and ethnographic research methods. Like other commentators, she has been at pains to point out that what would now be regarded as ethnographic research methods were by no means characteristic of sociology as it was practised at Chicago in the 1920s and 1930s. Chicago was the site for quantitative research methods. The close association between Chicago, qualitative research methods and interactionist ideas is a retrospective attribution. From this perspective, the Chicago tradition of interactionist-inspired ethnographic research and theorizing is a highly selective distortion of the historical facts.

These debunking revisionist histories are themselves problematic, however. In describing a Chicago style or tradition – whether in relation to the first or second Chicago Schools – we do not think that anyone has seriously claimed that there was nothing else in the Department of Sociology. Several of the commentaries – interesting though they are in their own right – seem to be arguing past each other. One does not invalidate the description 'a London bus' by observing that there are other means of transport in London, or by observing that the students at the University of California in Davis also operate a bus service using double-decker red London buses. The Chicago tradition(s) certainly did not exhaust all that was actually practised at Chicago. Equally, not all of the Chicago style of work was actually pursued at the University of Chicago itself. The diaspora of faculty and students in the post-war period meant that interactionist sociology inspired by people like Blumer, Hughes and Strauss was conducted and taught at other universities. One of the more robust and sensible statements of the position comes from one of the American revisionists, Deegan (2001). She concludes her essay on the Chicago influences on ethnographic research by suggesting that 'An easy way to refute the disputed and muddled claims over the existence of the Chicago School, its method and its theory is to read the hundreds of Chicago-style ethnographies. One could devote years to reading thousands of these studies in books and articles' (ibid.: 21). She adds that one could also gain a sense of the style of research and writing by paying attention to what she calls the 'core ethnographies' of authors like Whyte, Goffman, Strauss, Stone, Becker and Davis.

A very different kind of intellectual history is provided by Cappetti (1993). This provides not a philosophical or political matrix for Chicago sociology, but an aesthetic one. In particular, Cappetti discusses some of the literary models and influences that helped shape the Chicago representations of social worlds. The distinctive ethos of Chicago sociology was certainly influenced by explicitly aesthetic, literary models. For instance, Thomas Park made explicit his debt to writers of fiction. He suggested that writers like Emile Zola provided distinctive insights into modern urban life. He commended Zola's 'experimental' approach to fiction as a model for the disciplined exploration of social life. More generally, Chicago was a major centre for literary naturalism. One did not have to look as far as Zola's France for literary environment in which the everyday realities of modern life were explored, and in which a realist or naturalist style was used to represent such living. The sociologists and the authors were members of overlapping circles. The same urban environment, the same sense of social change and innovation inspired the literary as well as the sociological imagination. One of the classics of American realism – Dreiser's *Sister Carrie* – is an especially prominent and famous example of the literary exploration of the moral consequences of urban modernity. Cappetti's monograph traces the mutual influences and intersections of the sociological and the literary in Chicago. There were two-way influences. We have just alluded to the influence of literary models on the styles of ethnographic and other reportage in Chicago urban sociology. Equally, the sociological imagination exerted some influence in the other direction. James Farrell, author of the 'Studs Lonigan' trilogy read sociology at Chicago University. There was a close affinity between the novel of personal development – such as the 'Studs Lonigan' series – and the sociological treatment of the life-history and the recognition of the self as the central unit of sociological analysis. This history is a very different one from those that focus their attention on the concrete subject matter of social problems. It is also different even from most treatments of research methods in Chicago. Again this can be attributed to a sort of anti-intellectualism in the later development of interactionist sociology. A fairly self-conscious adoption of aesthetic, textual models in the development of a sociological style was perfectly congruent with interactionism's key inspirations and core tenets. After all, language – and symbolic means more generally – were seen as key mechanisms in the constitution of social processes.

25

Likewise, social research was predicated on the equivalence between everyday social life and the forms of inquiry. In principle, therefore, a reflexive attention to the possibilities of textual representation was entirely congruent with the main levels of interactionism. It appears, however, that the *conventional* character of realist writing was rather lost to view. The construction of realist ethnographic and similar texts was for many years a taken-for-granted feature: the conventions of naturalism became naturalized.

In recent years, of course, the development of interactionism has been affected by the rediscovery of textual and rhetorical conventions of academic and other genres. Atkinson (1983, 1996) identified the textual conventions of interactionist ethnography in an essay that narrowly anticipated the publications that most dramatically precipitated the so-called 'crisis of representation' in social anthropology and in sociology (Clifford and Marcus, 1986). John van Maanen (1988) also wrote about sociological ethnography as a collection of different genres, working within a broadly interactionist tradition. There is, therefore, an aesthetic history of Chicago sociology and of interactionism that stands alongside the institutional and methodological accounts. It is a history that, for instance, recognizes the significance of style in the work of key figures – most notably Erving Goffman (Atkinson, 1989) – and the role of textual conventions in establishing the characteristic works of interactionist ethnography (Lofland, 1974).

INTERACTIONISM TODAY

Interactionism – as we have indicated at several points already – has never been a narrowly sectarian strand in sociology. Admittedly there are authors whose prime interest is in the expression of an orthodoxy, a canon of works and the hagiography of founders. For the most part, however, its work has been fuelled by an engagement with empirical research programmes, and by a developing array of ideas. Notwithstanding attempts to define a more narrow 'symbolic interactionism', in practice the inspiration of the work has gone beyond narrowly sectarian boundaries. It has continued to change and to develop in a number of significant ways.

Some of interactionism's changing nature reflects the weakening of boundaries between interactionist sociology and other disciplines. This is especially noticeable in the flow of methodological influence from the confines of interactionism to a much broader audience within sociology, and – even more significantly – beyond sociology itself. To some extent the methodological commitments have become detached from any specific moorings in a specific theoretical school. The extraordinary spread of 'qualitative research' has seen its influence extend to domains like health and nursing research, educational research, management studies, human geography, discursive psychology and other areas. In some domains this has led to the establishment of new international research networks and academic journals – such as *Qualitative Health Research* and *Qualitative Studies in Education*. The methodological impulse has thus provided one avenue whereby an interactionist influence has permeated widely and informed empirical research programmes – if only at a second remove.

Equally, changes in the broader field of sociology itself have led to some areas of convergence between interactionism and newer interests. When interactionists felt themselves to be an embattled minority, the dominant motifs in sociology, especially in the United States, were structural and quantitative. Functionalist meta-theory was the dominant idiom. The epistemology was, if not strictly positivist, certainly 'scientistic' in the kinds of research designs that were implemented and criteria for validity that were invoked. There is, of course, still much work in that vein to be found, especially in American departments, research institutes, conferences and journals. Equally, however, sociology and the social sciences more generally have developed much wider interests that have made them potentially more open to interactionist thought. The turn towards more cultural issues has encouraged sociologists to take seriously semiotics and symbolic systems. Likewise the turn towards language has created areas of theorizing and research where the abiding interests of interactionism have been given renewed vitality.

In general terms, the cultural and linguistic turn have been closely related to the so-called postmodern moment in the social sciences. While it would be absurd to imply that all social scientists claim to be 'postmodern' in their own theorizing and research practice, it is undeniable that a variety of tendencies that are grouped under that rubric have helped to change the research agenda in ways congruent with some of interactionism's interests. Interactionist sociologists have in turn responded to these new intellectual currents. Authors like Norman Denzin (e.g. Denzin, 1989a, 1989b, 1992, 1995, 1997) have done much to transform the broadly interactionist programme. They have brought into conjunction interactionist perspectives with culturalist and postmodernist approaches. In the process, interactionism is partly re-defined and located afresh.

There is, for instance, a new juxtaposition of interactionist sociology and issues deriving from the cultural turn in sociology and other disciplines. Given interactionism's long-standing interest in matters of meaning and representation, through systems of symbol and gesture, one can argue that it was always, in principle, a 'cultural' form of sociological theorizing and empirical work. What is more, in its origins in

Chicago, the sociology was born of an interest in the mass media and a well-informed public. There was, therefore, nothing inherent in the tradition that would have precluded a strong interest in cultural themes. The recurrent interest in appearance and the self could have generated a more sustained interest in fashion, clothing, adornment and the body. As it is, these themes have become part of the contemporary mainstream of sociology. More generally still, cultural studies have been established as a disciplinary specialism in their own right. In important ways, the cultural turn has provided a fresh impetus for some contemporary forms of interactionist thought. In some ways, indeed, the interests have merged. In other ways, however, the relative neglect of interactionism has meant that current authors have not always paid sufficient attention to the interactionist tradition when locating their own work and searching for inspiration. Cultural and interactionist sociology share common perspectives and commitments, although the affinities are not always clearly apparent.

Similarly, recent interests in biographical and autobiographical practices have re-engaged a wider social-science constituency with interactionism. The life history has been at the heart of interactionism methodology since the early years of Chicago sociology. The intersection of the institutional career and the personal career has been a recurrent research topic. The transformation of the self has been one of the key preoccupations of interactionism. Recent interests in biographical work and narratives of personal experience have therefore opened a new bridgehead through which interactionist ideas can mingle with others. The contribution of Norman Denzin to the idea of 'interpretive biography' directly links the older strands of interactionism with contemporary interests in lives, voices and biographies (Denzin, 1989a, 1989b). There is, in other words, a long tradition of interactionist work grounded in the 'life history'. Some of the earliest classics of interactionist sociology and cognate work were based on the collection and analysis of documents of life, written and spoken. In recent years that interest has been refreshed and given a new impetus. Such renewed interest in lives and biographies has been a dialectical process between interactionism and the wider matrix of sociological inquiry. In many ways, biographical revival has emerged more or less independently of interactionism itself. There have been multiple sources of inspiration. They have included feminist and subaltern studies, in which the recuperation of muted voices have been of central significance (Plummer, 2001).

The imminent demise of interactionism has been proclaimed on several occasions. In his survey of research groups and networks in sociology, Mullins (1973) suggested that it was more or less moribund. Some of the leading lights of the Society for the Study of Symbolic

Interaction report taking delight in ringing him annually thereafter to assure him that they and the group were still alive and well. Others have suggested from time to time that interactionism was a dead end, was played out, or was irrelevant. Although the special interest in symbolic interactionism continues to be something of a minority commitment in American sociology and elsewhere, it continues to flourish as a well-established minority interest group. The Society continues to exist, and the annual meetings continue to be well attended. Moreover, they continue to attract younger scholars. The journal continues to publish theoretical, methodological and empirical contributions that help to renew the tradition, while Denzin continues to edit a series of yearbooks that contain major contributions to interactionist sociology. Part of the process of survival and renewal has been a widening of the boundaries of what counts as interactionism. Contemporary practitioners are not devoted to preserving the ideas of past interactionists or celebrating the ideas of Mead, Hughes or Goffman. Some of them do that, but there are much newer strands of thought that have been added. Some indication of these transformations can be detected in the contents of the annual Couch-Stone symposium, which is a relatively (by American standards) small conference. It has responded to the wider climate of social research by incorporating a broad range of materials, many of which arguably fall outside the scope of interactionism *stricto sensu*. These include varieties of 'new ethnography' that incorporate various forms of experimental textual forms, drawing self-consciously on literary models. They in turn reflect the kind of work published in the journal edited by Denzin – *Qualitative Inquiry*. This too is not explicitly 'interactionist' but it embodies the 'new' interactionism that reflects in turn the influence of postmodern and other more avant-garde modes of sociological investigation, reflection and writing. It includes the kind of research and reflection described by Denzin and Lincoln as characterizing the 'fifth' (and subsequent) 'moments' of their model of social research (Lincoln and Denzin, 1994; Lincoln, 1995). This is not driven by a single set of ideas, and certainly does not reflect one particular theoretical perspective, tradition or school. Rather, it reflects a much broader set of intellectual commitments that are often summarized as 'postmodern'. In our view, that term obscures more than it illuminates, and it is too often used to gloss diverse practices that are sometimes mutually contradictory. This is not the place to try to review postmodernism in contemporary sociology. For the present, suffice to say that its influence has helped to re-define the nature of interpretative sociology in general and interactionism in particular. The emphases include: a rejection of virtually all previous epistemological positions (including those of classic interactionism) as being unduly regulated by inappropriately objectivist criteria, grounded

29

in an unduly positivist view of truth. By contrast, the postmodernist position recognizes multiple criteria for the validity of research – allowing ethical and local criteria rather than universalistic criteria to regulate research. Further, it celebrates a multiplicity of perspectives. While accusing its predecessors of privileging a monologic account of the world, that inscribed the hegemonic rationality of the male and the West, the new paradigm seeks to represent multiple perspectives, giving prominence to otherwise muted or silenced groups. The avant-garde movement thus privileges multiple 'voices'. These commitments are reflected in the textual practices used to represent research and its outcomes. These include the use of different literary genres. Forms such as the short story, the play, or the poem may be used in order to transgress the taken-for-granted modes of representation. They are also used to create multiple voices and multiple perspectives. This 'moment' thus incorporates the outcomes of the radical critique of writing and authorship in the social sciences widely referred to as the 'crisis of representation'. The so-called crisis derived from a series of criticisms of conventional textual practice – most notably in anthropology – that produced monologic, single-perspective texts that constructed an omniscient author and an unwarrantably objectivist account of the social world in question. The positive response to such criticisms has included the exploration of literary alternatives. There has been an explicit recognition that the scientific, the aesthetic and the ethical have deeply intertwined relationships. The rediscovery of rhetoric in the human and social disciplines has contributed significantly to this development. Among interactionist sociologists and those espousing similar perspectives, these commitments have been translated into a 'new ethnography'. This enshrines various literary genres. It also includes a high degree of self-consciousness on the part of the researcher-as-author. There is, therefore, a strong element of autobiographical and confessional writing. This in turn reflects a similar tendency among sociologists and anthropologists: that is, the turn towards auto-ethnography. This latter term covers several meanings. It includes the study of one's 'own' immediate lifeworld. It can also mean the study of oneself. In general terms, the new ethnography and cognate aspects of the avant-garde are highly personalized. They resist the impersonal intellectual and literary style of modernism and science. (It is clear from this last statement that 'modernism' is as unhelpful a term as postmodernism: clearly modernist literature is quite distinct from realist or naturalist writing and can itself be highly personalized, idiosyncratic and stylized.) In the work and the professional activities of individuals such as Denzin, Clough (1992), Ellis (1995) and Richardson (1994), interactionism, new literary forms and reflective practice come together. In one sense this is a departure from interactionism. Viewed from a different angle, however, it can be seen as a renewal of interactionism, a re-statement of some of its recurrent concerns in a new guise. Moreover, it brings some aspects of interactionism into close intellectual proximity with more widely current and fashionable concerns of sociology and the cultural disciplines.

In other words, one can identify a number of different ways in which interactionism is represented in recent and contemporary sociology. First, there is something one might think of as the *longue durée* of interactionism in general. This is the sociology inspired by Park–Thomas urban studies, by the institutional studies of Hughes, Becker and Strauss, and by Goffman's explorations of the interaction order. Second, one can identify the much narrower line of 'symbolic interactionism' that derives from Blumer's exegesis of Meadian social psychology. Third, one can identify a much broader array of ethnographic studies that reflect the methodological inspirations of the second Chicago School without necessarily being explicitly interactionist in theoretical inspiration. Fourth, one can now perceive a much newer movement, partially overlapping with interactionism but also with links to a variety of other movements, that gives rise to various postmodern and other avant-garde tendencies. Interactionism can be engaged with through any or all of those strands of development.

Denzin's own work exemplifies many of these developments. His prolific output – substantive and methodological – provides an intellectual weather-vane, helping us to chart some of the changing intellectual currents. Denzin's recent work, for instance, incorporates contemporary aspects of cultural studies, which he explicitly invokes as a source of renewal for symbolic interactionism. Denzin sees this as an engagement with a more interpretivist and textual approach to social phenomena. Denzin's approach is to confront symbolic interactionism with newer forms of representation and interpretation – cinematic, and electronic modes among them – and new modes of engagement. The more traditional modes of social inquiry are now to be supplemented by transactions in the social world that are grounded in the emotions as much as in science, in relativist rather than objectivist epistemologies. This is, therefore, a symbolic interactionism that is nourished by dialogue with late modernity or postmodernity rather than a nostalgia for the earlier modernity of 'high Chicago' days. In place of the American pragmatism of the earlier decades of the last century, therefore, Denzin evokes late twentieth–century and contemporary ideas, culled from postmodern cultural analyses. Denzin outlines a programme for such a renewed interactionism, with three main strands: 'the production, distribution, consumption, and exchange of cultural objects and their meaning; the textual analysis of those objects, their meanings and the practices that surround them; and the study of lived cultures and lived experiences

31

which are shaped by the cultural meanings that circulate in everyday life' (1992: 81). This also includes a fresher commitment to modes of narrative. Denzin's own work has included an exploration of cinematic modes of representation: like his predecessors in interactionism he takes the existing genre of 'realism' and incorporates them within the sociological imagination. In doing so, and in applying the perspective to a topic like alcoholism, Denzin re-visits the earlier interactionist interest in the mass media and the creation of public knowledge. He thus reminds us that his is not always a radically new departure for interactionist sociology: in many ways it constitutes a return to long-standing ideas and approaches, but from a distinctively contemporary perspective.

However it is approached or defined, then, interactionist sociology has never been a single tradition. It has had diverse roots, and has incorporated within it a variety of perspectives. It has not been static. While it is helpful to periodize its development somewhat – especially in terms of the first and second Chicago Schools – this temporal division masks a process of continuous development and change. This process continues to the present day, when interactionist thought finds many affinities with other trends in the social sciences. Its main characteristics remain discernible throughout its now long history, however. They include the strong commitment to empirical research. While theoretical ideas have been important, the major impact of the research has derived primarily from the quality of the research that interactionists have conducted. There is something a good deal more enduring about the detailed empirical accounts of social institutions and processes than general sociological theories and propositions. (A similar claim could be made concerning the endurance of classic anthropological monographs over against general ethnological theory.) For that reason, writing on research method has endured and flourished, taking the general orientation of interactionist research to wider audiences, many of whom may not even recognize its origins within that school of thought. Indeed, ethnographic, life history and other 'qualitative' research strategies have now become so widely established in the social and cultural sciences that they often seem, metaphorically, to have broken free of any disciplinary moorings and traditions. None the less, the development of qualitative research is closely associated with the rise of interactionist sociology and its programme of empirical social inquiry. Moreover, the development of explicit methodological self-consciousness and expertise was directly associated with Chicago School authors. To that extent, therefore, the contemporary and widespread enthusiasm for qualitative research owes much to the interactionist tradition. The collective neglect of interactionist roots, however, can all too easily lead advocates and enthusiasts to believe that their methodological commitments are entirely separate from such disciplinary groundings. There is a clear sense, then, that the methodological character of interactionist sociology has had an effect on sociology far wider than any circles that explicitly identify with interactionism itself.

shall exemplify some of these themes and issues in later chapters of this book. We shall explore especially how the themes of interactionism have been interwoven with other strands of sociological thought in British intellectual life. This is no more a consistent development than is the history of interactionism itself. Indeed, the very nature of this syncretism creates a complex story. Some British sociologists have, like other European scholars, engaged with the intellectual history of symbolic interactionism, while others have paid attention to the Chicago School in general. British authors have also paid serious attention to the ideas of interactionism, incorporating them into programmes of empirical work in substantive research fields. Others have responded by integrating interactionism into a broader category of 'interpretative sociology' aligning it with other movements such as phenomenology and the study of language. Yet others have responded to interactionist authors in developing British contributions to methodological reflection. In the chapters that follow we shall trace out some of these complex interactions between American interactionism and British sociology. In all these responses and dialogues, however, the British sociological community has not been characterized by sustained schools of 'interactionist' sociology. The response has nearly always been eclectic, pragmatic and partial. It is for that reason that the next chapter explores the assertion that 'we were never interactionists'.

two

we were never interactionists

This book continues and ends in exaggeration, and in contradiction. We begin by arguing that British sociology has never had a consistent interactionist school of social research or social theory. We shall conclude by arguing that 'we are all interactionists now' in that many of the tenets of interactionist sociology have now become taken-for-granted features of contemporary social theory and social inquiry. British, European and American social scientists now work in an intellectual climate in which interactionist ideas have achieved a certain currency. Their origins in or congruence with interactionist thought are not always acknowledged. Indeed, they are often developed and used by scholars who overtly ignore or shun the interactionist legacy. While a good deal of interactionism has been neglected, however, many of its most significant features have now been incorporated into highly valued streams of social thought. To put it another way, some aspects of contemporary sociology have converged with or re-discovered issues that have been part of the interactionist world-view for many decades.

We were never interactionists in the United Kingdom in the sense that a distinctive approach to sociology and social psychology – namely interactionism – never became institutionalized in British academic life in the way it did in the United States. There were occasional attempts to establish research groups and networks, but they had only shallow roots and were short-lived in consequence. Whereas interactionism has had a long history in the US departments of sociology (while never becoming a numerically or intellectually dominant stream), interest in the United Kingdom has flickered, waned, and flickered back to life – only to be subsumed under new interests and enthusiasms.

In the main, of course, that imbalance is unsurprising. Interactionism or symbolic interactionism was born in American sociology, philosophy and social psychology. It has core features that have elective affinities with deeply embedded themes of American thought more generally. In the course of this introduction we shall provide some pointers to those key features, but this volume is not intended to be an overview of symbolic interactionist thought in general. There are plenty of books and papers that do that already, and such an outline is not the purpose of the book series of which this is part. Rather, we want to spend most of the book examining the influence of interactionist thought on key areas of empirical research and its conduct. Moreover, the focus of these books is on British sociology and its place in the wider intellectual context.

Hence the scope and purpose of this book will reflect that general rationale. The focus will be on sociological work in the United Kingdom. But it will not be – indeed it could not be – treated in total isolation. The flow of ideas in social science has, throughout the past century – been global and there has been a constant flux of mutual influence between Europe and North America. Indeed, from a general view of sociological thought, the United Kingdom has been something of a nodal point in this generalized exchange of ideas. With rather few indigenous sociological thinkers or movements of great originality (and several notable examples remarkable primarily because of their *lack* of originality), the United Kingdom finds itself something of an entrepôt for ideas. We can find in British universities a dialogue and, occasionally, a synthesis between different strands of theory and method, from continental Europe and from North America. The fate of interactionist sociology in British universities can thus be read as a specific case study of those more general trends in intellectual history. We can examine the interaction and the intersection of several intellectual traditions: symbolic interactionism and its intellectual roots; European social thought; British empirical research and its distinctive intellectual commitments.

Of course, our characterization of those general phenomena is coloured by how we choose to read and define 'interactionism'. Now the definition and exegesis of symbolic interactionism are a modest but well-established cottage industry in its own right. For the purposes of this book, however, we shall not be trying to define a single orthodoxy. We shall not attempt therefore to construct a canonical version of symbolic interactionism and then attempt to fit British research into that ideal type. Equally, we are not bothered as to whether British sociologists have reflected American inspirations faithfully and accurately. Rather, we shall explore how interactionist ideas were eclectically received and interpreted in various British research traditions, and their general fate in those domains. We shall, therefore, seek to document what versions of interactionist thought have been constructed by British scholars. In so doing we shall also take account of how various British authors have themselves contributed to the production of intellectual histories of interactionist sociology. There may not be a definitive British history, but it is striking that several of the major historical accounts of interactionist theory and method have come from British and other European commentators.

In examining how British sociologists have incorporated and used interactionist ideas we have cast our net quite widely. We shall certainly not confine attention to mainstream symbolic interactionism from the USA. Seen from the relative distance of Britain and Europe, American interactionism has not been a single, narrowly defined enterprise. Rather, it looks like a broader intellectual tradition, having affinities with a variety of other epistemological, methodological and theoretical perspectives. They have frequently been drawn on by British scholars in a catholic fashion, and our own treatment will reflect that approach.

Where relevant, therefore, we shall address work that incorporates the work of Erving Goffman without pausing for undue theological dispute as to whether or not Goffman himself should most appropriately be categorized as an interactionist sociologist. (It is a very telling irony, indeed, that the most original and prolific commentator in the interaction order perhaps is not an 'interactionist', and reminds us of the futility of many of the symbolic boundaries around intellectual fields and specialisms.) Likewise, the work of Aaron Cicourel and others with a close allegiance to ethnomethodology – especially in its earlier manifestations – will be addressed, as will work with inspirations deriving from phenomenology and other hermeneutic traditions, where relevant to the work's reception by British scholars and in a broader context of research.

Strictly speaking, of course, ethnomethodology falls outside the scope of a book on interactionist sociology. Notwithstanding some possible similarities and convergences, ethnomethodology has been a quite distinct form of inquiry, and its practitioners have – especially in the early years – been at pains to distance themselves from symbolic interactionism. Nevertheless, it is in the spirit of this book that we should consider how ethnomethodology has been selectively used by some sociologists in the UK working within a broadly interactionist frame of reference. The eclectic and flexible approach that has characterized much British work has been apparent in the way that ethnomethodological insights have been drawn on and incorporated into empirical research traditions. To that extent, therefore, it does make sense to make reference to those aspects of UK sociology where ethnomethodological inspirations have informed and enriched a more interactionist perspective. In dealing with the major empirical and conceptual developments in the chapters that follow, therefore, we shall discuss the significance of ethnomethodologically influenced work. We shall not, however, attempt to deal comprehensively with ethnomethodology itself. That is a topic that requires separate treatment: the diffusion of ethnomethodological thought – especially outside the United States – and its reception in different national and theoretical contexts certainly merit attention. One certainly cannot portray the development of ethnomethodology over the past thirty years or so as the preserve only of a relatively small coterie of specialists. Sometimes despite the intentions of those specialists themselves, the ethnomethodological movement has influenced a diverse array of sociological interests.

Clearly – as we have outlined in the previous chapter – 'interactionism' can mean several things in sociological work. On the one hand it can refer quite narrowly to that branch of sociological scholarship known as *symbolic interactionism*. This is a fairly well-defined area of specialization, with its own paradigm (we use the term loosely) consisting of key figures and founding heroes (George Herbert Mead, Charles Horton Cooley or Herbert Blumer among them), social networks (including the Society for the Study of Symbolic Interaction), its own canon of classic studies and publications, its own journal (*Symbolic Interaction*) and a distinctive approach to the study of social order, social actors and social action. On the other hand, it can be used more broadly and more inclusively to refer to the sociological study of social interaction and social encounters, the investigation of microsociological phenomena such as face-to-face interaction, the social construction of selves and identities, the structures of everyday knowledge, and the ordinary routines of mundane activity in social groups and institutions. In a broad sense it can also refer to a related tradition and set of texts, also deriving from Chicago sociology, with a distinctive focus on urban exploration, institutional ethnography, work and occupations, deviance and moral careers.

We shall be dealing with all connotations in this book. Indeed, as we shall try to demonstrate throughout, the attempt to make hard-and-fast distinctions is likely to distort the picture. That is especially true for a discussion of the British context. An 'impure' treatment of interactionist sociology is entirely appropriate when addressing the British context. It is a characteristic of British scholarship more generally that it has a tendency towards eclectic uses of theoretical traditions, and its disciplines are often syncretic in character. It is a feature of a good deal of British intellectual life that schools of thought that elsewhere exist in tightly bounded forms and in relative isolation can flourish in hybrid versions and in close proximity within the same institutional setting.

The British higher education system has traditionally been characterized by strongly classified segments. There are powerful boundaries round and within the academy. Those boundaries create very strong pressures towards academic specialization and subject loyalty. On the other hand, those strong boundaries or membranes – insulating academic disciplines and department from one another – create 'safe havens' within which competing ideas can co-exist and out of which syntheses can arise. Within well defined subject boundaries British academics can work across the frontiers of different

traditions or paradigms, relatively free from constraints of orthodoxy.

The British penchant for synthesis and hybridization is partly a
reflection of institutions and careers. Traditionally, the British academic
could gain a permanent, tenured position much earlier than her or his
American or European counterpart. Despite recent changes in career
structures and labour markets in higher education in the UK, this still
holds broadly true. Nowadays the aspiring academic may have to have
a series of short-term contracts before landing a regular post. But he or
she is unlikely to experience the kind of long-term uncertainty of the
American tenure system. The British lecturer has not had the same pressures as the American assistant professor or the European assistant (in
their various guises). Furthermore, the British pattern of research, especially at doctoral level, has placed greater emphasis on individual scholarship, with much less emphasis on prolonged socialization into particular
schools and traditions. To that extent, therefore, the British academic
has had a distinctive experience of research and academic socialization:
he or she has had the relative freedom to explore and assimilate ideas
from a diverse variety of sources. The cost has been relative isolation in
many cases, as the emphasis on the lone scholar or apprentice can also
prove somewhat anomic. In recent years British social sciences have
developed a 'mid-Atlantic' model of research training that incorporates
some of the more formal training elements that have characterized
American doctoral programmes for many years, but doctoral students
and others still enjoy relatively high degrees of autonomy. While British
university departments have fostered a high degree of subject loyalty
and early specialization, therefore, the fledgling academic has been able
to draw selectively on ideas locally and internationally without restric-
tions of strong collective adherence to particular orthodoxies and traditions. The British social scientist will not have been schooled in the
sacred texts of a particular tradition in as rigorous a fashion as some of
her or his international counterparts. Likewise, he or she is less likely
to be part of a group identified with one leading scholar and one clearly
defined school of thought. Comparatively speaking, British scholars
have not had a strong dependence on patronage and on membership of
a specific coterie. As a consequence, there have been relatively few stable departmental 'schools' of theory.

There is, therefore, a strongly pragmatic bent to the exploration and
use of ideas among British sociologists. Again, this reflects wider intellectual traditions and orientations. This is hardly attributable to a
national characteristic, although several decades ago Perry Anderson
suggested that the culture of British academic life had such a trait.
Anderson (1969) suggested that for a variety of historical reasons – not
least the influx of refugees from totalitarian regimes in Europe – British

academics have been typically suspicious of grand theory. This is reflected in a variety of different disciplines, that have been marked by a sceptical attitude and a firm commitment to empirical investigation rather than abstract theorizing.

It is a consequence of such a general academic style that exotic, foreign ideas can be accommodated through a process of domestication. This is true, for instance, of much European social thought. French structuralist thought was, in British circles, rendered accessible and usable through empirically grounded work. In anthropology, for instance, authors such as Edmund Leach or Mary Douglas used the ideas of Claude Lévi-Strauss as analytic tools rather than being completely seduced by his most general epistemological claims. Similar observations can be made of literary criticism, where authors such as David Lodge or Terry Hawkes took key ideas from the Parisian theorists and adapted them into a more pragmatic and empirical approach to literary criticism. Similar observations can also be made about varieties of Marxist thought: the general and abstract theoretical schemes of authors like Althusser, or the grand analytic sweep of the Frankfurt School have provided inspirations for British authors, but few in the United Kingdom have themselves engaged in such general theorizing. There are, of course, 'theorists' whose work is entirely or primarily theoretical in origin – in the United Kingdom scholars like Anthony Giddens or Zygmunt Bauman come to mind most readily. Their work, however, serves to illustrate the general point. Their work has been eclectic and synthetic. Moreover, there is little direct relationship between such theorizing and the conduct of empirical research. Likewise, the influence of continental European scholars such as Michel Foucault or Jean Baudrillard has frequently been domesticated, and incorporated into empirical research programmes.

We do not mean to imply that all of British intellectual life has been characterized by such an eclectic and pragmatic attitude, but it is a trait that is readily recognizable across many disciplines and departments in the social sciences and humanities. In the social sciences British universities have had relatively few purist groups. We have certainly not had groups working within an exclusively interactionist mode. On the other hand, interactionist sociology has lent itself to an eclectic and pragmatic approach to social inquiry. It is rather different from the kind of generalizing tendency of much 'grand theory' in the social sciences. It does have a coherent set of epistemological, theoretical and methodological precepts, and it has been remarkable for its resilience and durability while other theoretical perspectives have waxed and waned in popularity. Symbolic interactionism and various cognate strands in sociology have been especially adept at generating theoretical ideas of the middle range. Their strength has not resided in the sort of grand overarching theoretical schemas that one might associate with, say, functionalism, structuralism, or Marxism. Its strength lies in the capacity to furnish and replenish the sociologist's conceptual toolkit while engaging directly with the exploration of specific social worlds. It is, therefore, congruent with British sociology's recurrent interest in empirical social research and an eclectic approach to analysing and theorizing.

While relatively few British sociologists have, then, defined themselves and their work in terms of symbolic interactionism – or even a wider framework of interactionist thought – many have drawn on and used the repertoire of ideas that interactionism provides. In many ways, moreover, the most abiding contribution of interactionist thought has been to provide a warrant for empirical research of particular sorts. In its origins in the United States, and in its subsequent development there and elsewhere, the main justification for interactionism has lain in the programmes of work it has inspired. Further, when dealing with interactionist theories, British sociologists have typically done so by locating them within broader intellectual frameworks. They have often treated them as part of a broader stream of interpretative or hermeneutic sociology, or as a contribution to a more general research interest in social interaction and social identities, or as a distinctive contribution to an action-oriented sociological imagination. Whatever the precise mix of intellectual styles, the tendency has been syncretic rather than purist. We shall illustrate and develop this argument with reference to a few key authors later in this chapter. In subsequent chapters we shall also trace the fate of the British reception and interpretation in a number of key themes.

Equally, one must acknowledge that there have been and continue to be points of discontinuity between American interactionism and the recurrent preoccupations of British sociologists. We shall try to develop those aspects as the book unfolds, but it must be acknowledged that British sociologists have, collectively, been dominated by commitments that are not especially well addressed through the interactionist lens. While it is not a necessary equation, interactionism has often been identified with micro-level social analysis. The emphases on selves and identities, on situations and their definitions, on social encounters and their interpersonal management have been interpreted as precluding analysis of social structures, institutions and organizations. A British preoccupation with social inequality and demographic phenomena such as inter-generational social mobility owes very little to the intellectual roots of interactionism. For the origins of British empirical social research are to be found in the history of political arithmetic, with a strongly critical and reformist political ethic. Whether Fabian or more radical, a great deal of social research in the United Kingdom has been focused on the systems of class, race and gender differences that constitute the fabric of inequality in modern society. Variously informed by Weberian analyses of life-chances, Marxist analyses of social relations of production, feminist analyses of the structures of patriarchy, and so on, such analyses have had rather little time for what are too readily perceived as epiphenomenal issues of identity and interpersonal relations.

It is through the conduct of empirical research that interactionism and British sociology have found common interest. The affinity between interactionist sociology and ethnographic research methods has underlined a great deal of empirical research in recent decades. This affinity is not an all-or-nothing relationship. Interactionism does not depend entirely on the methods of ethnographic field research. Equally, ethnographic research can be grounded in a variety of theoretical and methodological approaches. Nevertheless, interactionist research has been a major inspiration for the promotion and development of ethnographic research. Ethnography has, in turn, spread far beyond the confines of interactionist sociology. Again, there has been an eclectic mix of theoretical and methodological traditions. Ideas derived from interactionism have interacted with methodological commitments associated with social and cultural anthropology, feminist scholarship, cultural studies, and the like. Again, therefore, interactionist sociology finds its widest expression not through the promotion of a purist theoretical school, but through a mix of ideas, inspirations and applications in combination with other disciplines and specialisms.

In those senses, then, sociologists in the United Kingdom can reasonably assert that 'we have never been interactionists'. Few have been, if by that we mean being committed to a single-minded pursuit of orthodoxy. There have been few sociologists in the United Kingdom to have espoused symbolic interactionist – or even more general interactionist – ideas exclusively. There have been few institutional groupings, networks, conferences and the like that have celebrated and reproduced interactionist sociology.

If we were never interactionists, then what is the subject matter of this book? Can there be an account of interactionism in British sociology if it has been such a minority interest? As we have indicated already, the impact of interactionism does not lie in the existence of exclusively interactionist research. Rather, it lies in how British sociologists have, at different times and with varying emphases, taken up and used interactionist ideas, and have incorporated them within various programmes of empirical research.

When we search for interactionism's main impacts, therefore, we shall find them in the major fields of empirical research – work and occupations, medicine, education, crime and deviance, for instance – and in the methodological perspectives that have emerged from that

41

research activity. In the course of this book, therefore, we shall examine the major themes that have come together to contribute to the consistent development of empirical research and methodological reflection. In doing so we shall also try to document how interactionism has become refracted through the particular preoccupations of British sociology. Ideas are not translated from one national context to another, or from one intellectual milieu to another, without becoming transformed in the process. Indeed, it is one of the more general lessons to be learned from such an exercise. The translation of ideas from American to British or European research provides an exercise in the sociology of knowledge in its own right.

Each national setting provides a site for the re-contextualization of ideas into a distinctive configuration. The flow of texts and ideas allows for the movement from sites of primary knowledge-production to new, secondary sites of reproduction and syncretic development. Ideas can undergo a series of transformations in that process. They may be simplified; they may become elaborated; they may be given new currency and force; they may be stripped of their original moral connotations and invested with new ones. As we explore the British reception and use of ideas we shall see some aspects of their re-contextualization within the national and intellectual context.

42

Of course, our main aim in this book is not simply to trace the British reception of one strand of predominantly American ideas. The main content of this exploration will be the research itself: how interactionism has informed our understanding of social processes and institutions. In doing so we shall trace a number of major research themes and empirical areas, in order to explore a distinctive British sociological tradition. We argue that there have been a number of recurrent motifs and preoccupations in that research tradition, spanning several decades, that impart a particular flavour to the study of social encounters and social institutions. We believe that the often 'impure' application of interactionist perspectives has not weakened those developments, but has proved a strength. The eclecticism that has marked British interactionism has allowed sociologists in the United Kingdom to draw on its strengths while taking inspiration from a broader intellectual context. In particular, it has fostered a specific tradition in which studies of the interaction order have been embedded in sociological analyses that owe a great deal to the critical and reformist underpinnings of much British sociology.

In this respect the British applications of American interactionism do not depart radically from the intellectual and political origins of symbolic interactionism. Interactionism was not born of an apolitical, de-contextualized research agenda. Nevertheless, the British re-contextualization of interactionist thought has given it a particular flavour – imparting a special stress on issues of social difference and exclusion, or institutionalized prejudice and discrimination. The analyses remain rooted in a sociological imagination that remains committed to analyses of class and gender and to the institutional framing of social encounters. In its British reincarnations, interactionist analysis combines a detailed attention to the interaction order with a sensitivity to more encompassing social phenomena. Again, while not uniquely British, the combination gives interactionist sociology a particular force.

A SECOND CHICAGO SCHOOL AND A FIRST BRITISH SCHOOL?

The force of interactionist sociology was felt in the United Kingdom at a time when sociology in general was expanding, and when the various strands of post-war sociology were beginning to unravel: the taken-for-granted orthodoxies of theory and research practice were, if not supplanted at least complemented by fresh perspectives. It is, incidentally, dangerously easy to over-simplify and exaggerate these points. The 1960s were not an especially 'golden age' for sociology's expansion: there are far more students and academics in British sociology at the end of the century than there were in the 1960s, for all the iconic significance of sociology in the mythology of that earlier period. Equally, it is easy to create a misleading picture of a monolithically orthodox sociology, dominated by functionalist theory and survey methods. Things were never completely dominated by a single paradigm. The fresh views emerged from and celebrated various European and American sources, sometimes being re-discoveries of older traditions rather than novelties in their own right. They included: phenomenology, ethnomethodology, Frankfurt School critical sociology, structuralism, and symbolic interactionism. Those various tendencies and others were certainly part of an intellectual ferment of the 1960s. By this we mean not just the special manifestations of student unrest and dissent in the academy – although they were in part symptomatic of intellectual challenges. Rather, there was a proliferation of theoretical and methodological approaches that both complemented and challenged prevailing orthodoxies. This was by no means confined to academic sociology. The social and cultural disciplines were the sites of remarkable innovation and debate. This was a period of genuine intellectual change, of which the popularization of movements like phenomenology and anti-psychiatry (Laing and Estersen), the Frankfurt School (Marcuse, Fromm), structuralism (Barthes, Lévi-Strauss) was a significant aspect.

Many of these renewed perspectives were not original to the 1960s or 1970s. Many already had a considerable intellectual history. In

43

sociology, for instance, Frankfurt-School critical sociology and social phenomenology were by no means new in themselves. They had pre-war origins. But they were given new impetus and became available to wider circles of students and scholars. Phenomenological sociology, for instance, was given renewed and wider currency by the publication of Berger and Luckmann's *The Social Construction of Reality* (1967) and by other publications of the same period that took up and developed the work of key authors like Alfred Schutz (e.g. 1967) and Maurice Merleau-Ponty (e.g. 1962). In the United Kingdom, key publications by Roche (1973) and others (e.g. Filmer et al., 1972) imparted a new urgency to the rediscovery of that philosophical and sociological tradition. It is noticeable that Roche himself suggests some key affinities between the social psychology of George Herbert Mead and that of Maurice Merleau-Ponty (Roche, 1973: 132-4). In a similarly eclectic spirit, Roche acknowledges the respective contributions of symbolic interactionism, labelling theory and Goffman to a 'humanistic' sociological perspective on psychiatry and mental illness. He thus recognizes a convergence between the phenomenology of, say, Binswanger (1963) and the interactionist tradition. In such intellectual contexts, the work of labelling theorists such as Lemert (1967) or Scheff (1966) was part of a more general intellectual ferment, that also included the work of anti-psychiatrists and other critics of modern treatments of insanity (e.g. Cooper, 1968, 1971; Szasz, 1962, 1971).

Much the same is true for interactionist sociology. Its intellectual roots were as old as the twentieth century, and in the United States there was a continuing tradition of symbolic interactionism, with significant centres of research and publication, a substantial body of empirical research, its own professional society, and even distinct 'schools' within it (the Chicago and the Iowa Schools in particular). Yet the reception of interactionist thought in the United Kingdom was not rooted in quite the same tradition. In many ways it derived from the influence of members of the so-called 'second Chicago School' of symbolic interactionism that had developed and was continuing to develop – not just in the Department of Sociology at the University of Chicago itself, but in other American institutions, in the Mid-West and in the University of California system. This was combined with and reinforced by the reception of work that was, if not 'symbolic interactionist' in the pure sense, readily assimilated to an intellectual project to re-focus sociological inquiry on the interaction order and – more broadly still – on an interpretative perspective, with an emphasis on the close scrutiny of forms of social action and the sociology of everyday life. In this melting pot of ideas and empirical research the work of Erving Goffman was a significant point of reference and an inspiration for many pieces of empirical research. Indeed, it was one of the strengths of interactionist work that is adherents were relatively indifferent to doctrinal disputes within and between different schools and approaches, and were thus able to assimilate ideas from rather different traditions in the construction of an interactionist sociology.

As we have already suggested, the influence of phenomenological and existential perspectives was also significant. Authors like Berger and Luckmann were drawing on very different intellectual traditions from the symbolic interactionists in the United States. The phenomenological movement was grounded in European philosophy, with rather different German and French strands. But in its sociological guise – especially when applied to empirical research interests – it had important resonances with key themes in interactionist thought. Likewise, the early work in and proximate to ethnomethodology was readily assimilated to the broader sweep of work that began to come together in the 1960s.

The American influences percolated through various routes and channels. It was not altogether unlike the influence of some American music. While mainstream popular music reached Britain through equally mainstream media and the commercial activities of record labels, less mainstream music such as blues, rhythm-and-blues or soul came through more personal routes and via more peripheral entry points such as ports (such as Liverpool). So the Americanizing influence of interactionism, together with the English-language secondary sources on phenomenology, had multiple points of entry, often on the basis of just a few individuals and a few personal contacts. The combined effect of Goffman was less obscure in origin. His major works such as *Stigma*, *Asylums*, and *The Presentation of Self in Everyday Life* were commercial successes. Published in paperback by Penguin they achieved something of the status of 'cross-over' books, migrating from specialist academic reading lists to becoming general trade books.

The initial impact of interactionist sociology was to be felt in major areas of empirical research that were themselves undergoing rapid change and expansion towards the end of the 1960s and early 1970s. They included: the sociology of crime and deviance; the sociology of education and professional socialization; the sociology of health and medicine. The intellectual impact arrived primarily – though by no means exclusively – through the application and extension of interactionist methods and concepts to a diverse array of social problems, settings, institutions and processes. It was, and continues to be, one of the abiding strengths of interactionist work that it remains close to the 'coal face' of empirical research, and so often bypasses the more arid terrain of theoretical exegesis and the recapitulation of sacred texts. In comparison with other domains in the social and cultural disciplines, interactionism has – mercifully –

45

been fairly free from the vacuous and scholastic poring over the founding fathers and mothers. While secondary texts and expositions of major theorists do exist, of course, within the field as a whole they have never substituted for the real work of research and the exploration of actual social worlds.

The sociological study of deviance was one key domain in which interactionist and related ideas were significant in the UK context. An institutional focus was the National Deviancy Conference. The collection of papers edited by Stan Cohen (1971) gives a very clear representation of the work of the later 1960s and early 1970s, and includes contributions by major British scholars in the field (Jock Young, Maureen Cain, Mary McIntosh, Ian Taylor, Max Atkinson, Mike Hepworth, Laurie Taylor and Paul Walton). The general spirit of the collection is permeated by American influences, including those of interactionism and labelling theory. The editor and the contributing authors positioned themselves in contrast to the then prevailing criminological perspective – attempting to define the particular characteristics and predispositions of deviants – by exploring the processes of societal reaction and deviance amplification, the meanings of deviant acts, the socially organized processes of becoming deviant and the pervasiveness of deviant actions. These perspectives were explicitly indebted to the American literature, most notably interactionism and closely related perspectives (e.g. Becker, 1963, 1964; Lemert, 1967; Matza, 1964, 1969; Rubington and Weinberg, 1968). Goffman (1961, 1963) also featured prominently. Becker's work on deviance was especially influential, capturing the interest of a generation of students as well as engaging researchers. It brought to the attention of many outside the United States the general style and substance of second Chicago School interactionism.

While interactionist ideas informed the emergent sociology of deviance in the United Kingdom, they were rarely transported unalloyed into the British intellectual context. British research, for instance, retained a strong sense of social class and an abiding interest in working-class cultures. For example, within the programme of deviance research there was a strong commitment to themes of resistance and the expressive order of working-class identity. Among the National Deviancy Conference papers already referred to, Ian Taylor (1971) explored processes of societal reaction and deviance amplification in response to the phenomenon of soccer hooliganism, and he also discussed the topic in terms of supporters' resistance and estrangement from a game increasingly dominated by millionaire directors, commercial sponsors and the mass media. Laurie Taylor and Paul Walton (1971) described acts of 'industrial sabotage' in terms of their meanings for workers, which could include attempts to render work more manageable – tampering with industrial processes to render them easier and quicker – or attempts on the part of workers to assert control in the workplace.

The British studies of deviance did not, then, deal exclusively with the purely 'interactionist' wing of Chicago-inspired sociology. Influence was also drawn from the ecological strand of urban sociology: Mays (1954) and Parker (1974), both working in Liverpool, located deviance within local urban territories, their material and cultural circumstances. The National Deviancy group were certainly not defined solely or even primarily in terms of interactionist tendencies. The Conference umbrella drew together a loose coalition of interests, including Marxists and phenomenologists (Sumner, 1994). In the UK the study of deviance gave rise to a series of influential monographs, the impact of which went beyond the specialist study of deviance *per se* and were themselves eclectic in intellectual style. Young's account of illicit drug use in London (Young, 1971) is 'steeped in interactionism' (Hobbs, 2001: 209), but is eclectic in terms of data and theorization. So too is Cohen's (1973) study of mods and rockers and the 'moral panics' that derived from the dramatization of their symbolic and physical antagonism. This too deployed interactionism within a more diverse theoretical framework that took account of class differences and the meanings of subcultural style.

Interactionist ideas were also introduced via the study of educational settings. Among the most influential of American resources were also the American interactionist studies of higher education and professional socialization. The work deriving from the second Chicago School was especially influential. *Boys in White* (Becker et al., 1961) was a type case for making sense of student cultures in educational settings. So too was the same group's monograph on undergraduate students, *Making the Grade* (Becker et al., 1968a). The former was especially influential for those working on professional socialization and professional knowledge (e.g. Atkinson, 1981). To those influences was added the equally important study of nurses' professional socialization, *The Silent Dialogue*, by Olesen and Whittaker (1968). What did these sources have in common? They reported detailed, long-term ethnographic field research in educational and professional settings. They documented how students took an active role in shaping their own work and effort. Of the medical students, for instance, Becker and his colleagues wrote how they set their own 'level and direction of effort'. That is, in terms explicitly derived from industrial sociology, how students collectively negotiated strategies to limit the volume of work they faced to manageable proportions, and how they were selective in what they concentrated their efforts on. These aspects of student culture resonated with the themes of research on students in higher education from outside interactionist circles – notably Snyder's work on students at

MIT. Snyder wrote in terms of 'selective negligence' to capture how even the most highly motivated and selected students at an elite institution could engage in a kind of 'soldiering' (to use another phrase derived from shop-floor studies) in order to engineer an unofficial or alternative subculture that ran counter to the explicit expectations of faculty members.

The interactionist contribution that was derived from these classic works of Chicago was rapidly incorporated into the Edinburgh University programme, together with other influences that derived from elsewhere. Several of the group (including Delamont, Atkinson and Torode) were graduates of social anthropology from Cambridge. Michael Stubbs brought a background in linguistics (also from Cambridge) and the developing specialism of discourse analysis. His work on the discourse structures of classroom pedagogy was a pioneering contribution to the formal analysis of spoken interaction in such an institutional setting. Brian Torode's interests brought an early acquaintance with ethnomethodology, together with the phenomenology and existential sociology that we have already referred to. Symbolic interactionism was introduced through the increasing availability of texts and anthologies. Notable among the latter were the collections of classic papers and contemporary research exemplars edited by Manis and Meltzer (1967) and by Rose (1962). The appearance of those volumes did a great deal to disseminate the American tradition and its more recent applications in substantive fields of research, such as work and occupations, socialization and subcultures.

Here it is worth recollecting that there was no indigenous interactionist tradition available to younger British researchers. There was probably less transatlantic contact than in some other areas (such as deviance studies). Many of the British students and younger academics had no formal training in interactionist sociology. Indeed, some were drawn from disciplines other than sociology. The Edinburgh group were perhaps unusual in having so many with first degrees in anthropology (though there were plenty of other research students in the same group with backgrounds in other subjects too) but in general it was by no means uncommon for research students and others to come to sociology from other disciplinary backgrounds. Hence an eclectic assimilation of ideas, refracted through the needs and interests of empirical research rather than purist theorizing was a shared characteristic.

The way in which a broadly interactionist sensitivity was infused into the field is perfectly illustrated in Sara Delamont's (1976) synoptic view of school and classroom research *Interaction in the Classroom*. This presented a thoroughly interactionist synthesis of the emerging speciality of classroom research, and in turn helped to promote the reception of such ideas in the United Kingdom and beyond. Drawing on Goffman and Chicago School authors, richly illustrated from her own and others' fieldwork in school classrooms, Delamont portrayed the school classroom as a site of self-presentation on the part of teachers and pupils, and as an arena in which a precarious negotiated order is generated, sustained or threatened. The classroom is portrayed as an interactionally busy setting, where pedagogical and other relationships are forged through the enforced intimacy of schools and classrooms. This interactionist view of classroom realities stood in sharp contrast to more behaviourist accounts generated from social psychology.

At about the same time as the Edinburgh University group were incorporating and developing interactionist work on educational settings, a similar movement was being promoted and disseminated through the Open University. From time to time the OU has been in a position to encourage and foster particular perspectives. Its distance learning materials have been distributed widely and have reached readerships even beyond the large number of registered students. During the earlier years of the Open University the use of television and radio programmes was a prominent part of its distance-learning strategy. Courses and degrees in Education were a significant part of the OU's output from its inception: many of the early student cohorts were drawn from the teaching profession. The early OU courses and associated course materials did much to encourage the appearance in the UK of American interactionist and other interpretative work, including phenomenological and early ethnomethodological perspectives. The Open University academics themselves were, of course, far from being passive transmitters of those influences. Figures such as Martyn Hammersley and Peter Woods, together with later colleagues, did a great deal to develop empirical research of their own, working on educational settings in an explicitly interactionist vein. Hammersley in particular went on to make major contributions to the methodological literature of ethnography and interactionism, not least through his work on Blumer (which we discuss elsewhere in this book). The Open University thus provided a locus and a mechanism for the diffusion of interpretative sociological ideas. One of the earliest edited collection of previously published papers ('readers') brought together a rich mélange of sources that were exciting and influential: *School and Society* included a wide range of sources – interactionist and phenomenological work being especially well represented. It helped to bring these intellectual perspectives to a wide readership in the United Kingdom and helped shape the research climate for a generation. Its contents well beyond the specific subject matter of schooling, including a large variety of background theoretical contributions.

It must also be acknowledged, however, that the general climate in which these interactionist ideas were developed was highly variegated.

49

Here, as in other contexts, phenomenology and ethnomethodology were part of the mixture. There was an important London axis, institutionally based at Goldsmiths College and at the Institute of Education. Their interests were partly aligned with those of the more overtly interactionist researchers, not least in their shared aversion to the dominant sociological approach to education – especially a systems-oriented approach that attempted to identify the antecedents of educational success, the determinants of educational failure, the impact of educational attainment on occupational destination and social mobility. The London group drew on phenomenological perspectives, in stressing the need to address the social construction of student ability and the construction of pedagogical knowledge. Processes of interaction in educational settings were part of the research agenda, but a wider array of theoretical perspectives were brought to bear. The construction and reproduction of educational knowledge were a central plank in this collective approach. The collection of papers edited by Michael F.D. Young (1971) was in effect the manifesto for this grouping. Containing papers by Basil Bernstein and Pierre Bourdieu – that owed more to a Durkheimian or structuralist heritage than anything else (Atkinson, 1985) – as well as more phenomenologically inspired chapters (notably by M.F.D. Young himself), this was a coalition of mixed interests. They included a Marxist element – most significantly addressing the problem of educational knowledge as a form of commodity, alienated from students and teachers alike. These innovative approaches were, however, constituents of a British sociological climate in which various forms of interpretative inquiry – including interactionist-inspired work – could take root and flourish.

The impact of interactionist thought on empirical research in the United Kingdom has been especially evident in the sociology of medical settings. The sociology of medicine (more latterly referred to as the sociology of health and illness) has been numerically the most vigorously flourishing fields of British sociology since the early 1970s. It has been marked by a consistent output of empirical research studies, many of them based on ethnographic research and a broadly interactionist inspiration. Its themes have included the systematic study of medical encounters and their moral order. Medical settings have been explored as sites of moral work as well as technical professional decision-making. Indeed, one of the significant contributions of the sociological tradition has been to demonstrate the intersection of technical and moral work. The clinic has been characterized as the outcome of social interactions through which medical and personal identities are ascribed and negotiated. Technical processes of medical diagnosis and management intersect with the construction of moral categories.

While the sociological analysis of medical settings and clinical encounters developed in multiple centres in the United Kingdom, the University of Aberdeen was the home of the most influential single grouping in the 1970s. More precisely, it was the research unit funded there by the Medical Research Council. This was directed by Raymond Illsley, who encouraged a younger generation of researchers to develop a distinctive sociological imagination within the empirical domain of medical settings. It was by no means exclusively interactionist in inspiration or qualitative in research strategy. Its origins lay with more epidemiologically oriented work, associated with the study of birth-cohorts in Aberdeen under the influence of the obstetrician Sir Dougal Baird. There developed a school of sociologists who developed a recognizably consistent approach to the conduct of medical sociology, who were in the forefront of UK ethnographic research, and whose ideas played a pervasive role in the formation of the sociology of health and illness in the United Kingdom more generally. (The MRC unit itself migrated to Glasgow in later years, where it continues to be a major centre of excellence; Scotland more widely retains a strong influence in the sociology of medicine, health and illness.) The generation of researchers in Aberdeen included Sally Macintyre (Illsley's successor as director in its newer Glasgow incarnation), Philip Strong, Alan Davis, Michael Bloor, Mildred Blaxter, Margaret Voysey. Michael Bloor's essay on the ethnography of medical settings helps to convey some of the intellectual atmosphere of the Medical Sociology Unit, where the interactionist ideas of Goffman and the second Chicago School were part of the intellectual stimulation of the environment (Bloor, 2001). Bloor specifically cites the interactionist hospital ethnographies *Boys in White* (Becker et al., 1961), *Psychiatric Ideologies and Institutions* (Strauss et al., 1964), and *Timetables* (Roth, 1963). Goffman's *Asylums* had been republished by Penguin in the UK (Goffman, 1961), and exerted considerable influence at Aberdeen (as elsewhere among British social scientists). Eliot Freidson's *Profession of Medicine* (1970) – also a product of the second Chicago School preoccupation with work and occupations – if not precisely a symbolic interactionist ethnography – was also influential. Bloor also cites David Sudnow's ethnographic account of the construction of death in American hospital settings, *Passing On* (Sudnow, 1967), that also helps illustrate the joint influences of Chicago and social phenomenology – a combination that in the early 1970s was seen as a perfectly obvious approach to interpretative sociology, and one that was reflected in Bloor's own work (Bloor, 1997).

In these areas of empirical research, therefore, one can readily see the considerable influence of broad interactionism – with a much stronger influence of the second Chicago School work of Becker, Geer, Hughes, Strauss and others, together with the very considerable impact

51

of Erving Goffman's work on the interaction order. We shall return to these and other studies in the following chapters, where we deal with recurrent themes in British interactionist and cognate research. The impact of American research in this vein was also felt – and perhaps has its most lasting influence – in the context of research methods, where earlier Chicago traditions were also invoked in justifying and legitimating aspects of ethnographic research. There were direct personal influences as well as the more diffuse impact of trans-Atlantic flows of literature. Howard Becker, Anselm Strauss and Julius Roth were among the American scholars to spend time at British universities. Virginia Olesen maintained close working relationships with a network of British researchers, mainly in the sociology of health and illness and feminist studies. The influence of interactionist work helped to give considerable impetus to the development of lively research traditions at a time when British sociology was undergoing a period of growth and revitalization. The contributions were by no means confined to the empirical areas we have just discussed, but they were certainly among the most lively and populous of the research fields to benefit from interactionist ideas, and from a wider range of interpretative sociological perspectives. They helped in turn to lead to a British sociology that was marked by high levels of empirical research, often with an explicit interest in classic themes of interactionism, and grounded in a vigorous tradition of field research.

52

In later chapters we shall be returning to some of these earlier themes and studies, and also tracing some of the succeeding work, in order to trace some of the most important analytic themes. Our remarks so far in this chapter are not intended to be comprehensive historical overviews of the reception and use of interactionist sociology in the United Kingdom. At this point we aim to provide an introductory gloss on how and where some of the ideas made their way into British sociology. They help to set the scene for the more detailed descriptions that follow. They also illustrate our contention that 'pure' interactionism has not been a widespread feature of the British sociological landscape. From the outset, interactionist and related ideas were assimilated within a matrix of more diverse sociological perspectives. These included various approaches to interpretative sociological thinking, some of which included interactionism, while others did not. Again, we illustrate some of these approaches in the section that follows.

INTERPRETATIVE SOCIOLOGY

The theoretical reception of interactionism in the United Kingdom can be understood against a more general background of theoretical analysis.

They include the work of Zygmunt Bauman, the contributions of Arthur Brittan, the meta-theoretical framework of Alan Dawe, and the reception of Goffman. In different ways these themes illustrate how ideas have received distinctive treatment in the United Kingdom.

One of Bauman's theoretical exegeses outlines a series of contributions to what he glosses as 'hermeneutic sociology' (Bauman, 1978). Under this rubric he collects a series of theoretical schools that share significant family resemblances. He does not include symbolic interactionism within this tradition. He deals with a broadly defined sociology of knowledge that includes Karl Mannheim, Alfred Schutz and Harold Garfinkel. He does not dissolve the distinctive characteristics of each theoretical school, but he does emphasize a broad continuity of social theory that incorporates symbolic interactionism together with other theoretical strands. The broad sweep of hermeneutic sociological theory represents a major line of continuity that runs through all of modern sociological thought, from the *verstehen* tradition that derives from Dilthey and Weber, and continues in various disguises onwards throughout the twentieth century. The *verstehen* or interpretative tradition is concerned with the intentionality of social action, with the motivation of social actors, and the socially shared systems of meaning through which concerted social action is undertaken and understood. This is a tradition that was given a particular direction by the phenomenological movement. A number of theorists contrived a synthesis of *verstehen* sociology with ideas derived from the philosophical tradition founded by Edmund Husserl. In doing so they transformed many of the philosophical ideas, transforming them into analytic tools for sociological analysis. Alfred Schutz made the most sustained of such contributions. He explicitly grounded his work in Weberian sociology. A starting point is the Weberian emphasis on social action. Action is distinguished from mere behaviour. The latter is an unmotivated response, whereas action is meaningful. Schutz developed the Weberian approach by incorporating and adapting Husserlian phenomenology, to the effect that the interpretation of social action necessarily directs analytic attention to the character of everyday life and common-sense reasoning. There is, therefore, a major emphasis on the methods and structures of everyday life and mundane reason. Schutz insisted, for instance, that everyday social actors engage in the construction of typifications: the creation of ideal types is not the preserve of the social analyst. The sociologist develops secondary analytic constructs that take account of the primary constructs of everyday life. Everyday life is, therefore, the domain of social phenomenology. This is the world of immediate social relations. It is a world of shared experience, or reciprocal perceptions and perspectives between social actors. Bauman's collection of sociologies under the rubric of hermeneutic theory is

53

characteristic of a particular period of British sociological writing. It is synthetic, and it draws together American and European strands of thought. It identifies this broad strand of interpretative or hermeneutic sociological reasoning. Notwithstanding Bauman's complete neglect of the Meadian and Chicago tradition (there is but passing reference to Znaniecki), his book is symptomatic of the intellectual context of the British reception for much interactionist work. Later in the book, we shall also note how the content of Bauman's own writing has altered in the intervening years, suggesting that this general shift is also symptomatic of the treatment (and partial neglect) of key ideas in interpretative sociology in contemporary writing.

Similar observations can be made of the contribution of Alan Dawe (1967). Regrettably, his contribution to the published work of British sociology was curtailed. But his ideas were undoubtedly influential, not least his thesis of the 'two sociologies'. He argued that there were two countervailing tendencies in sociology, that had been there from its earliest years, and that continued to colour sociological thought throughout the twentieth century. He called these polar types theories of 'constraint' and 'control'. He suggested that each of these ideal-typical emphases did not separately characterize theorists or theoretical schools. Rather, he suggested that there was a constant tension or dialectic between the two. Sometimes social theory could veer toward one polar type, and at others could be steered in the opposite direction. Moreover, constraint and control could be said to represent different alternating or contending tendencies within any given school of thought, or indeed within the *œuvre* of any one major theorist. Indeed, given their ubiquity and their longevity, one might even suppose that sociology itself is constituted out of the forces generated between these two poles. By theories of 'constraint' Dawe meant sociological ideas that placed primary stress on impersonal or supra-individual social or historical laws, forces, or structures that constrain the actions and identities of social actors. Such ideas are likely to be couched in terms of social systems and inexorable social processes. By contrast, theories of 'control' emphasize the degree of autonomy of the social actor, exercising control over her or his own social action (the term 'control' itself is potentially confusing, of course, as notions of social control are likely to engender notions of coercion rather than relative autonomy). Constraint ideas portray the individual as a social product; control ideas portray society as a collective achievement. In the former, the social actor is the incumbent of a position or role that is defined in terms of the overall social system; in the latter, the actor is engaged in a creative process of self-creation – role-making rather than role-taking. Dawe did not use his polar types to classify different types of sociology. As we have said, he suggested that they represented an abiding tension within the discipline as a whole. Clearly some constellations of theoretical ideas stressed one or other more strongly. They could also characterize different aspects of the same author's work – early Marx versus late Marx, or the Talcott Parsons of social-action theory versus the Parsons of social-systems theory, for instance. Dawe's collection of various strands of social thought under the rubric of 'control' helped to crystallize a response to and reception of a series of influential ideas, all of which could be counterposed against theories of social structure and constraint. They provided, along with the rubric of interpretivism or hermeneutics, a rhetoric for the promotion of such ideas. They chimed with other inspirations – such as those provided by Berger and Luckmann – that suggested the possibility of a sociology of action, of meaning, of everyday life and conduct. They equally suggested a sociology that was much more engaging than anything offered in the sterile discourse of structural-functionalism, or the dry facts of Fabian political arithmetic. Moreover, they provided intellectual means to undermine those positions.

We are not suggesting, incidentally, that Dawe's work was in any sense unique in pointing out the dualisms at the heart of the sociological endeavour. In his own influential work – *Meanings and Situations* (1973) – Arthur Brittan pointed out that such contrasts were ubiquitous in sociology, whether between positivism versus idealism, or structure versus process. He stresses the continuity between the German tradition of cultural disciplines and their profound difference from the natural sciences. In doing so he invokes a tradition of humanistic sociology, which in turn means that 'The empirical world which sociologists study is the world of symbols, meanings and consciousness' (ibid.: 18). In this he aligns himself with Herbert Blumer, arguing that sociological inquiry must be faithful to and respectful of the social world, A given social world can only be understood in its own terms, Brittan argues – and that means 'an interactive symbolic world where men [*sic*] are capable of interpreting their own conduct, as well as interpreting other people's conduct' (ibid.: 19). Brittan's inspiration clearly incorporates not just Blumer, but also the general spirit of symbolic interactionism. He also relates his commitment to interpretivism and phenomenology.

Brittan's account of symbolic reality and social interaction is not confined to a recapitulation of symbolic interactionism, however. His argument proceeds through a dialogue with Simmel among others. Brittan uses symbolic interactionist ideas to develop Simmel's formalist account of patterns of social interaction. He canvasses several models of interaction. From Goffman, Burke, Mead and Duncan he constructs a general account of interaction as drama – not just the dramaturgical metaphor of Goffman's self-presentations, but a more general sense of the social as tragic or comic enactment. Likewise, he explores the dimensions of interaction that reflect game, exchange, strategy and power. Here too the approach is eclectic – including Garfinkel as well as Goffman, Homans and Blau. Brittan is critical of any and all models of interaction and the self that are unduly behaviouristic, ignoring the principle of reflexivity, and that are unduly rationalistic. He argues for a perspective that retains the Meadian insistence on reflexivity and that allows for the emotional aspects of intentions and actions. Perhaps the most significant aspect of Brittan's work is his treatment of interaction as the negotiation of identity. Models of identity creation suggest, Brittan argues, that a fragmentation of the self is an inescapable consequence of the social conditions of contemporary modern society: 'Today, the rate of geographic and social mobility is so great that I never have the opportunity to establish social relationships of any great duration or meaning' (ibid.: 165). The relationships between interaction, selves and social fragmentation are the culminating themes of Brittan's book. He is in fact sceptical about the wider implications of the fragmentation thesis, and enters reservations concerning the construction of the self as a microcosm of society writ large. Brittan also argues against the over-socialization of the self to the extent that the psychological and the emotional are entirely subsumed under social constructions. Indeed, citing Dennis Wrong's arguments concerning over-socialized views of the social actor, Brittan insists that the 'body' (in a very general sense) must not be erased from the sociological account of selves and the social. Brittan's stance is a shifting one. He is not an advocate or a spokesperson for any one theoretical school. He draws together American and European thought in exploring different models of social interaction and self creation. Interactionism is but one of the perspectives that is treated sympathetically but critically in that conceptual exploration.

The same can be said of Brittan's other work in a similar vein. In *The Privatised World* (1977) Brittan deploys a wide variety of theoretical frameworks. Again, he draws on a wide variety of ideas and theoretical perspectives; they include phenomenology, Meadian interactionism, and Goffman. Brittan returns to the theme of fragmentation, now in the context of a discussion of the privatization of everyday life in contemporary society. The humanistic sociology of everyday life and the construction of the self are thus embedded in a much broader consideration of embourgeoisement, the division of labour and the divide between the private and public realms. Brittan argues that the emergence of sociological interest in the self, biography and consciousness was itself a reflection of the cultural significance of the privatized world for sociologists and other intellectuals in modern societies. The sociological interest is thus symptom and diagnosis simultaneously.

In both these major works of the 1970s, then, Brittan offers a critically sympathetic reading of interactionist ideas alongside a range of others. He does far more than recapitulate and celebrate any one of the theoretical positions he examines. He retains a critical faculty in addressing them all. He ranges widely: Marx and Marxists; phenomenologists and ethnomethodologists; interactionists and Goffman. He uses these ideas to reconstruct humanistic or interpretative sociology, while remaining attentive to the social conditions that give rise to such a sociology itself. In this wide-ranging and synthetic approach, therefore, Brittan is characteristic of British approaches to social theory.

These broader treatments of interactionism are characteristic of non-American perspectives. Authors from the United Kingdom, Europe and elsewhere have been less directly implicated in the contested loyalties and mythologies of their American counterparts. They have, therefore, been relatively more free to explore the broader picture and to transgress the boundaries of specific traditions. Goff (1980) looks boldly at a synthesis of George Herbert Mead and Karl Marx. Goff suggests that there is the possibility of a critical sociology of knowledge that draws on the two figures, despite their apparently very different orientations. Goff concludes that both authors construct human actors as men and women of 'praxis':

57

> That is to say that his [sic] reality is a reality of dialectical engagement with the world in an active, self-conscious and co-operative process of producing what is required to maintain the species or to fulfil needs. It is to recognize that man [sic] creates what he requires: conceptions of his physical world, objects of consumption, technologies, forms of co-operation or social, institutional structures. Furthermore, the idea of praxis contains the recognition that these products are and remain contingent and passing, and that man is capable, through his emergent reflexive capacity, of the necessary refashioning of his products whether this be as a result of the experience of problematics or of the recognition of new potentialities implicit in the present mode or production. (1980: 113)

Such a perspective, that also engages critically with Durkheim, Mannheim and other significant themes in the sociology of knowledge, inserts Meadian pragmatism into the mainstream of European sociological thought.

THE FUSION OF THEORY AND METHOD

It was very much in that spirit that interactionism made its first impact in British sociology: as part of an eclectic programme of interpretative sociology, with a strong emphasis on empirical research in fields of empirical inquiry. The ideas of interactionism, not least its repertoire of middle-range analytic concepts, fed directly into the rapidly expanding research programmes of British sociology in the 1960s and 1970s. In turn they encouraged a particular style of research, with particular emphasis on qualitative field research. Although there was never a single 'paradigm' in play at any given time, British sociologists – like their counterparts in Chicago and California – espoused a broadly ethnographic approach to the detailed exploration of social institutions, encounters, careers and identities. The fusion of theory and research, for instance, was the key feature that Robin Williams identified as the defining characteristic of symbolic interactionism (Williams, 1976) although he is far from uncritical in his discussion of the notions of 'theory' embedded in the formulations of 'grounded theory'. Williams was one of the relatively few British sociologists to discuss seriously the inspirations of interactionist sociology for the practice of sociological research (see also Williams, 1981).

Taken in conjunction with phenomenological and other radical inspirations, interactionism also fed the growing popularity of constructivist perspectives on knowledge and belief. The British interactionists repeatedly documented the 'social construction' of problems, facts, diagnoses and dispositions, across a wide variety of professional and organizational settings. This was a characteristically eclectic approach, owing much to the inspiration of Alfred Schutz and to the emergent ideas that became associated more firmly with ethnomethodology.

It would, however, be wrong to attribute everything to the importation of ideas from the United States or elsewhere. Some British sociologists might with reason disclaim any close affiliation with American symbolic interactionism. The institutional manifestations of the distinctively American school of thought have never taken deep root in British academic circles. There has never been a branch of the Society for the Study of Symbolic Interaction, despite one or two tentative attempts to create one. More significantly, there has never been a core set of devotees to disseminate the ideas and to recruit disciples in academic departments in the United Kingdom. As we have suggested already, interactionism has made itself felt through its practical application in empirical research. It has not been received and reproduced primarily as a major theoretical tradition alongside the major European schools of thought. Mead and his successors enjoy a somewhat uncertain place in the Anglo–European canons of social theory. Equally, influential ethnographic work, such as that of Willis (1977) was conducted independently of the interactionist tradition (see Willis, 2001).

To that extent, therefore, the British might well claim that 'we have never been interactionists'. For there have been few single-minded adherents of symbolic interactionism *per se*. On the other hand, the

58

influence of interactionist thought has been consistently fruitful in British empirical research. At a time when key areas of empirical research were developing and expanding, interactionism was among the newer and fresher of the influential sets of ideas. The rapid growth of deviancy studies, for instance, or the extraordinary expansion of the sociology of medicine, or the development of research on educational processes, or the close examination of scientific knowledge and work – these were all nourished, sometimes indirectly, by a broadly interactionist sociological imagination.

The strength of those influences and links lies primarily in their somewhat diffuse and pragmatic nature. If few of the British sociologists felt total allegiance to a purely interactionist theoretical perspective, then their empirical research was less subject to the changing fads and fashions that so often characterize theoretical disputation in the social and cultural disciplines. Symbolic interactionism was never an especially voguish theory. It lacked the continental chic of European ideas, the moral fervour of critical stances, or the outrage of ethnomethodology. It has had fewer enthusiasts than, say, Althusserian structuralism or Foucauldian post-structuralism. One could indeed argue that it has been marked by a distinct lack of enthusiasm and fervour by even its most loyal exponents. Unlike some of the more modish positions it has rarely been proclaimed as *the* answer to sociology's problems. It has never enjoyed that reductive or totalizing effect whereby its adherents have proclaimed it as the *ne plus ultra* of sociological thought. Its merits have been sought and proposed in more downbeat ways. Its virtues have been demonstrated through research rather than through theoretical systems. Interactionism thus stands in sharp contrast with those essentially empty modes of sociological discourse enunciated by authors conspicuous by their virtually complete innocence of empirical inquiry. Interactionism does not commend itself readily to those 'theorists' who theorize in the absence of direct exploration of social realities or sustained experience of research activity.

Equally, however, we shall go on to argue towards the end of this book that many of the ideas that are *au courant* at the end of the twentieth century and the start of the twenty-first, and that are often celebrated as especially novel, owe much to the general perspectives of interactionist thought. Many of those insights that are categorized as 'postmodern', implying a discontinuity with the past, display considerable continuity with the interactionist tradition. Often the apparent novelty of postmodernity reflects authors' and students' relative ignorance of the past rather than genuine novelty. It is, after all, easier to re-invent past ideas and claim them as new-found land than it is to pay one's dues to past thinkers and previous research. Contemporary sociological literature is populated by the work of semi-scholars who adopt just one

59

fashionable author (Foucault, Baudrillard, Beck, Giddens) or one fashionable concept (postmodernity, globalization, post-structuralism). They can then save themselves from the irksome business of knowing about a wide variety of other ideas; they can claim that the world of significant ideas began with 'their' school or sprang fully armed from the head of their particular parent figure. (Such semi-scholarship almost always does a disservice to those founding figures, who almost always have wider views and greater historical depth than simplifications and adulations imply.)

Although this book is not the right vehicle in which to explore this theme in any detail, any observer of a major substantive field in the discipline should have noticed the transformations in terminology that indicate the shifting allegiances of fellow sociologists. Apparently identical phenomena become invested with special significance through the adoption of newer and newer vocabularies. Successive generations will bring 'hegemony' or 'discourse' to bear where once they or others were content to talk of 'power' and 'culture'. In the process ideas and their origins are submerged beneath a palimpsest of ill-digested concepts and 'theories'. That fate has overtaken a good deal of interactionist inspiration. Interactionist ideas have been rediscovered, renamed and appropriated in the process of theoretical recycling. That is not to imply that interactionism is 'really' the *fons et origo* of many contemporary ideas. In fact, of course, there is a constant flux of ideas. There is a generalized exchange of concepts and terms between different schools of thought and among different research centres. Ideas and their justifications are particular to national cultures and to different generations of scholars. When we return to this particular theme towards the end of the book, therefore, we shall not argue that the key ideas of, say, postmodernism or post-structuralism were all pre-empted by interactionist sociology. But we do suggest that there are many affinities that are too rarely acknowledged. We shall also propose, therefore, that contemporary European sociologists (including the British) could learn something from a sympathetic and constructive reading of interactionist research. The relative neglect of authors like Everett Hughes and Erving Goffman – despite the influence of substantial published output in their lifetimes – is a waste of our shared intellectual capital. Authors with the quality of sociological imagination they had to offer should not be discarded in the frantic search for novelty or because a small number of influential synthesizers neglect them in their secondary works of sociological exegesis.

Interactionist sociology was never universally accepted in British sociology, even within the framework of newly constituted interpretative or humanistic sociology. By no means all British sociologists were receptive to it. Some were explicitly dismissive of interactionism in particular and interpretative-humanistic sociology in general. In his early work, for instance, Giddens had little time for sociological perspectives on what he described as the 'triviata' [*sic*] of everyday life. His early commitment to the exegesis of classic sociological theory left virtually no room for interactionism or any cognate sociological work. His dismissive attitude is all the more striking in retrospect, given that he is one of the most obvious examples of sociological theorists rediscovering key themes in interactionist thought without due acknowledgement of their sources. We return to this topic later in the book. Here we note simply that Giddens was merely one among many sociologists who paid little serious attention to interactionism in the 1960s or 1970s, or who did so only in order to attack any influence it might exert. In one of his many general treatments of sociological theory, for instance, Giddens had little to say about symbolic interactionism beyond rather faint praise for Mead's identification of the reflexive self, and a much stronger dismissal of the tradition for its inadequate treatment of social structure (Giddens, 1984). One would not know from such slighting (and slight) discussions that there was a substantial body of work from Chicago and elsewhere that was precisely aimed at a sociological analysis of selves and institutions, or that examined the personal and interpersonal consequences of major historical transformations. Because Giddens decontextualized aspects of interactionism, he assumed that the sociology itself was equally lacking in historical or social context. We shall return to the work of Giddens later, where we discuss the transformations in sociological thought that seem to have incorporated interactionist ideas, while paying scant attention to their interactionist origins – a point where our argument is reunited with that of Maines (2001).

61

The most frequent form in which such attacks were mounted came from British sociologists committed to a methodology derived from the political-arithmetic tradition, and who were guided by Marxist or Fabian intellectual commitments. Seen from such a perspective, interactionism could seem divorced from the core interests of sociology. British sociology in the post-war years was dominated by research that addressed a restricted set of issues. In the 1960s it was limited to a degree unimaginable in today's climate of proliferating subject matter and research strategies. Contrary to the myths cherished by older members of the profession in the UK, it was not a golden age of the discipline. There were many fewer departments, many fewer professors, many fewer students, fewer research projects, fewer journals. It inhabited an intellectual landscape of humourless drabness, dominated by a preoccupation with social class, social mobility and social justice. It had little or no interest in the disciplined analysis of selves and identities, in language and meaning, in the interaction order. It was against such a background that perspectives derived from phenomenology, interactionism, linguistic philosophy and other perspectives provided a breath of fresh air. These newer and epistemologically more sceptical or radical orientations were joined by feminist analyses of various sorts. Their cumulative impact was to change British sociology irreversibly. They were, however, felt as deeply threatening by a substantial number of British sociologists who attempted to discredit them and render them marginal to the discipline. Uncomprehending attacks were mounted from various quarters. The core preoccupations of sociology were thus reaffirmed, as were its roots in structural analysis. While interactionist ideas have since become 'domesticated' within the mainstream of sociological research, and while qualitative, ethnographic research has become taken-for-granted within the methodological canon, one must not forget that in an earlier generation, the reception of interactionism in the United Kingdom was seen – in some quarters at least – as part of a wider and more radical assault on the cherished subject matter, ideas and procedures of sociological thought.

In the following chapters we lead on from that observation that 'we were never interactionists' by exploring the legacy and context of British studies and empirical research. As stated earlier, we will examine a range of studies that, while not always exhibiting an explicit identification with the interactionist school, reflect the influences and character of interactionist work within British sociological work. The following chapters explore this legacy in terms of two principal domains of enquiry; namely the practical morality of types and learning, becoming and career. These chapters are then followed by an exploration of the interactionist legacy and influence within the methodological sphere of the sociological tradition. In each of the following chapters we also recognize the continued relevance of 'collective amnesia' to the contribution and relevance of interactionist ideas, concepts, themes and studies to contemporary sociological work and 'emerging' fields of theorization and empirical investigation.

three
the practical morality of types

The analysis of types, typifications and associated processes has been a prominent and important idea within the human sciences. In terms of the social phenomenology of Schutz, the notion of types, typification and so forth have represented important foundational concepts that have fuelled a number of intellectual enterprises. The precise inter-relationship between phenomenology and symbolic interaction is not a topic of this chapter. However, it is clear that the notion of types has played an important role in both traditions. In terms of *interactionism* the notion of types has been grounded in terms of everyday practices and activities. Furthermore, such activities have been articulated in terms of the normative apparatus of social interaction. Thus, one is able to contextualize such matters in terms of the practical morality of types. It is this set of concerns that we explore during the course of this chapter.

The interactionist analysis of work and lives, people processing and organizations has repeatedly documented the practical morality of everyday life. In particular, interactionist studies of categorization or classification processes constitute a substantial corpus of material that concerns the moral production of biographies, and the personal conse-quences of that biographical work. The practical morality of types is, in one sense, a foundational concept within the interactionist tradition. It bears repetition and reaffirmation that these studies constitute a sus-tained series of attempts to generate a sociology of personhood and the moral work that constructs or undermines social actors' identities. Equally, it merits emphasizing that this does not equate to an individu-alistic approach to social life and the moral order. Personhood and identity are inescapably social, collective and cultural processes.

While it has affinities with a broad range of sources and inspira-tions, this research domain owes much to Goffman's approach to the 'moral career'. Here, of course, the notion of 'moral' refers not to everyday connotations of morality but to a broader sociological con-cern with the achievement of a socially organized identity and the construction of actors as moral agents, responsible for their actions and subject to the evaluations of others. Based on his observations in a mental hospital (St Elizabeth's) Goffman described the moral career of the mental patient. This 'career' – like any career sociologically viewed – has temporal markers and is socially shaped by the interpretative work of family members and by the formally organized work of medical and other practitioners. The most striking of Goffman's contributions was his vivid characterization of the *rites de passage* that mark the transition from the status of 'inmate'. Goffman described them in terms of the 'mortification of the self' and the processes of 'role stripping'. The ideal-typical account of the ritualized entry into the total institution brings into conjunction with micro-sociological, ethnographic observation of organizations and their members a more classic sociological sensitivity to the collective observances and rituals through which social identities as a specific form of typification and careers are shaped and transformed.

The significant point is *not* that the ritual transformations of the self mysteriously *cause* mental illness. Goffman was not a vulgar determinist. Rather, they capture the intersection of institutions and persons. Opportunities for action and self-creation are progressively curtailed while expression is channelled into institutionally prescribed avenues. The moral career is the personal counterpart to the moral order of the organization. Both are to be thought of as part of the same process of negotiation and accommodation: there is a dialectical relationship between institutions and the identities of their members. In Goffman's treatment the 'asylum' offers an especially stark exemplar of those more general social phenomena.

Processes of social classification or categorization are therefore of fundamental importance to the machinery of social life. Those processes are, as we have suggested, part of the practical morality of social life. But they are not identified merely in order to disparage the inevitable: social typifications and their consequences are inherent features of everyday, practical thought and action. In the following sections of this chapter we will seek to explore a selection of studies that represent interactionist-influenced work in the United Kingdom. More specifically we will seek to explore this influence by focusing on one particular core theme, namely types and the activity of people processing. We note that there is a strong affinity between types and people processing. Thus, before embarking on a consideration and reflection of relevant studies, some consideration of people processing in relation to types will be conducted.

TYPES AND PEOPLE PROCESSING

The impact of interactionist thought on empirical research in the United Kingdom has been especially evident in the sociology of medical settings. The sociology of medicine (more latterly referred to as the sociology of health and illness) has been numerically the most vigorously flourishing field of British sociology since the early 1970s. It has been marked by a consistent output of empirical research studies, many of them based on ethnographic research and a broadly interactionist inspiration. Its themes have included the systematic study of medical encounters and their moral order. Medical settings have been explored as sites of moral work as well as technical professional decision-making. Indeed, one of the significant contributions of the sociological tradition has been to demonstrate the intersection of technical and moral work. The clinic has been characterized as the outcome of social interactions through which medical and personal identities are ascribed and negotiated. Technical processes of medical diagnosis and management intersect with the construction of moral categories.

The joint study of children in clinical settings, conducted by Philip Strong and Alan Davis (1978), is a notable case of the Aberdeen school. It was an interesting collaboration from several points of view. The fieldwork was conducted jointly, in British and American clinical settings. Several of the key papers were co-authored, but there was no jointly authored monograph: each wrote his own. Of the two, Strong's monograph has had the more enduring influence. The existence of the joint papers and the two monographs presents in itself a fascinating methodological and representational case study (that to our knowledge nobody has yet essayed). Together Strong and Davis described the moral order of the children's clinic, and the socially accomplished distribution of competence and moral agency within such clinical settings. To begin with one of their best-known formulations, they discuss the implicit cultural proposition – sometimes explicitly articulated in the clinic – 'aren't children wonderful?'. Children, as a cultural category, are by definition innocent of blame and are not accountable for their actions. Unlike those of adult actors, any and every action by a child can therefore be treated as evidence of how intrinsically 'wonderful' they are. In such contexts, children's inherent moral innocence contrasts with the moral accountability of adult actors, such as parents.

Strong's own monograph – *The Ceremonial Order of the Clinic* (1979) – was notable not only for its general approach, but also for its sustained use of Goffman's sociological perspective and ideas. While many authors have used Goffman's concepts within eclectic interpretative frameworks. Strong saw his as one of the few not merely to borrow from but also to develop and extend Goffman's sociological insights in the context of a major ethnography. Strong's 'ceremonial order' related forms of politeness to 'role formats' in the clinic. These were in turn embedded in an analysis of the organizational framing of the respective clinical settings. Strong's formulation of role formats prefigured, and was then assimilated to, Goffman's frame analysis (Goffman, 1972). Significantly, Strong used the analytic strategy to relate the forms of social encounter with the institutional order of organizational settings. These in turn generate distinctive kinds of moral work and the construction of social identities. Parents are constructed in terms of normal or 'natural' parenthood. The social resources and conventions available to social actors in the clinic in accomplishing this work include the right to criticize and question the competence of others. This technical and moral work is embedded within the relatively invariant forms (Goffman's frames, Strong's role formats) of most clinical encounters. For the most part, Strong describes encounters framed in terms of the 'bureaucratic' format.

Davis's parallel monograph, *Children in Clinics: A Sociological Analysis of Medical Work with Children* (1982) differentiates itself from Strong's in a number of particulars. He prefers to examine the local differences in children's clinics, while suggesting that Strong preferred to develop more generic analyses. He draws on Goffman in describing each clinical setting as a kind of 'workshop', developing Goffman's characterization of the 'tinkering trades' that includes medicine (Goffman, 1961). He discusses the interactional management of the clinic, including the strategies deployed to exclude the child as an active participant, so that clinical encounters with children are encounters with parents (in practice usually mothers). Davis's detailed ethnographic narratives include accounts of the construction of normal children in screening sessions, including the routine screening of the newborn. The moral work performed on children and their parents in such contexts includes the normalization of any possible deviations. Even in settings where frank illness was managed, medical staff attempted to construct as positive a version of normal childhood as possible. In contrast, Davis also documents clinical settings in which children were admitted to spoiled identities, and where the routine admiration of children is withheld. In such settings, not only is the performance of the child in question, but the moral status of parents can be subject to questioning as well. The latter are not automatically assumed to be credible witnesses of their child's condition. Throughout these different clinical settings, then, the medical work is also moral work. The contrasting encounters described by Davis are sites for socially organized and technically informed identity work.

The moral work of medical practitioners on children and their families, described by Strong and Davis, is paralleled by the work of families in constructing normal family life. This is the theme of yet another of the Aberdeen studies – Voysey's (1975) monograph *A Constant Burden*. This was a study of a series of families with a handicapped child, Voysey reversed the prevailing analytic assumption in a study that drew on an eclectic array of interpretative perspectives. The ordinary social-science perspective assumed that a handicapped child implied that parents would have 'problems' of coping and adjustment. Their interview accounts were taken to indicate processes of disavowal and other coping mechanisms. Voysey, by contrast, scrutinizes the parents' descriptions of their children and their family life as accounts that perform a particular kind of moral work. In particular, they construct the parents – the tellers of the accounts – as moral agents and their families as 'normal'. It is, Voysey argues, neither necessary nor legitimate to peer 'beneath' these parental accounts in order to reveal the 'real' problems with which they are coping. Rather, one should examine the interview accounts in order to understand the moral work and identity work that they enact. Voysey's work shares the same interactionist inspiration as that of other Aberdeen sociologists. It draws also on the early ethnomethodological inspirations concerning the construction of 'normal appearances'.

In the clinic and in the family, then, the categories of 'normality' and of normal troubles are constructed. These are treated as sites of identity work. The interactionist tradition, established in the Institute of Medical Sociology at Aberdeen, clearly aligned the rigorous empirical analysis of medical settings and encounters with 'mainstream' sociological analysis. The work of Strong and Voysey was clearly formulated in response to several strands of sociology. On the one hand, there was the interactionist – most notably Goffmanesque – influence; second, there were the phenomenologically informed versions of early ethnomethodology; third there were the prevailing preoccupations of medical sociology, including the work of Talcott Parsons on the social position of the sick person. Parsons had provided a sociological starting point for some aspects of sociological inquiry, but his particular approach was far too limited to be theoretically satisfying or to inform rigorous and detailed ethnographic research. Rather than the arid formulations of social systems, therefore, the British interactionists insisted on an action frame of reference in formulating their analyses of sickness as a medical, moral and social category.

The social production of moral types, as discussed previously, was forcibly analysed in Roger Jeffery's (1979) account of 'normal rubbish' in accident and emergency settings. Jeffery describes how medical staff members categorize their patients through the folk term 'rubbish'. In this work setting, rubbish includes a variety of possible clinical presentations. They include: self-inflicted injuries; effects of alcohol and other substance abuse; diffuse psychological troubles; conditions with no observable medical cause. Jeffery's invocation of the concept of 'normal' rubbish does two things. First, it alludes to Sudnow's category of 'normal crimes' (Sudnow, 1965). Sudnow discusses normal crimes as the outcome of definitional work within the American criminal justice system. Agents such as district attorneys and public defenders attribute typical or 'normal' crimes to characterize 'normal' types of perpetrator. Such attributions and their resulting official processes generate stable categories of crime and criminal from the myriad of local events and personal particularities. Second, it affirms that such moral categorizations as 'normal rubbish' are embedded in the practicalities of everyday organizational and professional work. In the context of accident and emergency work, rubbish reflects intractable and troublesome cases that place special stress on the clinical setting and elude the diagnostic or management routines that would ensure the relatively untroubled production of clinical categories and the relatively smooth accomplishment of work. The category and its use echo the American equivalent of 'gomer' (sometimes back-translated as standing for 'Get Out of My Emergency Room'), which also refers to a rather diffuse category of patients who display ill-defined conditions. Analytically, Jeffrey's sociological contribution is not to be found in an emotional response to the pejorative categories and their implications. It is to be found, in part at least, in the professional attribution of *legitimacy* to their clients and their complaints. Medical practitioners grant or withhold medical categories and in doing so convey certain other kinds of rights and obligations. (The latter have been rather blandly explored under the rubric of the 'sick role' and its variants.) Would-be clients who are deemed to be 'rubbish' do not have their medical status legitimated. Equally, clinic presentations by 'rubbish' implicitly neutralize or undermine the legitimacy of the medical practitioner. 'Patients' who have no strictly defined medical problem pose a symbolic threat to the categories of medical work and medical knowledge. Hence normal rubbish is a recurrent problem in such settings, in that it encapsulates some of the phenomena that escape the normal categories of professional expertise. Hence, in a way reminiscent of Mary Douglas's (1966) structuralist discussion of purity and danger, objects and persons that are interstitial entities in the classificatory systems of culture are re-categorized as a collective entity of 'dirt' ('rubbish').

The action orientation to illness itself was ably synthesized in Dingwall's influential work. Dingwall was another of the remarkable generation of young sociologists in the early 1970s who developed sociological perspectives on medical encounters and institutions in Aberdeen. From the early days of medical sociology the notion of 'illness behaviour' was a recurrent theme in the intellectual programme to carve out a distinctively social domain for sociological analysis – especially in American medical sociology. It was, however, poorly integrated with more mainstream sociological ideas. There was a tendency to regard illness as culturally regulated, unreflective behaviour. Dingwall took the opportunity to re-draw the approach, using the interactionist and other interpretative work that had been published, to integrate the understanding of health and illness with the analysis of *social action*. Among other things, this stressed that illness is meaningful and that becoming a sick person is purposeful, grounded in everyday common sense and practical actions. Like Bloor and Voysey, Dingwall blended the various kinds of interactionist inspirations of Aberdeen. A second domain in which types and people processing has been explored can be found in the field of labelling theory and its co-constructed concept of deviance. It is to this domain of enquiry that we now turn.

TYPES, LABELLING AND DEVIANCE

Labelling theory, closely aligned with key features of interactionist sociology, has in the past enjoyed remarkable popularity and subsequently suffered equally remarkable decline and eclipse. It deserves attention here from both perspectives. Its popularity was probably just as undeserved as was its later rejection: both derived from unwarrantably crude versions of the theory. This general perspective derives initially from the work of several key American sociologists of deviance in the 1960s, including Lemert (1967), Kitsuse (1962) and Erikson (1962). They were all critical of a great deal of the prevailing orthodoxy about crime and deviance that assumed that deviance or criminality were to be explained primarily in terms of the characteristics of the perpetrators. Criminality was readily accounted for as an inherent property of specific sorts of acts and the characteristics of particular actors. The labelling theorists, on the other hand, avoided the prior assumption of inherently deviant acts, or of essentially deviant persons. In an attempt to render a comprehensively *sociological* account they shifted the focus onto the social processes and responses whereby acts and actors are treated as deviant or criminal. Lemert, for instance, explained his interests by contrasting previous sociological or criminological thought – that proposed that 'deviance leads to social control' – with the labelling perspective that proposed that 'social control leads to deviance'.

In pursuing this analytic reversal, Lemert distinguished between primary and secondary deviance. The distinction is problematic, to be sure. In the original formulation, primary deviance refers to rule infraction irrespective of societal definition and response. Indeed, Lemert's model depends on the *a priori* assumption that rule breaking exists independently of any witnessing, denunciation, or accusation. Primary acts of deviance do not in themselves create deviance (such as mental illness) or criminality. The secondary processes of identification, diagnosis, detection, definition, and disposal can create deviant identities.

They are embedded in the activities of legal procedure, police action, medical diagnosis and the like. Lemert argued that of all the many ways in which social actors differ from one another, some result in negative sanctions, rejection or condemnation. The collective responses of social institutions or collectivities have a dynamic effect in shaping the deviation and constructing a deviant identity. Deviant identities are, therefore, created not by actors' deeds *per se* but by the processes of societal reaction, and the institutional arrangements through which careers and identities are shaped.

Now it is clear that from one point of view primary deviance is all but a contradiction in terms. In the absence of societal response it is unclear how any attribution of primary rule infraction can reasonably be made. If we assume that attributions of deviance are not attached to observed or reported actions on a random basis, then we cannot readily sustain the distinction between primary and secondary deviance. On the other hand, once we recognize that the *sociological* interest in these approaches lies specifically in the biographical work of accusation, diagnosis, denunciation, disposal and management, then we can safely overlook some of the manifest problems discovered in 'labelling theory' at large. Indeed, we can, we think, start to appreciate that labelling theory (and its applications in empirical research in particular) is far from being a uniquely deviance-based strand in sociological thought. It is more usefully thought of as a specific series of applications of a much more pervasive interest in moral careers, biographical work, the social management of identities, and the practical morality of typifications.

Among the influential examples of research in educational settings to cross the Atlantic was *The Educational Decision Makers* (Cicourel and Kitsuse, 1963). This empirically-based monograph was not a strictly symbolic interactionist work. Its authors – Aaron Cicourel in particular – occupied an interstitial space, somewhere between the early days of ethnomethodology, interactionism and cognitive sociology. Their joint research on educational careers owed much to the general inspiration of a sophisticated version of labelling theory. The research was based on field research in a Chicago high school that had a well-developed system of professional student counselling. The cadre of pastoral professionals exerted considerable influence over the high-school students' careers. They shaped students' organizational identities. They could identify students as 'under-achievers' – if their actual performance fell below professional expectations based on the results of aptitude tests; they could equally identify them as 'over-achievers' if they did better than their perceived characteristics predicted. The professionals could manage the organizational reality in such a way as to bring expectations and performance more closely into line when such discrepancies were identified. Those definitions thus had real consequences: students could be channelled into different curricular tracks, and thus have future opportunities widened or narrowed. Thus 'labelling' was not viewed as simply an interactional or 'linguistic' tag, but a temporal process that had material and concrete effects on individuals.

The management of student careers, and the consequent social shaping of their identities, explored by Cicourel and Kitsuse, helped to draw together the American interests in labelling and similar processes and the British interest in processes of differentiation and polarization in schools. Again, the key issue here was the notion of *typifications*. This in turn linked the interactionist with the phenomenological: an emphasis on typifications aligned the analysis with the conceptual framework of Schutz. Schutz had stressed the role of types and typifications in the forms of everyday practical reasoning: the phenomenological emphasis on practical reasoning had extended the Weberian perspective, stressing that ideal types are not the sole preserve of the social scientist. Everyday actors too construct types in the organization of their mundane, practical understanding of the world about them. In constructing their professional typifications of high school students, the counsellors studied by Cicourel and Kitsuse used standardized psychological assessments. But it was clear that they were not relying on them as definitive guides for action. They resorted to a variety of *ad hoc* personal judgements in order to align the 'objective' test results with their own and others' impressionistic judgements of the students. In the course of such professional assessments the school counsellors were engaged in organizational biography-building. These biographical constructions were in turn located in the organization's system of records – case notes, records and reports. Those fragmentary sources of information could be read and interpreted by the school's professional staff members in constructing their biographical interpretations.

Rather than a vulgar version of 'labelling', therefore, Cicourel and Kitsuse aligned organizational ethnography with the phenomenological interest in typifications. They documented the biographical work done on the high-school students by the professional counsellors and their biographical consequences for the students themselves. They made an important contribution to the sociological approach to biography as well as to the sociological study of moral careers and organizational identities.

Some of these ideas influenced a number of important British 'interactionist' studies of deviance within educational and other settings. These studies include *Deviance in Classrooms* (1975) by Hargreaves et al. Within this study a theory of types and typification in relation to classroom deviance and interaction is advanced. For Hargreaves and his colleagues, Rosenthal and Jacobson's (1968) notion of self-fulfilling prophecies in classrooms and labelling theory are relevant. Hargreaves et al. noted that labelling theory has tended to be tied to deviance theory while the notion of the self-fulfilling prophecy had been traditionally tied to the realization of 'positive' behaviour, e.g. good academic progress. For Hargreaves et al., the fundamental dynamic to understanding deviance in classrooms is the interactional characteristics and practices that constitute 'typing'. They argue that typing constitutes a form of 'person formulation'. (1975: 143). This study advances the notion that the typification of pupils (and persons universally) into deviant categories is realized through a number of stages through a period of time. These stages include 'speculation', 'elaboration' and 'stabilization' (ibid.: 145). Central to this idea is the notion of impressions that are picked up from visual resources (e.g. appearance), conformity to role expectations and peer group relations. This interactional matrix forms the resource through which teachers type pupils in particular and specific ways. These types can be 'de-typed' or 're-typed' and are therefore subject to modification over time. However, such processes are firmly located within the interactional order and milieux of the classroom. Thus the notion of the moral career is evident and is conceived as one that is characterized by a number of non-rigid but observable, interactionally realized and accomplished stages. This is both an elaboration and promotion of the analytical link between typing and social/moral processes. A further example that illustrates the importance of the notion of types to studies of interaction within British sociology can be found in those studies that have explored deviance in relation to crime and criminal activity.

CRIME, DEVIANCE AND TYPES

Perhaps the most important book that deals with crime, deviance and types can be found in David Matza's book *Becoming Deviant* (1969). It is clear that the distillation and articulation of interactionist and neo-Chicagoan ideas within this book had a great influence on sociological and criminological studies of deviance. In terms of the United Kingdom an important manifestation of these influences can be found in a range of studies that include *Images of Deviance* (1971) edited by Stanley Cohen. This collection represents an attempt to counter administrative criminology, on the one hand, and 'ivory tower' sociological theorizing, on the other. Cohen identifies a number of themes that drive this collection and programme for a 'new criminology'. These involve a requirement to be intelligible and therefore connect with the public both in terms of its perceptions and concerns, to be sceptical of official versions of deviant types, to embrace a conceptualization of deviance as both a structural and interactional process, an appreciation of the definition of meaning, i.e. an ability to take the deviants' points of view and experiences as an important topic, a potential to appreciate the similarity between deviant values and accepted values within different settings and the political implications of studying deviance. What is striking about these studies is the prominence of interactionist thinking. For example, the opening chapter by Young on the police as amplifiers of deviancy explores W.I. Thomas's dictum concerning the definition of the situation as it relates to social epistemology and processes in the context of drug control at the Notting Hill carnival. The process of reality negotiation and deviance relies heavily on the use of types and their grounding in specific forms of practical morality and predication that produces, what Leslie Wilkins describes as, an amplification of deviance. This involves, in Young's example, a process in which the police act against drug-takers in terms of specific types or 'stereotypes'. Members of the drug-taking group are placed in a new situation and interpret, make sense of, the changes in policing and life on the street, in the community and general encounters. The police react to the changed behaviour of the defined group. The drug takers then react to this change, and so on. Central to this process is the notion of types and the moral inferences of two groups in relation to behaviour and the censure or control of the behaviour. Young also notes how the amplification of deviant acts are also connected to wider social processes and institutions that effect the process of typing and stereotyping. Prominent among these is the role of the media who are integral in producing a situation in which the reality of drug-taking and its fantastic portrayal mix, merge and mesh. In terms of the control of drugs, Young concludes that deviancy amplification can only be tamed through reference to the health issues surrounding drug use rather than the moral issues surrounding unwarranted pleasure and excitement. Other studies in this collection include Maureen Cain's study of the beat and interactions and relations with the community in both rural and urban police forces and Max Atkinson's societal reactions to suicide and the role of coroners' definitions. The final chapter by Laurie Taylor and Paul Walton explores the phenomena of industrial sabotage. In this chapter the meaning of industrial sabotage is contextualized in terms of three ideal types of moral reasoning that help to explain industrial sabotage by workers. This represents a Weberian methodological strategy that nevertheless grounds various seemingly sporadic social actions in an explanatory context. Jason Ditton's interactionist ethnography of crime, interaction and organizations links the process of types and labelling to the process of 'becoming' in relation to petty pilfering and 'fiddling' in a medium-size bakery business. He calls this process 'learning the fiddle' (Ditton, 1977: 30). This process involves the

73

careful co-ordination of managing customers and the presentation of product and self. This process of 'learning the fiddle' was seen by Ditton to be an entrenched and inexorable process that initiates were interactionally compelled to adopt as a means of negotiating and surviving in the interactional order and moral organization of the 'shop floor'. The management of customers and the presentation of self are, according to Ditton, central to understanding this process of 'becoming' deviant. Ditton states: 'Two basic conditions of sales existence operate to modify how the well-bred salesman will use the moral licence for illegal activity he was coerced to adopt during socialisation, and persuaded to retain in everyday sales life' (ibid.: 81).

Thus, as we shall see in the next chapter, the relation between types, self-presentation/labelling and 'becoming' in terms of both deviant and sanctioned careers are intertwined features of a mutually constitutive process. In terms of this chapter we have seen how a number of studies took seriously the concept of the practical morality of types and applied it vigorously to medical and criminal practices and formal institutions such as the school and the hospital. The manner in which the sociology of types and the related process of moral careers has impacted upon the study of organizations and work will figure prominently in the following chapter. However, in terms of this chapter, a further set of studies that have reflected a concern with the practical morality of types can be found in interactionist studies and ideas that focused upon issues and processes related to social differentiation. A discussion of this field of enquiry and its use of the concept of types will now be explored in terms of interactionist core themes and relevant studies that have impacted upon the British sociological landscape.

INTERACTION, TYPES AND SOCIAL DIFFERENTIATION

The influence of interactionism within British sociology was mediated by the crumbling edifice of functionalist modes of sociology during the 1960s and 1970s. While interactionist ideas were clearly a means of questioning the prevailing orthodoxy of the time, through its promotion of voluntarism and social action, such questioning was taking place within a context where issues of inequality, class and struggle were also becoming increasingly important within the sociological and political landscape. In some cases this resulted in the operationalization of well-established interactionist ideas as a means of contributing to this new configuration of sociological horizons. In particular the concept of (urban) subcultures presented a space within which such concerns could be readily pursued. The Chicago School and the work of Robert E. Park provided a base within which the moral and cultural organization of urban settings could be fruitfully explored as a vast array of lived practices. The provision of 'micro-sociological' accounts of the hidden lives of the disadvantaged has a long pedigree within interactionist studies. In the British context this was reflected in a number of studies which demonstrated the manner in which interactionist ideas have been percolated, disseminated, utilized and synthesized within the realm of sociological enquiry in general and other forms of enquiry in particular.

An example of this form of work can be found in Phil Cohen's paper entitled 'Subcultural conflict and working-class community'. For Cohen, like other subcultural analysts of the time, subcultures were to be understood as 'symbolic systems' (1980: 78–87). Furthermore, these symbolic systems are characterized by a number of sub-systems; these sub-systems include 'plastic forms' that do not originate from the sub-culture *per se* but are utilized and absorbed e.g. dress and music and 'infrastructural forms' that are more resistant to change and include argot and various rituals. However, while Cohen's study takes on some of the clothing of interactionist ideas (including a submerged concept of types and typification), it also conceives of subcultures within a wider set of macro-sociological and economic concerns. Furthermore, the symbolic texture of subcultures is one in which the structuralist concept of signs and signification was seen to have increasing analytic purchase and prominence.

75

The introduction of structuralist concepts into the investigation of subcultures is not one that possessed a historically distinct 'moment'. However, Hebdige's work, *Subculture: The Meaning of Style* (1979) provides a good example of the synthesis of ideas that were taking place. Within this work, Hebdige notes how subcultures represents a form of the 'other' in relation to dominant cultural forms. Drawing on the work of Stuart Hall (1977), Hebdige notes how subcultures are returned through a process of 'recuperation'. This process involves the commodity form (i.e. the conversion of subcultural signs) and the ideological form (labelling and redefinition of behaviour by dominant agents, e.g. the media, the judiciary, and so forth). In terms of the Birmingham School of Cultural Studies, this represents the increasing focus upon subcultures as an ideological object.

The upshot of this development and the success of this form of sub-cultural analysis was a dropping back and receding of interactionist ideas that had once permeated any conceptualization of subcultural forms. Of particular significance here was the Centre for Contemporary Cultural Studies' use of structuralist ideas and the synchronic approach to understanding subcultures which relegated the concept of time, and therefore 'career', from analytical view. Furthermore, the lived character of subculture and its relation to space and place, a prominent concern of previous interactionist studies, becomes obscured. The sign and the emergent concept of 'discourse' begin to substitute the notion of types and typifying as a grounded interactional practice. The emergent properties of subcultures are re-articulated within the domain of the discursive or ideological sphere, within which representation takes on more and more importance. The theoretical begins to transcend the empirical and/or observational attention of interactionist ethnography. The subcultural becomes a resource for theoretical development within the field of cultural studies. It may be argued that this was because the interactionist studies of subcultures as *process* had achieved their objective and that new work and new domains of enquiry were an inevitable result, including the relationship between subcultures, signification and representation. In many respects this move also provided ground for the emergence of the various sociologies of identity. Furthermore, this drive towards the sign and representation was, in many respects, also justified by the accusation that interactionist approaches fall short in providing credible accounts of 'power'. At this stage of sociological theoretical development, power had become synonymous with a sense of wider social structure. Power was seen to be incarnated through social inequality and socio-economic relations that were reflected or articulated through ideological forms. The future re-investigation of micro-dimensions of power was, curiously, enabled through the reception of the Foucauldian analogy of micro-capillaries through which power circulates within the social body. However, with the demise in influence of the Marxist enterprise and the rise and rise of 'theory', the focus upon matters of representation and signification were intensified. This intensification represents, in our opinion, the 'postmodern moment' within British sociology, that has been characterized by a form of willed amnesia in addition to many useful and innovative forms of enquiry and theoretical development. This 'willed amnesia', as it were, did not represent a break in the use of ideas and concepts that had been circulating within sociology for many years, instead it represented a fashion for not acknowledging 'modernist traditions', a category that imposed a particular reading of modernity and social theory through a simple conceptual bifurcation. The positive benefits of this manifesto remain to be fully experienced or appreciated.

Consequently, in recent years the moral character and organization of subcultural types or 'identities' and so forth have been sidelined in favour of more fashionable concerns. The theory of moral and epistemological relativity that stands at the heart of the postmodern was used as a means of ignoring the classic sociological question of how it is that social order(s) are possible altogether. It may well be that the notion of types, interaction, moral careers and so forth are part and parcel of a 'modernist tradition'. However, this periodization of sociological enquiry will not do due to the fact many interactionist ideas are, in fact, alive and well. However, in terms of the central point of this chapter the moral organization of types and categories is, we believe, of central importance to many of sociology's (enduring) questions. In particular, as Giddens has noted, identity and types are of central importance in beginning to understand the macro-micro levels of social and moral order. The notion of the interpretative dimension in human action, a central concern of the theory of structuration, is a Schutzian and inter-actionist pillar upon which the theory of structuration is partly built. Indeed, identities, types and typifications are a fundamental way of understanding the moral machinery that is necessary for social action and organization. Of relevance to our discussion and exploration of interactionism in terms of the practical morality of types is the renewed interest in topics such as trust, identity and organization, that are of extreme importance or feature heavily in those studies broadly con-ceived of as interactionist. However, in recent years the demise of the notion of moral machinery and the allocation, negotiation and accomplishment of self and social order have left a vacancy for an under-socialized concept of the individual. In part, this is due to the unfashionable notion of social organization as an emergent property of human agency, action and understanding. The Newtonian conceptual-ization of social structure remains firmly intact despite paradigm shifts within other human sciences. The security blanket of a clearly dis-cernible social structure remains a more comforting picture for those committed to social critique and change if only for the reason that, at first glance, a conceptualization of social organization as an emergent property problematizes the efficacy of modernist tools of social ame-lioration. However, despite the attempts at synthesis, the filtering process of macro/micro theorizing has buried much that was of importance within the interactionist tradition. The result has been the development of certain concepts that may well benefit from a recon-sideration of their sociological heritage. An example will perhaps illustrate what is meant here.

A useful example can be found in the rise of interest in consumption and lifestyle as opposed to subcultures or forms of life. In recent years, the transcendence of the form of explanation that includes issues of types, typing, moral careers and so forth has led to a situation within which the grounded realities of the lived experience of the lifeworld have been theoretically glossed over. Leading on from subcultural theory and notions of identity, it has been argued that the concept of 'subculture' should be substituted for a concept of postmodern 'youth culture' or 'neo-tribes' (Maffesoli, 1996). This is because the notion of a *sub*cul-ture lends itself too readily to pre-postmodern attitudes, in the sense that it serves to maintain a binary relation between dominant cultural forms and the 'other' and because of the alleged changing nature of the social within which consumption has taken on an increasing level of sociological and cultural importance. In turn, the 'authentic' subculture is now seen as an object of the past. The concept of lifestyle is, in one sense, continuous with the older concept in the sense that subcultures were always visible *stylistically*. However, this concept is transformed via notions of lifestyles and neo-tribes that are contextualized within the framework of consumer culture. Neo-tribes, it is argued, are fluid entities that are in a constant state of flux. Members of such a tribe 'belong' through a visible form of voluntarism centred on fashion and various forms of aesthetic practice. Individuals may move between many neo-tribes negotiating and displaying various forms of social identity that stand outside traditional concepts of class, race and gender. Maffesoli asserts, however, that the internal social organization of such entities are unimportant due to the fact that their existence is their *a priori*. According to Maffesoli, one should submit analysis of such phenomena at the surface level due to the assumption that this is their primary *raison d'être*.

This is an interesting transformation of the concept of subculture from interactionist theory to postmodern theorizing. The notion of neo-tribes affords further purchase upon the practical process of theorizing social reality and associated rhetorical activities. The definition of the concept ensures that such phenomena can be used for further declarations concerning consumer/material culture and the wider society (e.g. Bauman, 1992). Indeed, Bauman asserts that neo-tribes are a refuge for alienated souls in an increasingly fragmented and privatized existence. In a sense, Maffesoli almost seems to attempt to inoculate the practices of such groups from observational scrutiny. Of central concern here is the way in which types and typification become the privilege of the theorist rather than an interactional product of social actors grounded in the mundane and exotic texture and practices of the lifeworld. Are the 'lads and lasses' of such 'neo-tribes' so inert? Passively governed by wider social processes in an unreflective structural or semiotically determined manner? Furthermore, if we are to accept such an assertion, then the internal dynamics of such phenomena are obscured and relegated to a series of intellectual/descriptive footnotes: mere illustrations of a semiotic/discursive mosaic of cultural forms; a new canvas for the broad sweeps of sociological generalization rather than the careful appreciation of actors' meaningful actions and rich social worlds, lives and processes. While it may well be the case that the social formations such as neo-tribes are transitory, it does not mean that they are not observable. Furthermore, if it is the case that these represent new and interesting social forms it would seem that the interactional character of such forms and the process of categorization, style, type and career should be explored. In one sense the above provides a good example of how the substantive domains of interactionist enquiry have been colonized by 'theory' and sealed by the portcullis of periodization.

Of course, the picture painted above is not as distinct as it may first appear. A number of studies have made use of 'ethnographic' and 'interactionist' ideas in exploring these 'new social phenomena'. In many respects the practice of ethnography within the United Kingdom has provided a vehicle through which both interactionist ideas and new waves of theory have jostled, intertwined and been synthesized, to varying degrees of success.

This process of synthesis has also been punctuated by an early, but considered, interactionist critique of the form of subcultural theory promoted in the work associated with the Centre for Contemporary Cultural Studies. The North American interactionist authors Fine and Kleinman (1979) argue that the conceptualization of subculture within CCCS-type studies assumes that such phenomena are merely 'an aggregate of persons'. Furthermore, members of subcultures are conceptualized, it is argued, in a one-dimensional manner. The multi-layered and shifting character of affiliations is, according to Fine and Kleinman, overlooked. Furthermore, for Fine and Kleinman, such a glossing over of such concerns reduces our ability to appreciate the character of cultural change.

79

In response to this particular ontological 'frameworking' of subcultures, Fine and Kleinman argue that an interactionist framework can provide a more holistic account of variation between subcultures, cultural change and the movement of cultural ideas, elements and practices. For Fine and Kleinman subcultures are, fundamentally, interactionist products. The notion of subcultures as groups or gangs may be seen to be ineffective in explaining the distribution of subcultural types across cultural and social spaces. However, Fine and Kleinman invoke the notion of interaction and *networks* in advancing their argument. Thus, interaction not only refers to group membership but also casual conversations (that may now include electronic communication) and more explicit structural roles that link disparate groups and the media. Central to understanding the interactional characteristics of networks, in relation to subcultures, is the concept of communication. This call to take account of (or make reconnections with) interaction in understanding and exploring subcultures has more recently, been taken up and explored. It is perhaps worth reiterating at this point how the emphasis upon communication and interaction re-introduces the notion of the centrality of types and typification and career. While it is not explicitly stated it remains implicit to this approach.

For example, in some of the recent studies (few in number) that have attempted to return to the interactional character of subcultures and so forth, the consumption of 'cultural forms' is prominent. In particular, this form of popular consumption focuses upon a particular type; namely 'the fan'. Jenson (1992) notes how much discourse surrounding 'the fan' presents them as deviant. The fan is is viewed as 'fanatical', obsessed, a loner, one who sublimates or projects feelings upon remote but materially immediate entities and phenomena. These typifications of fandom have, from Jenson's point of view, detracted from the interactional and career-like character of how individuals relate to the media and cultural forms.

Camille Bacon-Smith's (1992) study of 'Trekkies' explores the interactive production of fan-based texts and materials. These include novellas, paintings, music videos and dress at gatherings. Bacon-Smith's study, while not presenting the level of detail associated with interactionist studies, does emphasize the role of types and careers in the collective production of fan-based materials. Jenkins (1992) also explores the world of *Star Trek* fans in a manner that accommodates interactionist ideas. The popular view of *Star Trek* fans as sad and alienated individuals is contrasted with a study that reports upon a network of extensive communication and collective production of fan-based materials for 'group' consumption. This study also facilitates the concept of interactional networks through a discussion of the role of computer-mediated interaction within such networks. Clearly, Internet chat rooms, sites and electronic communication have greatly enhanced the interactive and communicative dimension of such forms of life. Fandom is therefore conceived not only as an interactional activity but also a creative one. Central to understanding the career of the fan is not only the typing of fans in particular ways but the immediacy and use of cultural types and typification in making sense of the world and fulfilling various needs (e.g. social contact, friendship) or resisting unpalatable aspects of contemporary life, through fan-based networks and groups. The trajectory of these studies is echoed by those who draw attention to the way in which recent cultural theory has ignored the meaning of subcultures for the actual members of such collectivities (e.g. Muggleton, 1997; Widdicombe and Woofit, 1995).

The studies briefly discussed above do represent a break from recent theoretical accounts of subcultures and forms of life. Central to these studies is an exploration of the interactional and creative character of extensive communication networks. However, it is crucial to note here that the concept of networks is not akin to that propagated by 'actor-network theory'. Rather, 'networks' refer to the lived practices, biographies and interactive resources that actors use in a creative and meaningful manner. Actors are not merely constituted through networks in a constitutive 'top-down' manner. Networks are emergent properties of social action.

A related area that has also, we will seek to demonstrate, exhibited a sometimes obscured continuity with certain core interactionist themes can be located within those studies that have focused upon the 'body'. In particular the notion of types (and the related concept of career) have been of particular significance. This field of enquiry serves as a further exemplar of the way in which the notion of social types continues to have significance while its roots in a wider theoretic often remain unacknowledged.

TYPES, THE BODY AND SEXUALITY

An important and sustained domain of enquiry within which interactionist ideas have relevance can be found within the context of the 'body'. In some circles a concern with the 'body' in sociology is viewed as a relatively recent field of investigation, a product of the influence of Foucauldian studies and, to a lesser extent, the theoretical work of Norbert Elias. In the case of the work of Foucault, interest in the body has centred on a concern with the proliferation of discourse through which the raw materials of the individual, collective and body have been utilized as a means of shaping and managing the social conditions of populations. The body and 'bio-politics' become an important domain of enquiry due to the manner through which discourse is impinged upon the body (e.g. health, psychological profiles, rights and obligations, disease, lifestyle, credit rating). Thus the concepts of power, knowledge and 'the civilizing process' are seen to be central to understanding the relationship between the body and society.

81

This theoretical grounding of the body has spawned a number of studies that have discussed and explored the body in relation to representation. For example, Dick Hebdige develops the structuralist/culturalist approach to understanding subcultures in his book *Subculture: The Meaning of Style* (1979). Hebdige focuses upon the semiotic/symbolic characteristics of subcultures as a means of interpreting them. As noted earlier in this chapter, this represents a distinct move from a concern with subcultures as systems of interaction to subcultures as forms of representation; in this case *style*. Hebdige notes that subcultures are subject to a number of social processes that include 'moral panics' and media hysteria. Style is both celebrated through fashion, body work (hairstyles, tattoos, piercing, movement, bio-chemical experimentation) and other activities and reviled as a social problem. Subcultures represent a fracturing of the social order, a breaching of convention. This fractured order, argues, Hebdige, is routinely subject to a process of recuperation through which the subculture is incorporated within the dominant mythology. The move to representation is realized through the development of concepts that focus on style and lifestyles as forms of representation at the semiotic and ideological level as opposed to phenomena that are interactionally produced, recognized and utilized as everyday practical resources. Further work on the body has extended the representational move. For example, work carried out in relation to gender and the body (Featherstone, 1990). This is related to a number of different studies of the body and gender in relation to advertising, fashion, pornography, sport and other cultural forms within which gender distinctions and representation figure prominently.

However, recent work has acknowledged the limitations of the 'representational' approach. These studies acknowledge the importance of earlier work on the body, for example, the work of the French anthropologist Marcel Mauss (1872–50) on 'body techniques' and embodied methods for body work within cultural frameworks and the concept of body and performance promoted by Erving Goffman within his interactionist sociology. Thus, in one sense studies that have explored 'the body' in terms of post-representational analyses have made some reconnection with earlier anthropological and interactionist work and their implicit concern with types and typification. For example, studies that have explored emotional labour in relation to the body (e.g. Hochschild, 1983) explore the artful management of body work in relation to various interactional specifics and practical types. In this case the display of emotion (smiling and courteous body movement) by flight attendants working for a large airline. These body techniques and methods are the product of various forms of training but are produced and negotiated within the interactional setting of the workplace. Clearly, such body work is firmly located within interactional specifics through which various culturally available types (posture, facial expression, movement, and so forth) are central to the task of managing passengers. Furthermore, the reciprocity of typing work necessitates that the flight attendants' emotional work responds to and recognizes the possibilities of the 'contented passenger', the 'angry passenger' or the 'anxious passenger'. Thus the process of typification within the interactional milieux is explored.

More recent work has focused on the process of performance in the age of 'narcissism' (Lasch, 1980) where 'beauty', 'youth', 'health' and 'fitness' have become dominant and defining societal values. Within this context the project of the self is oriented to specific goals and constructed forms of 'lifestyle'. As Giddens states: 'The consumption of ever-novel goods becomes in some part a substitute for the genuine development of self; appearance replaces essence as the visible signs of successful consumption come actually to out-weigh the use-values of the goods and services in question' (1991: 198). Within this framework of normative valorization the body becomes a strategic and performative site through which appearance and the performance begin to constitute identity. Furthermore, in terms of the societal values of health, beauty, youth and fitness, etc. the more the performance and display of the body approximate to these values, the higher the 'exchange value' (ibid.: 177). A further example of the theorized approach to the everyday, the self and the body can be found in the work of Alberto Melucci (1996). Within the context of this work the phenomenological perspective is brought to bear on notions of performance and 'the playing self' within which related concepts such as identity and the materiality of 'the body' and so forth are conceptualized and contextualized within a system of relations and representations. In terms of this theoretical turn, the interactionist concerns of the body in terms of type, meaning and performance are evident. However, this is synthesized with new forms of theoretical enquiry, political economy and understandings of consumption. Further examples of such synthesis and continued focus upon types and people processing can be found in the related domain of sexuality. In terms of the early sociology of sexuality in the United Kingdom, one of the most important ideas that has been generated within the broad interactionist tradition was of supreme significance: the concept of stigma. Goffman's notion of stigma was a crucial step in forging self, types, interaction, and career into an analytical concept with methodological purchase. Clearly, 'stigma' is but one example of a number of potential formulations. In terms of types and interaction and sociology in the United Kingdom an influential study that made significant use of this concept was Ken Plummer's *Sexual Stigma* (1975). In this book Plummer adopts an interactionist approach to exploring forms of sexual behaviour that have been labelled as 'deviant', in particular homosexuality. Plummer's book is contextualized in terms of possible audiences and archaic discourses in which homosexuality is unproblematically linked to deviance. However, Plummer's study of homosexuality and 'deviance' is, in one sense, an important contribution to the questioning of established prejudices through interactionist work. Central to his approach is the idea that sexuality is characterized by a problematic and socially constructed array of meanings. As Plummer states:

> Commonsense and research definitions alike frequently assume that 'everybody-knows-what-sex-is', that 'sex-as-we-know-it' exists independently of its social construction, and that when members talk about 'sex' the categories used are not problematic to the users. But such assumptions cannot be taken-for-granted by the interactionist perspective long ago. (1975: 29)

In this version of interactionism sexuality is only sexual in and through the meanings attached to specific forms of behaviour. Clearly, biological specifics and functions are not dismissed, rather sexuality and experience for human beings is realized through meaning. While fantasy and the like may also be important psychological aspects of sexuality, the encounter and interaction remain central, for Plummer, to understanding sexuality. Plummer does acknowledge constraints upon this position, for example, biological, cultural and interactive constraints. In terms of his case study Plummer notes that the major way in which various interactional practices are associated as deviant is through the process of societal reaction. Thus the experience of being homosexual is intimately connected to societal reaction. For Plummer homosexuality is a way of life rather than a condition or state of mind grounded in friendships, relations, lifestyles and encounters. While Plummer notes societal reactions as a means through which formal conceptualization of deviant behaviour are reified, he also explores how individuals pursuing practices that are deemed 'deviant' react to such societal conditions. Of course in terms of homosexuality like other sexual types (identities), the process of becoming and various rituals are central to the experience (e.g. coming out), etc. A related process is collective responses, for Plummer, this is crucial in understanding the character of gay subcultures. Central to this world, like other subcultures, are symbolic systems, normative organization, argot, the interaction network, behavioural patterns, self-concepts and identity and material organization.

Plummer's analysis briefly presented here represents a clear interactionist examination of a particular sexual typification as a lived category. The interactionist approach to this world is one in which meaning, practices and subcultures or lifestyle figure prominently. In many respects this work represents one of the more explicit examples through which interactionist studies contributed to a substantive domain of sociological enquiry. It is interesting to note that during the 1970s this domain was highly under-researched. Plummer provides much ground for further work in which many of the concerns flagged and explored in his book give way to analytical accounts in which identity, lifestyle and narrative become more visible analytical concerns at the expense of other domains of lived categories as a way of life. Thus issues of material resources or networks slide further into the background as forms and ways of speaking and self-concept and societal reaction move to the fore.

Plummer's later work, as pointed out earlier in this book, provides a neat example of this mode of theoretical and analytical development. Plummer's later book *Telling Sexual Stories* (1995) is explicit in its orientation towards one particular field of ontological practice and

84

performance. Plummer explores the culture of story telling and its centrality to understanding sexual identities and experiences. He relates the work on sexuality and story telling in terms of the 'narrative turn' in sociology. For Plummer, stories and narrative can be understood as a form of negotiated order which is characterized by 'a constant flow of joint actions circulating between tellers, coaxers, texts, readers and the contexts in which the stories are told: tellers can only select, coaxers can only sift, texts can only sieve and readers can only interpret' (1995: 95). For Plummer this process is not a literary exercise but is one grounded in social practices and organization. Plummer continues by exploring the importance of narrative in understanding sexual suffering and survival, as well as the power of narrative as resources for combating sexual violence, prejudice and other forms of discrimination within the emerging domain of lifeworld politics. Furthermore, in terms of 'coming out' or sexual experiences Plummer explores the power of narrative in mobilizing desire and exploring new avenues of being. *Telling Sexual Stories* is an important work that has direct links with his earlier work. It provides an elaborate and detailed framework for exploring sexual identity within a narrative frame grounded in practices of social construction, reception and consumption. However, it also serves to illustrate how the concerns of symbolic interactionism have been developed. In this case, a particular aspect of interaction (here ways of speaking, telling and representing) is re-examined and recast in terms of the narrative turn in sociological enquiry. However, this concern, while developed, has clear links with the characteristics of the sexual worlds explored in his earlier work. What is different, striking and compelling is the extent to which the wider concerns and characteristics of the lifeworld documented in earlier work give way to a focus and radical development of one particular frame of being in the later direction and study of sexual lives, types and processes. Meanings and types and other related lived sexual categories and experiences are re-explored through a focus upon narrative and telling. In one sense, in terms of types and sexuality, this represents an important domain of study through which a core theme and concern of interactionist enquiry continues to sustain its relevance. Closely allied to this notion of narrative and identity is the concept of discourse. This has also represented a domain in and through which core interactionist themes and ideas continue to have, not always acknowledged, relevance.

TYPES, TYPIFICATION AND DISCOURSE

The explosion in interest in language and the social has spawned a range of analytical methods that aim to explore the importance of language to understanding social structure, representation and interaction. The concern with types in the interactionist sense has not figured prominently within the linguistic turn. We tend to associate the linguistic turn with the semiology of de Saussure and its use by the post-structuralist and postmodern movements. However, an earlier manifestation of the linguistic turn can be found in the work of Harvey Sacks (1992a, 1992b) and Garfinkel's study of jurors' deliberations (1967). In the work of Sacks we have the beginnings of conversation analysis and its concern with the sequential organization of talk, members descriptive conceptual machinery and categorization. The relationship between ethnomethodology/conversation analysis and interactionism has never been fully articulated, partly due to Garfinkel's commitment to a position of incommensurability and an alternate (indifferent) vision of social enquiry. However, in the work of Sacks, we have a clear connection with interactionist ideas. This connection is visible through the influence of the work of Erving Goffman on Sacks's work.

Goffman (1959) extended interactionist ideas into the realms of face-to-face encounters, impression management and character work. Unlike other analysts of the time (e.g. Bales or Homans), Goffman did not focus upon laboratory data and 'experiments', rather, he focused on naturally occurring behaviour in the field. It was this material that was, for Goffman, the key to understanding and exploring people's social interaction. Sacks's engagement with Goffman also focused upon the role of 'ritual' and 'ceremony' in everyday impression management and life. For Sacks, the ceremony was honed down towards a greater level of detail that ultimately found expression through a concern with the sequential organization of conversation in various settings (e.g. a call to the police). However, Sacks's concern with descriptions and categorization in everyday life also develops certain phenomenological and interactionist concerns. It is perhaps difficult to ascertain the extent to which a concern with types influenced Sacks via Goffman or through other sources. In any case, the fact that Sacks's work, as part of the post-war milieux in which interactionist ideas found new life, can be connected to a theory of types and descriptions is one that should be noted. Indeed, the development of membership categorization analysis in recent years represents one form of 'discourse analysis' within which the practical and everyday use of types as resources for understanding, making decisions and other activities is of primary interest. Clearly, in many respects the ethnomethodological concerns of membership categorization analysis (MCA) and the interactionist tradition remain problematically bound and intimately connected. While a rendition of this connection remains outside the realms of this book, MCA's capacity to explore the role of types in interaction has often pitted it against representational and theorized accounts of social phenomena. For example, the discourse of national identity has often been explored at the representational level (e.g. Bhabba, 1994). However, recent studies (e.g. Hester and Housley, 2002) have also explored how categories and types of national identity are interactionally deployed and accomplished for a variety of purposes in a number of mundane and banal (Billig, 1984) settings. Categories of national identity are not fixed but are occasioned in terms of various performances and activities e.g. within the context of the UK debating proposals for constitutional reform, voting rights and matters of taxation across boundaries. To this extent the practical morality of types has found concrete expression within the realms of discourse studies. While the lineage of this type of work to the classic concerns of symbolic interactionism may be less than clear-cut, the particular preoccupation of these studies means they promote an interactionist focus and have, in one sense, developed a discourse analysis of types and typification that is grounded in the interactional accomplishment of social organization. Thus the notion of types advanced by Schutz, and the space of interactional analysis developed by Goffman and Sacks in different but interrelated ways, represent a clear demonstration of how the practical morality of types remains a central concern of a variety of sociological approaches to understanding discourse, language and interaction. This provides a final exemplar through which we hope to have rendered visible the continued relevance of the interactionist concept of types and people processing in contemporary sociological thinking.

87

CONCLUSION

In the course of this chapter we have seen how interactionist ideas within a number of different domains have been characterized by a firm connection with interactionist sociology and studies, punctuated by a theoretical turn and, at a later stage, characterized by some reconnection with the lifeworld and actors' practices. In many respects, the theoretical turn, drawing on some tenets of post-structural theory, produced a form of representational sociology within domains formally occupied, in some part, by interactionist forms of social enquiry. Why? In part this was due to the perceived inability of interactionist accounts to *account for* power. Clearly, in the case of CCCS, a focus on representation and discourse/ideology enables a space within which the power of representation and the sign can be fully illustrated. Furthermore, through the identification of the powerful sign with a form of representation that extended or downgraded social groups, a first step in resisting forms of 'power' was initiated. Forms of counter-imagery,

narratives of resistance and new forms of expression deployed as technologies of liberation, though often ignoring their obvious interactional
consequences. The observational concerns of interactionist sociology
can therefore be viewed as a distraction from the task. However, as
recent work and studies have begun to acknowledge, such a strategy
falls short in a number of ways.

First, the outbreak of 'theory' in a rapidly changing world can often
overlook the social texture and, for social actors, reality of the lifeworld. Furthermore, representation, forms and types are both utilized
and mediated by social actors, groups and networks as a necessary, creative and artful accomplishment of the world (this may well include
forms of resistance). Consequently, sociological understanding cannot
ignore the interactional dimensions of subcultures, consumption, the
body and so forth due to its fundamental relationship to the processes
which constitute such phenomena, and some contemporary work in
this area vindicates this position. The theoretical reification of these
phenomena ignores the interactive process; the notion that interactionist studies ignore power can be challenged by exploring the practices
associated with its manifestation, e.g. resistance, subcultures, mundane
practices of discrimination and prejudice.

Second, a preoccupation with power relations has (sometimes) produced accounts that deride and run roughshod over the social actors'
capacity to mediate, interact with and interpret various relations, experiences and messages. In one sense, the point of audience theory and
Hall's concept of negotiated de-coding within media culture studies is
to balance the representational model of televisual discourse and communication with approaches and ideas that note the capacity of individuals to negotiate texts in a variety of, some unexpected, ways. Thus,
the theorized expected reading of various forms of representation has
been questioned by observational studies, ethnographies that have
emphasized not only the reception of images, texts and so forth but
their creative and interactional articulation in various forms of activities (e.g. fan bases, to living room discussions).

However, while interaction, networks and 'lived experience' (surely
all experience is lived!) have had some limited re-exposure, the role of
the practical morality of types has not been explicitly discussed nor
acknowledged as a potent and relevant concept within most descriptions of contemporary sociological matters. Clearly, the role of types as
an interactional device and resource remains integral to many of the
phenomena that form the staple of contemporary social and cultural
studies. To this extent, the practical morality of types, their social
and moral accomplishment and use in doing social phenomena, stand
in contrast to semiotic calculus and its limitation to the analysis of
representations.

four

moral careers

learning and becoming

The themes of learning, becoming and career have had a wide resonance within the human sciences and within the context of British sociological work. These themes have impacted upon both theoretical and empirical work in a number of areas and domains of enquiry. Clearly, these themes are interconnected with the other thematic frames explored in the course of this book. In this chapter, we will explore institutional and organizational settings associated with education, medical practice and work. These areas have been characterized by studies influenced by interactionist ideas. Indeed, the concept of socialization, institutional identity, action and organization form a common bedrock of interactionist conceptualization in studies associated with institutions and organizations. The domains of education, medicine and medical practice in particular also represent exemplars through which British sociological work has exhibited its debt to and inspiration from ideas that can be understood as specific manifestations of the interactionist spirit.

Processes of socialization are of fundamental significance to interactionist research. George Herbert Mead's original programme of social philosophy was grounded in a vision of 'mind, self and society' as *process*. Indeed, his sociology was not based on the attempt to reconcile *a priori* categories of structure and agency, of mind and society, or of the individual and the collective. The three elements of his triad – mind, self, and society – are all to be understood as aspects of the same general process of development, change and evolution. The social self is not an entity, it is a process. Selves and identities are never fixed. Processes of socialization or enculturation do not have a determinate end-point. Socialization is not viewed in interactionism as the preliminary to some final state. The processes of becoming – of the flux of identity and biography – are the very stuff of social life.

It is, therefore, no accident that interactionist sociology has been especially lively and influential in the study of educational processes, and in processes of socialization in occupational or professional groups. The sociology of education has a fairly long history in the United Kingdom and there have been some distinguished names among its practitioners. It has, however, enjoyed a rather lowly position and has been for the most part a somewhat 'provincial' pursuit, conducted away from the most elite centres of the British academy. Its association with teacher training (in reality a loose one) has done no good to its standing over the years. Sociologists in the UK have been happy enough to study workers and professionals, but close association with them (by contributing directly to their training) seems to carry the same stigma as did social intercourse with 'trade' for less intellectual snobs of previous generations: leading sociologists are as likely as any others to adopt the detached aloofness of the 'State Nobility' as Bourdieu (1996) calls them.

Given the general affinities we have already alluded to, it is not surprising that sociologists of education were among the first groups of specialists to adopt and disseminate interactionist approaches to the empirical investigation of educational processes and institutions. It is characteristic of the British context in this aspect of interactionist research, as in others, that it should have mixed origins and inspirations, and should remain eclectic in character. Its story is not one of diffusion from a single site of origin, nor even from a single discipline of origin. It had multiple origins, converging on similar research problems and drawing on common methodological principles. The study of educational processes and settings in the United Kingdom in retrospect can be made to look like a very coherent development – as a series of responses to major changes in the parent discipline – with an unfolding research agenda. In reality, however, the development of a broadly interactionist sociology of education and socialization was far from that. It certainly was not a conscious attempt to embrace sociological innovations based on a consistent and sustained reading of interactionist sociology. Interactionism was certainly brought in, and in many ways furnished many of the key ideas and the language of research in which the work was couched. Interactionism was less the single inspiration as one of various intellectual currents that fed into the British experience.

In many ways social anthropology was as formative an intellectual experience as any other. Indeed, the study of educational settings was one of the first attempts to undertake anthropology 'at home' in a modern organizational setting, in that the research was done by people trained in anthropology or working in an anthropology department. When contemporary social anthropologists write about anthropology at home, however, they seem to treat it as a more recent phenomenon and make little or no reference to the educational research. This is, perhaps, because it was no more purely anthropological at the outset than it was purely interactionist in its outcomes.

Among the earliest attempts to document educational institutions and the processes of socialization within them were three related projects undertaken simultaneously at the University of Manchester.

Anthropologists there, such as Valdo Pons, were promoting the ethnographic study of local institutions and cultures. There was an ambitious, if ultimately under-productive, Greater Urban Manchester research programme, which would have produced a series of major studies in urban anthropology. The three educational projects were conducted in parallel by Colin Lacey, David Hargreaves and Audrey Lambart, to which more detailed reference will be made below. It is also noticeable that one of the other centres in which the ethnographic study of educational institutions took root was also influenced directly by social anthropology. Liam Hudson had been researching and teaching in social psychology at Cambridge when he was appointed to the Bell Chair of Education at Edinburgh University in the mid–1960s. He recruited a number of graduate students who had read anthropology at Cambridge in trying to reconfigure the Edinburgh department as an innovative research-led centre. He was joined by Malcolm Parlett who had been influenced by a period at MIT with a research group committed to the use of naturalistic observational methods for the evaluation of educational innovation.

The research students at Edinburgh carried some of their anthropological interests and commitments to the study of educational topics. It was a partial reflection of their background that they individually and collectively interpreted 'education' in a broad way. The main intellectual commitment that they derived directly from Cambridge anthropology was the assumption that ethnographic fieldwork was a valid way to undertake research. Indeed, there was a recurrent pattern to the research projects undertaken by a number of the ex-anthropologists. Under the influence of Hudson's social psychology, which included fascinating work on the intellectual and personal differences between arts and science specialists, there was a tendency to try out various techniques that included pencil-and-paper tests, such as Kelly's repertory grid technique, the semantic differential, sociometry, the twenty statements test and the like. To a considerable extent, however, those techniques were either abandoned or reduced to the status of supplementary data sources. Participant observation and ethnographic interviewing re-asserted themselves.

Among the research projects that took this turn was Delamont's study of an elite girls' school. The original research design was based on an interest in contrasting learning styles, based in part on an inventory of study habit: this in turn reflected Parlett's work on university students who were 'syllabus bound' and 'syllabus free'. As the research developed, however, the elements of participant observation and interviewing, together with sociometric methods, took over and the study reverted more closely to the anthropological and sociological than to the kind of social psychology practised by Hudson and Parlett. Brian

91

Torode's work was an even more extreme version of this intellectual journey. He collected a vast amount of data in the course of his field research with working-class pupils. He undertook extensive data collection using Kelly's repertory grid, for instance, in order to explore the school pupils' self-perceptions and perceptions of others. He also collected detailed sociometric data, and interviewed pupils' parents. His doctoral thesis and the subsequently published monograph version were derived exclusively from relatively brief extracts from ethnographic work on classroom encounters. Torode did not restrict his analytic insights to interactionist perspectives, however, he drew on a rich and diverse range of philosophical and theoretical resources in order to theorize the language practices and the work of reality-construction in pedagogic encounters. His personal research developed further in terms of language practice – including the co-authored monograph with David Silverman (Silverman and Torode, 1980).

Atkinson's doctoral research on medical education followed a similar trajectory. The doctorate was originally intended to focus much more abstractly on language and identity: the immediate influences were Dell Hymes, Basil Bernstein, Alfred Schutz and Maurice Merleau-Ponty. Acquaintance with Liam Hudson's work led to an interest in unpublished data Hudson had collected – based on semantic differentials – in which medical students had rated different medical specialists (surgeon, paediatrician, general practitioner, and so on). These data were ultimately unsatisfying in the absence of a close ethnographic understanding of at least some aspects of medical education. Atkinson therefore proceeded (with no little difficulty and after protracted access negotiations) to conduct an ethnographic study of the Edinburgh medical school (Atkinson, 1981). This provided a direct UK parallel with the Chicago School ethnography of medical education at Kansas (Becker et al., 1961), although the Edinburgh study had a much more explicit focus on the management of knowledge in pedagogic encounters in the teaching hospital.

These were just three of the projects that were undertaken by anthropology graduates, that passed through a phase of social-psychological methodology, and came to rest in an interpretative sociology, informed by interactionist and phenomenologically inspired traditions. They help illustrate the eclectic and messy processes whereby interactionist ideas could become assimilated in a context of ethnographic research and interpretative social science. In the mid–1960s the circle of doctoral students at Edinburgh (much more extensive than we have identified by name here) introduced one another to the emerging literature of phenomenology, existential sociology and interactionism. For instance, Schutz was supplemented by and extended by the publication of Berger and Luckmann's (1967) *The Social Construction of Reality*:

this was a remarkably influential event in the publishing history of sociology, bringing together the European tradition of phenomenology and Anglo-American social science.

Goffman's work, while escaping easy categorization and open to numerous re-contextualizations in different sociological traditions, was enormously influential in the 1960s. While sociologists of the time were by no means blind to the limitations of his dramaturgical and strategic metaphors, *The Presentation of Self in Everyday Life* (1959) was revelatory. It offered an account of culture and social action that had not been approached by any other scholar working in his or her own society. It rivalled – and in some respects surpassed – the best products of detailed ethnography from the anthropological tradition. Goffman's capacity to turn detailed observation into a kaleidoscopic array of concepts and tropes provided a remarkable resource for younger researchers searching for their own interpretative vocabularies. At the same time, work in a specifically symbolic interactionist vein became part of the analytic framework available to the Edinburgh group.

We have already made reference to the very considerable significance of the Open University group in the development of sociological studies of schooling and educational processes. The Open University collection of papers edited under the title *Schooling and Society* included a number readings from celebrated interactionist works. It also included phenomenological accounts and the developing approach of social constructionism alongside Marxist-influenced accounts of ideology, curriculum and selection, for example, studies included an analysis of role and interaction in teaching. Geer (1971: 4) examines the accomplishment and recognition of authority and the process of bargaining between teacher and pupils as well as issues surrounding the recruitment, training and professional status of teachers. Geer takes notes of issues concerned with the architecture of the classroom, and the character of situated interaction as well as issues concerned with the public affirmation of the teacher as an embodiment of objective forms of knowledge and hence the legitimization of control, claims making and assessment. The study also explores the moral bargaining between teacher and pupil, its spatial organization and rule negotiation/generation. A further study in this collection resonates more readily with interpretivist approaches. Berger's 'Identity as a problem in the sociology of knowledge' (1971: 107) explores the relationship between the Meadian tradition of symbolic interactionism and the phenomenology of Alfred Schutz. The notion of types and typifications and the 'stock of common-sense knowledge' provide an additional resource for exploring the dialectic between social structure and psychological reality. Drawing on Schutz, Berger suggests that the Meadian dialectic can be developed or complemented through the invocation of a related process, namely between 'social structure and the comprehensive organisations of reality within which individual experience can be meaningfully interpreted' (1971: 108). Central to this process is language as the means through which interpretative schemes, cognitive and moral norms, value systems and theoretically informed 'worldviews' are constructed and realized. Central to the enterprise of 'world building' is the concept of identity, indeed a repertoire of identities. In this sense the introduction of the concept of identity (as opposed to the triadic notion of mind, self and society) provides a conceptual keystone for the development of a possible research programme that Berger's interpretivist/symbolic interactionist dialectic suggests and points toward. Thus, the inclusion of this piece represents a manifesto for an acknowledged synthesis between the two traditions of interpretivism and phenomenology with the symbolic interactionism of Mead.

A third study in the OU collection represents the third influence in this specific collection, namely a concern with the ideological and political context of educational activities and organizations. The section includes contributions from Marx and Engels and studies carried out on the concept of equality of educational opportunity and social movements and political action. These studies and reading do not slot in so directly with the other themes, issues and topics covered by the other readings. However, the studies and readings in this section of the reader are here for a purpose. In short, they represent a claim that any interactionist perspective on education must still take account of ideology and the political in making sense of educational processes.

Despite this diversity of approaches and ideas the reader was described as interactionist in orientation. This may, from a contemporary perspective, appear to be a misnomer. However, it reflects the particular brand of interactionism that was being distilled, developed and promoted within the Open University at this time. This was an interactionist approach not only grounded in the work of Becker and Goffman, but also a developing strand of enquiry that was making connections with interpretivist traditions and critical perspectives in a synthetic fashion.

Thus, interactionism informed the sociology of education in the UK throughout the 1970s and beyond. The career of interactionism itself can be traced, selectively, through the development of this research field. We have already made some reference to the early years in Chapter 2. Interactionism is identified by Peter Woods – one of its most consistent adherents and advocates – as one among several key influences that informed the sociological study of schools and classrooms (Woods, 1979). Woods includes interactionism with phenomenology, ethnomethodology and social psychology among the intellectual precursors. He aligns himself with interactionism itself in justifying and informing his own ethnographic study of a secondary school. He does so, in part, on the basis that interactionism gives credence to social actors' own accounts; directs attention to processes of interpersonal negotiation; and pays due regard to the social context of action. In his own empirical work and its analysis in that monograph. Woods emphasizes – in the same vein as other ethnographers of schooling – processes of adaptation to the circumstances of schooling, including the development of students' shared frames of reference and group perspectives. Different modes of adaptation lead to the differentiation of student identities and careers. Individual and group styles or biographies are thus crystallized out of these adaptational strategies. Processes of adaptation within the school thus create the organizational conditions within which identities and reputations can diverge and stabilize in stable and predictable ways. Personal identity – especially for students – can be threatened in various ways. Most notably, Woods describes classroom encounters in which humiliation or degradation are brought to bear on students – reminiscent of Harold Garfinkel's account of degradation (Garfinkel, 1967) or Goffman's (1963) treatment of spoiled identity – when teachers 'show them up', making criticism a personally threatening matter. By contrast, students value 'having a laugh' in class, and humour may be a source of resistance and the expression of student autonomy.

95

Interactionist accounts of adaptation and identity-formation in education settings – mainly secondary and primary schools – have recurrently dealt with similar themes. In particular, they have treated schools as organizational settings within which biographies are shaped and progressively differentiated. Schools and colleges are portrayed as settings that are interactionally 'busy' places in which personal reputations circulate. Teachers and pupils are thrust together in enforced intimacy. The classroom is portrayed as an enclosed arena in which teachers and pupils find recurrent problems of establishing a *modus vivendi*. Teachers' identities can be interactionally fragile, when they are confronted by a relatively large group of students some of whom may not wish to be present and who withhold unconditional respect for the teacher. Students' identities are equally constructed through displays *vis-à-vis* teachers and fellow students. Within this micro-system, teachers and students are engaged in a process of mutual surveillance, testing out of each others perceptions, responses and interactional routines. The school and its various locales (classrooms, laboratories, gymnasia or playing fields) are thus rich environments in which social selves are forged, reputations established, and moral character worked on.

These perspectives were by no means restricted to interactionist ideas nor derived uniquely from them. In work published in the late

1960s and early 1970s one can readily detect the arrival of interactionism as an overt influence within a field that had already identified relevant themes and research strategies. One can, moreover, see the growing
influence of interactionism within the work of individual authors. We
have already seen that the intellectual climate in which interactionist
ethnographies of schooling were carried out was already in place virtually independently of interactionism itself. The three studies of secondary schooling by Hargreaves (1967), Lacey (1970) and Lambart (1976)
were part of the Manchester University programme in urban anthropology. They owed more to the tradition of community studies than to
American interactionism. The substance of their school-based fieldwork, however, prefigured some of the interactionists' themes.
Hargreaves notably went on to develop an explicitly interactionist allegiance (before moving away and pursuing other intellectual agendas
subsequently). The two monographs by Hargreaves and Lacey – dealing with a boys' secondary-modern and a boys' grammar school
respectively – were published in close proximity. Lambart's study was
a parallel account of a girls' grammar school, but she interrupted her
academic career so that the equivalent monograph was not written, and
her publications appeared some years after those of her male colleagues. The research programme documented processes of what Lacey
specifically identified as 'differentiation' and 'polarization' within the
school. The same processes were at work across the schools. Schools
differentiated their students, most overtly by assessing them and assign-
ing them to streams. In response to these organizational arrangements,
students developed increasingly contrasted, even mutually hostile, student cultures and increasingly separated social networks. Successful
students generated pro-academic, pro-school perspectives, while those
identified as relative 'failures' within the school became increasingly
estranged from it. There was, therefore, an ironic parallelism within the
UK selective schooling system of the period: even among the most able
and successful students, who were selected for the grammar school at
the age of eleven by public examinations (the 'eleven plus'), a substantial number were turned off schooling, becoming disaffected and
antipathetic to the values of the school and its academic content. The
more successful of the eleven-plus failures, on the other hand, could
align themselves with the school and its values. These processes were
not based on measured ability and attainment alone. There was also a
strong element of social selection within the school, and personal conduct was also evaluated by the school's teachers as part of the insitu-
tional shaping of reputations and careers within the organization.

These studies thus mirrored accounts of labelling and deviance
amplification from elsewhere. In particular, they described the amplification process whereby differentiation in the early years of schooling

generated subcultures and identities that became increasingly distant and hostile. Schools could thus be understood as institutions that reproduce social differences through these processes of subcultural formation and the associated distribution of social identities. The school system could also be represented as embodying a self-defeating principle – generating as many, if not more, students antipathetic to its content and its ritual forms as those endorsing them and succeeding within the academic culture.

In retrospect it is easy to read the highly influential Hargreaves and Lacey monographs as if they were interactionist ethnographies. Yet it is absolutely clear that they were not explicitly informed by the interactionist literature to any great extent. In a sense, both authors seemed to 'catch up' with the theoretical and methodological tradition that their own work prefigured and paralleled. The transformation of the work into a more interactionist programme can be identified in two ways. First, there is the subsequent work of Hargreaves and Lacey themselves. Second, there is the work that they influenced directly or indirectly.

Hargreaves himself went on to couch his own views on the sociology of education in specifically symbolic-interactionist terms. This is explicit in his general, synthetic work published three years after his first research monograph (Hargreaves, 1972). The work itself is an extensive and general review, drawing on sociology, social psychology and other sources (including literary exemplars) on social relations in educational settings. By this stage Hargeaves's work was thoroughly suffused with ideas derived from and attributed to 'classical' symbolic interactionism. For instance, the discussion of the self and socialization is grounded in a wide array of sources that include Mead, Shibutani, Blumer and Strauss. His discussion of 'perceiving people' is an essentially interactionist account of the reciprocity of perspectives between social actors such as teachers and their students. Hargreaves also deals with the processes of categorization that go on in educational settings, drawing on interactionist and phenomenological analyses of typifications (cf. Hargreaves, 1977). Throughout, Hargreaves emphasizes the need for analysts of educational settings and processes to treat seriously the definitions of the situation that are negotiated and sustained by students and teachers.

Interactionism had thus become the most important single justificatory framework for detailed analyses of schools and classrooms, with a distinctive emphasis on the categorization of students and the organizational shaping of educational careers. Interactionism pervaded the various edited collections of papers that were published throughout the 1970s and 1980s. Hammersley and Woods (1976), for instance, brought together previously published papers by American interactionists (including Becker and Blumer) and original papers by British authors in the same tradition (Hammersley, Woods, Hargreaves, Delamont and Atkinson). We have already made brief reference to Delamont's overview of classroom processes (Delamont, 1976) which was highly influential in disseminating interactionist ideas to a wide audience. Delamont drew together the emerging research literature and placed it within a symbolic interactionist framework, stressing the processes of mutual perception and evaluation between teachers and students, the negotiated order of the classroom, and the emergence of different student groupings and subcultures. Delamont's account was informed by her own ethnographic study of an elite girls' school, in which she – like other researchers – undertook ethnographic fieldwork, as well as conducting structured classroom observations (Delamont, 1984a). Delamont's ethnography differed from many sociological accounts of educational processes, in addressing the educational experiences of young women from backgrounds in middle-class and intellectual families. It thus contrasted with many of the preoccupations of British sociologists of education, who were and continued to be more preoccupied with lower-class or deviant males (Delamont, 2000). Among Delamont's elite young women, differential group perspectives on schooling and classroom life reflected the intersections of gender and cultural capital – the daughters of the intelligentsia and the 'new middle classes' had quite different collective orientations and strategies from those of the daughters from bourgeois backgrounds (Delamont, 1984b).

By the time that Stephen Ball published his monograph *Beachside Comprehensive* (Ball, 1981) the interactionist frame of reference was clear and explicit. In substance, Ball's school-based study was in direct line of descent from those of Hargreaves and Lacey. Indeed, the doctoral work from which it was derived was supervised by Lacey. The research itself showed that the introduction of comprehensive secondary schooling in England and Wales had little or nothing to eliminate the processes of differentiation, polarization and social selection that had been described in the pre-comprehensive era by the Manchester group. Whereas Lacey's monograph had but one reference to Howard Becker's early work on the teacher in the school system (Becker, 1953b), Ball's work pays explicit acknowledgement to Chicago School interactionism, as well as to the Manchester group and community studies more generally.

Similarly, interactionist work continued through further published research studies. Pollard (1985), for instance, developed the research tradition further by investigating processes of mutual accommodation and coping strategies within the primary school. Pollard again explicitly locates his work within a tradition of symbolic interactionism as well as phenomenology, stressing their recurrent interests in the development and maintenance of 'selves' in school settings. In common with other British authors, Pollard places considerable analytic emphasis on the coping mechanisms that students and teachers develop in order to render classroom life manageable and the strategies employed in the negotiated order of the classroom and its everyday routine practices.

Pollard's is thus one example of the widespread analytic perspective among British sociologists of education, in describing schools and classrooms as sites for the deployment of strategic interaction (cf. Woods, 1980). This in turn reflects a broad and distinctively British approach to the sociological study of educational settings: an emphasis on schools and colleges as places of work, accommodation and survival (see Delamont and Atkinson, 1995, Chapter 3, for a comparison of this perspective and American studies that have been much more overtly preoccupied with cultural differences within schools and classrooms.)

British interactionism and its wider influence have helped to create a sustained and cumulative research tradition. This has never been a purely interactionist one, as we have seen. It has drawn on and incorporated different intellectual strands. It is a distinctively British synthesis that has consistently provided one of the most lively and research-active domains in which interactionist thought has flourished. It has consistently demonstrated the power of interactionist ideas to inform and sustain a major programme of empirical studies. While each of those studies may be self-contained and often (though not always) conducted by a lone researcher, they are far more than a series of isolated case studies. One does not necessarily have to engage in a systematic review or meta-ethnographic exercise (cf. Noblit and Hare, 1988) in order to identify the continuities across the studies and the presence of a strong collective orientation across the research community towards the promotion of a common understanding and a set of common research problems.

This does not mean that all UK researchers in the field have stuck slavishly to an identical research agenda, and it certainly does not mean that they have all been in thrall to American interactionism. We have already seen that most of the British authors have brought to bear a variety of theoretical traditions. Here, as elsewhere – and as we stress repeatedly throughout this book – interactionism in the United Kingdom has nearly always been part of a syncretic research tradition. The combination of perspectives has differed from researcher to researcher and from local grouping to local grouping.

The interactionist study of face-to-face social interaction in classrooms or laboratories has, for instance, been aligned with approaches derived more explicitly from the sociology of knowledge (cf. Delamont, 1989), including the sociology of Pierre Bourdieu and Basil Bernstein. Delamont and Atkinson (1995, Chapter 6) provide just one example of an analysis that suggests a fruitful synthesis of work on socialization (in that case the socialization of teachers) from an interactionist perspective in the tradition of Everett Hughes, and the ideas of Bourdieu, among others, on the social organization and distribution of knowledge itself (e.g. Bourdieu and Passeron, 1977). Likewise, the sociological analysis of pedagogic discourse (Bernstein, 1990), they argued, needed to be aligned with the sociological study of educational processes.

The British syntheses of interactionism and other approaches led some commentators subsequently to conflate them all into a single perspective, sometimes attributing them all to the so-called 'new sociology of education' (Young, 1971) to which we have already referred in Chapter 2, and which pulled together phenomenological, Marxist and structuralist analyses of the organization and reproduction of educational knowledge. Karabel and Halsey (1977) made this blunder, for instance (cf. Delamont and Atkinson, 1995: 21).

In some ways the British use of interactionist ideas in the sociology of education was – like much of the interactionist tradition – an 'understated' one (Rock, 1979). It informed field research and it helped to generate empirical generalizations about educational processes, moral careers and collective responses to institutional demands. However, as early as 1978 David Hargreaves was asking – by no means rhetorically – 'whatever happened to symbolic interactionism?' (Hargreaves, 1978). Hargreaves was drawing attention to the relative failure of sociologists of education to develop new theoretical contributions to interactionism itself. To some extent Hargreaves was justified in voicing some reservations. As we have seen, he himself had attempted to articulate a sustained account of educational processes that placed interactionist ideas centre stage. The developing array of empirical research appeared to suggest, however, that while ideas and general orientations were being used fruitfully, they were not being developed into a specifically interactionist sociology. The ideas were still derived from Chicago for the most part.

On the other hand, Hargreaves's strictures should not be interpreted to mean that interactionism's influence on educational research was stunted or still-born. Indeed, there are several possible answers to the question Hargreaves posed, and they are by no means negative. One is – as we have outlined – that interactionism continued to inform sociological studies for many years; indeed, it continues to do so. Another answer is that the most abiding influence of interactionism (and its related sociologies) lies in the methodological justification it provided for extensive empirical research – not just in education, of course, but in many sociological fields. This is a major theme to which we return in Chapter 5. At this point we note that the close study of educational settings and processes has become widely conceptualized and legitimated

100

in terms of *method*. It is now commonplace in the United Kingdom and elsewhere to refer to the 'ethnography' of schooling. The methodological approach – with its attendant analytic commitments and orientations – is the force that articulates and synthesizes the research and the ideas, rather than one or other particular theoretical tradition or school. We do not altogether endorse that view. We think it is a mistake to equate a methodological perspective (and a very broad one at that) with a theoretical position – much less one or more 'paradigms' (Delamont and Atkinson, 1995, Chapter 11). None the less, the force of the ethnographic perspective cannot be avoided, and in its inspirations and development it owed more to interactionist thought than to any other sociological tradition.

The vigour of the interactionist tradition in educational sociology, not least in the study of careers, identities and institutions, means that it is far from coincidental that a substantial amount of methodological writing concerning ethnography and qualitative research generally has derived from researchers working on educational processes. Robert Burgess, for instance, was one of the first to write a systematic introduction to field research (Burgess, 1984), and it reflected Burgess's own field research in a Roman Catholic secondary school – 'Bishop McGregor' – (Burgess, 1983). Burgess also edited an influential collection of papers on field research (Burgess, 1984) that anthologized a wide range of materials from various disciplinary and theoretical traditions, including the interactionist one. Burgess went on to edit several series of edited collections on qualitative method as well as having a very considerable personal impact on the development of research methods and research methods training, not least through his work with the Economic and Social Research Council. Martyn Hammersley's own empirical research specialism was (and is) the sociology of education. His contribution to the development and dissemination of ethnographic methods and their associated epistemological issues has been second to none (Hammersley, 1983, 1989, 1991, 1992; Hammersley and Atkinson, 1983, 1995).

101

WORK AND ORGANIZATIONAL CAREERS

The sociology of work and organizations has, from the very beginning of interactionist thinking, always been an area of interest and intense focus for sociologists associated with the interactionist tradition. In conventional terms the world of work and sites of work (in institutions and organizations) has provided a setting in which individual social actors and wider social processes have been thought to intersect. In short, the substantive interest in work and human activity is also complemented by an opportunity to explore one of sociology's classic questions, namely, how is social order possible? The study of work, organizations and institutions provides a clear opportunity to pursue such central sociological concerns. Within the tradition of the Chicago School, Everett Hughes and Howard S. Becker both, through intense forms of participant observation, explored various organizational settings and occupational identities. Their work, as pointed out in an earlier chapter, developed the concept of career and type and applied it to an understanding of occupational lives and processes. This concept of work as a moral career enabled an examination of the opportunities, dangers, sanctions and rewards that characterized the living world of the work setting. It also represents a field of enquiry that has much in common with interactionist approaches to educational organizations and activities.

It is perhaps in the later work of Erving Goffman that the concept of an 'interactionist' approach to institutions, work and organizations finds a momentum that was to have a profound effect across the human sciences. Goffman's work on the presentation of self and 'back' and 'front' regions provided penetrating insights into the moral and social organizations of 'establishments'. For example, in a study of waiters and restaurant establishments Goffman noted how the polite manner of the waiter/waitress would change once they had moved from the front region of the dining table to the 'back' region of the kitchen, where displays of resentment, boredom or anger with customers could be displayed. Goffman's work brought forward the concept of the moral career, and the theory of types through his penetrating examination of total institutions and identities. In *Asylums*, Goffman examined spaces and places where back and front regions were of far less significance. He noted that, despite official descriptions, mental institutions were usually characterized by forms of practice that were oriented to the dilution of individual identity, sense of self and personal respect. These interactional orders were observed as working in ways that were often disciplinary and oppressive in practice.

Studies in the sociology of health and illness were one of the most fruitful domains in British sociology to document the intersection of individual identities and institutional arrangements in the development of *moral careers*. The notion of the 'career' has been a central one in interactionist accounts of individual and organizational experiences. Many aspects of health and illness lead to such a perspective, and medical sociologists gave currency to the career-perspective. Sally Macintyre's (1977) account of pregnant single women captured the perspective thoroughly and elegantly. The research design was itself described as a career study, explicitly acknowledging the inspiration of Goffman and Becker. A series of single pregnant women were followed from an early stage in their pregnancy to its outcome. In tracing the women's careers, Macintyre invoked the interactionist notion of the 'definition of the situation' in order to account for how the women perceived and interpreted their circumstances at crucial stages in their pregnancy. She documented the different interpretations that could be operative, avoiding essentializing the experiences of pregnant women, while also avoiding an over-rationalized version of decision-making processes in acknowledging the significance of chance events. Macintyre documents the moral work and character attribution that are done by and on pregnant single women, including the moral work of women's lay and professional advisers. The pregnancies and their outcomes are thus portrayed fundamentally as moral careers. See also Macintyre (1976) on the social constructions of motherhood and the 'maternal instinct'.

In a rather different series of Aberdeen studies, Bloor et al. (1988) put together a number of ethnographic studies of therapeutic communities. (The work is remarkable, if not unique, for its synthesis of multiple ethnographic sites.) Among other things, the authors document the processes of status passage and notions of 'progress' among the therapeutic community residents. They explore processes whereby residents' talk and behaviour are subject to 'redefinitions' by the staff and other residents. Depending on the therapeutic regime in play, residents' progress may be defined in terms of their acquisition of appropriate vocabularies and narratives, or by the acquisition of competence in specific daily tasks. Such therapeutic redefinitions therefore rest on the careful and detailed surveillance of residents: any and every action and speech event is potentially available for evaluations and redefinition in evidence of progress or its absence. There are, of course, opportunities for residents to engage in resistance against such surveillance and the moral categorizations that may ensue. Here and elsewhere (e.g. Bloor and McIntosh, 1989; Bloor and McKeganey, 1986), there are clear debts not just to the interactionist tradition, but also to Foucault's historical accounts of institutional regimes of surveillance and discipline (e.g. Foucault, 1973). Indeed, there is an expansion of the ethnographic and interactionist imagination here that encompasses early ethnomethodological work, Foucauldian analysis of regimes and technologies of the self, married to detailed ethnographic reportage. It is yet another example of the eclectic use of interactionist styles of research by UK scholars working in substantive fields.

Within the context of British sociology a series of studies, published by the Cambridge University Press during the early 1970s, topicalized issues surrounding work, identity and occupation. Some of the most famous of these published works included the famous studies by Goldthorpe et al. on the affluent worker. They also include work by

Beynon and Blackburn on workers' perceptions, Wederburn and Crompton on workers' attitudes to technology and Salaman's account of working lives in *Community and Occupation* (1974). Salaman's account provides an interesting framework for the sociology of work and organizations at this time. Within it Salaman notes a number of theoretical influences that inform his study; they include the ideas of Marx, Weber, Durkheim and Tönnies but also the tradition of symbolic interactionism. Drawing heavily on Hughes, Salaman explores the components and determinants of occupational communities.

The components of occupational communities are seen as those that constitute forms of life and practices associated with various occupational activities. In essence, occupational communities are those that are characterized by little separation between people's work and 'the rest of their lives' (1974: 19), in short, between occupational activity and friendship, family and leisure activities. A further dimension of the occupational community is the importance of the Goffmanian concept of self-image and presentation of self. Within the context of the occupational community this is, more often or not, expressed primarily through occupational identities (e.g. fisherman, musician, academic, and so forth). This form of 'occupational membership' (1974: 24) necessarily involves what Becker and Carper (1956) identify as a form of occupational ideology or culture. Drawing on the work of Polsky, Box, Cotgrove and others, Salaman notes that occupational cultures identify the value system of particular occupational forms, orientations and activities.

The determinants of occupational communities are, for Salaman (1974: 27), of three types. These include the involvement in work tasks, stratification position and inclusiveness of the occupational setting. Salaman's use of interactionist ideas is developed through a consideration of a number of occupational communities. These include shipbuilders, the police, fisherman and jazz musicians. Drawing on earlier work in each case, for example, in the case of the police, Salaman draws on Banton's work on police in the community (1964), Salaman provides an interactionist account of occupational communities and membership, interactional co-ordinates and determinants, in short, an interactionist account of various occupational lifeworlds. Salaman's account provides an almost 'classical' interactionist account of occupational communities. While acknowledging the influence of social theory, it locates the study of work, occupations and their organizational context within a space inhabited by living, breathing, thinking social actors. However, Salaman's work represents a contribution to the interactionist tradition whose level of formality (associated with the high point of symbolic interactionism) was not matched in future studies or contributions. In part, this is due to the drive away from formalization to sensitized and more grounded concepts.

A further contribution to the interactionist approach to work and organization within the United Kingdom was provided by Silverman's work on *The Theory of Organization* (1970). In this book, Silverman identifies four key approaches to understanding institutions and organizations. These include structural functionalism, organizational psychology, social-technical systems theory and the action model of organization. The action model of organization can be understood to include Weberian concepts alongside more fully distilled accounts of action theory in the guise of symbolic interactionism and the influence of the Chicago School. However, Silverman's advocacy of an action perspective, with respect to a sociology of organizations, opened up a space through which the workplace itself, and not just the broader conceptualization of occupational communities, was opened up for inspection. Expectations, perceptions, organizational roles and so forth became an area of interest and legitimate research. Silverman (1970: 170) notes that an action model of organizational enquiry may enable the study of the interactional differences and similarities across and between institutions. Thus, the idea of a comparative interactionist account of organizational work settings is announced. In many respects Silverman's work provided space in which subsequent work, focusing on discourse and interaction in institutions, builds upon.

Silverman (ibid.: 185) notes that the Chicago School's sociology of work did not, at this stage, have much of an influence on British social scientists. However, he notes the importance of types, moral career, role and interaction to the understanding organizational sites. Central to these concerns is the reciprocal character of interaction and 'the definition of the situation'. As Silverman notes (ibid.: 193), drawing on the work of Goffman, any study of organizations should pay attention to the 'bounded' character of the rationality that provides the context for action in any given setting. Silverman's discussion culminates in a powerful vision of the importance of interaction to understanding organizations. Silverman argues:

> The nature of the attachment by the actors to any existing norms is shaped by the orientations that they bring to the situation (especially taken-for-granted worldviews) and by their subsequent experience of the situation itself. The actor's definition of his condition is therefore an *emergent* characteristic which is continually reshaped by his experiences. (ibid.: 212)

It is this concern with the emergent properties of action, leading to formal and informal modes of social organization, that betrays Silverman's interactionist concerns. A precondition for the existence of organizations is located within the realms of actors' orientations to such an entity in the first place. Institutional identities are therefore a starting point for many interactionist explorations of organizations, institutions and the workplace.

There are a number of other important pieces of British sociology of the workplace during the late 1960s and early 1970s that have exhibited core interactionist themes and concerns. However, these concerns were not interactionist *per se* and were often tied to other programmes, normative principles and theoretical ideas. This cross-fertilization of approaches, concepts and principles remains a core feature of British sociology. However, as indicated in early chapters, the incorporation of core interactionist principles provides an interesting feature of the sociology of sociological knowledge in the United Kingdom. One of the most famous of these studies of work can be found in Huw Beynon's *Working for Ford* (1975). As is suggested above, this does not represent an 'interactionist' piece of work. It provides a cogent Marxist account of working on the assembly line in a large multinational automobile factory. The work provides a historical account of the Ford company in relation to the changing profile of capital in the United Kingdom and trade union organization and activity. It also represents a case study in the sociology and the history of industrial relations in the United Kingdom. However, the book is also concerned with the lives and occupational 'living world' of working-class men, a world that had often been hidden from view within structural-oriented accounts of agency, class organization, opportunities, hardships and experiences. As Beynon states: 'One of the most obvious criticisms of much that passes for social science is that it drastically underestimates people's intelligence' (ibid.: 113).

This clear commitment to taking the actor's point of view is bolstered by an awareness that people are able to make accurate and informed assessments of their life chances (1975: 113). This position has clear, critical, Weberian resonances with the work of Goldthorpe on the affluent worker and, though not explicitly, introduces the distinction between structurally generated attitudes, on the one hand, and the meaningful character of the living world of workers and the values of the lads at the factory, on the other. This position is also complemented by the account provided by Beynon that is highly ethnographic in character. For example, accounts from various informants, 'the lads' working at the plant, rich descriptive narrative that draws on first-hand observation of the assembly line and the wider occupational community, the lives and leisure pursuits of the Ford workers. While this work does not provide a methodological framework for its claims, nor does it refer to literature that can be located in the interactionist domain, it exhibits a sense of the ethnographic that is visible and tangible through the immediacy of the prose and narrative. This is a work that provides a cogent analysis of the motor industry and the *lives* of working people. The formal account of organizations is contrasted with accounts of the dangers, opportunities, relationships, dilemmas, interactions and techniques that workers use to get by and survive; the sheer grind of working life in a demanding industrial environment. An example of relating the lived processes of work with wider concerns can be found in Beynon's account (1975: 109) of 'going blank' as a means of coping with the tedium and monotony of the assembly line. This is related to the alienating effects of the labour process in question and is also exemplified through further examples that include workers' desired preference for cars other than the Ford marque. This is not to say that all of this account of working for Ford conforms to an ethnographic approach or approximates to a complete concern with types, processes and relationships. It does not. However, it does represent the seepage of core interactionist concerns into the mainstream of British sociological work, to the extent that they are not viewed as particularly deserving of attention, nor are they seen as notable or distinctive, instead, they have become taken-for-granted procedures and ideas circulating within the broad mass of social scientific ideas, methods, principles and practices. To this extent it expresses the level at which core interactionist ideas had penetrated the British sociological establishment. It also represents a framework within which ideas associated with the liberal critique of capitalist America could be employed in the service of more radical critiques of capitalist organization in other parts of the world.

In terms of additional developments in studies of work and organizations a later wave of more explicitly interactionist-oriented studies can be discerned. This pre-empts the explosion of interest in interactionist ideas via the fashionable rise in interest of qualitative methods during the late 1980s within social science. An interesting example of this type of work can be found in a number of ethnographies of occupations and work identities. One such study by Richman (1983) examined the working lives and daily round of street wardens. Published by the Manchester University Press, it can be viewed as a reflection, an interesting token, of the concentration of interactionist scholars and research that was identifiable in Manchester University and Manchester Polytechnic (as it was then, now Manchester Metropolitan University) at this time. The work, by Joel Richman (1983) explores the occupational lives of street wardens within the context of a neglected area of study, namely, the street. The book draws explicitly on the Chicago School, symbolic interactionism, the work of Simmel, the work of Mayhew and the wider sociological tradition. Thus, while the work is explicitly ethnographic in character, it does not seek to locate itself inside one particular theoretical tradition. The account of the work of street wardens is presented in terms of modified field notes gathered through direct observation and accompaniment of the street warden during their daily patrols. Organizational features of traffic wardens' work is not viewed as one that is subject to formal categorization. However, the identification of roles and hierarchies is discerned as resources through which the administrative design of street warden work is accomplished. In a chapter entitled 'Getting a Ticket' the importance of types (e.g. 'bad parkers'), speech (the display of swearing or rudeness by the potential offender) and interaction (good reasons for questionable parking) is identified. To this extent who gets a ticket and who does not is one that is couched within a framework of negotiated interactional practices. The centrality of face work, the presentation of self, account work, motives and mundane morality were central to this task. Further factors that are seen to effect the production of bookings is the concept of career. One tactic observed by Richman was that high ticket producers were often, though not always, oriented to a career-oriented script, as opposed to just getting through the day. A further account of street wardens' work is the use of common-sense geography as a means of organizing surveillance and placement during the day. The rhythms and activities of the street are practical concerns for street wardens as is time of day and so forth. This 'working knowledge' and other contingencies form a central aspect of the occupational socialization of street wardens. Furthermore, Richman notes that such occupational socialization is not a formal process but draws on the collective and individual experience of workers and is made manifest through shared knowledge, stories, accounts and so forth. Richman notes: 'Although industrial society is developing more and more mechanisms for the recording and transmission of knowledge, the cultural importance of the story in its interpersonal settings must be recognised' (ibid.: 112). Often these stories could be understood in terms of types that relate to different kinds of motorist. They sometimes function in order to display an identifiable moral lesson or rule, for example, how the most routine of situations is unpredictable and can escalate 'out of control'. Richman's study also demonstrates how the contested nature of the street intersects with the work of the street warden; to this extent the working lives of the street warden are contextualized in terms of wider social processes.

A much earlier, and more influential, interactionist-oriented study, that focused on occupational lives and practices can be found in Paul Rock's *Making People Pay* (Rock, 1973). This study explores the occupational life and career of debt collector and debtors. Central to the process of debt collection is the moral constitution and typification of debtors, these include 'the professional debtor', 'the feckless debtor' and the 'unfortunate debtor'. The process of enforcement and execution is realized through an interplay between moral assessments and the artful deployment of threats. Certain threats for specific debtors may not be appropriate or practical in terms of the recovery of outstanding debts. Thus, the trouble, work and time expended in gaining a legal order in order to seize assets are only appropriate if there are goods or property to seize. This is not always a very easy assessment to make as solicitors or those standing on behalf of debtors are reluctant to occupy a state of being knowledgeable or being seen to be knowledgeable about debtors' circumstances. A further aspect of the debt collectors' career is the management and display of 'the working personality'. This involves careful role work and negotiation in discharging work duties that may invite troubling, difficult and sometimes violent responses from clients. In terms of difficult cases, this may involve the management of deception in order to produce threatening circumstances (e.g. debtors' prison) as a means of securing payment or enforcing moral expectations. For example, persistent debtors who refuse to respond to an increasing level of threat may be paid 'a visit'. During the course of friendly talk and interaction it may be suggested that the debtor accompany the collector to a phone box in order to negotiate circumstances with the organization or individual to whom money is owed. Once outside the debtor's abode, the debt collector may continue jovial conversation, as a distracting measure, while conveying the unaware debtor to the debtors' prison. These strategies also help frame interaction within an apparent space of informality, and this is an important means of avoiding violent or difficult responses to unpalatable sanctions. *Making People Pay* documents the difficult and moral hazardous character of debt collection, it documents the manner through which role – negotiation, typification, face work and discrepant roles are central to the moral work of collecting outstanding debt. Debt collection and the career of both debtors and debt collectors within the cycle of collection and the avoidance of collection are characterized and suffused with practical moral and social processes. As Rock states:

109

> debt collection sets up a drawn-out career based on weak forms of social control. Collectors operate with a threefold classification of defaulters which is linked to two features of enforcement: the need to predict a defaulter's intentions; and the particular information that a process involving variable amounts of time and effort generates. The career is drawn out because it is subject to legal constraints which prevent precipitate action; it relies on bluster and the creation of impressions rather than direct sanctions; and it has to be both complicated and simple. It must be complicated enough to cater for a variety of types of default and response. It must differentiate between the feckless, the unfortunate and the professional. Having established a means of differentiation, it must further incorporate appropriate strategies for each type (ibid.: 294)

Rock's account provides a rich and detailed account of occupational lives and professional processes in which interaction is of central importance to understanding 'how the system works'. The complex co-ordinating strategies and role work associated with the enforcement of sanctions necessarily involve complex, yet recognisable procedures, for getting the work done. A central process, central to the career and cycle of debt collection, as well as the impression management associated with the 'working personality', is the process of typification. This process provides the means through which the perception and under-standing of potential 'victims' and the justification of harsh sanctions can be dealt with on a daily basis. Thus, once again, this study displays the close relationship between the practical morality of types and occu-pational lives and careers.

Other studies that have drawn on interactionist ideas via specific methodological commitments can also be found in work by Marxist and feminist ethnographers during the 1980s. An interesting, and relatively unknown, example of such modes of normative ethnogra-phy is the work of Kate Purcell, *More in Hope than Anticipation: Fatalism and Fortune Telling amongst Women Factory Workers* (1988). In this ethnographic study, the role of fortune telling in rela-tion to time, fatalism and the everyday experiences of female factory workers is explored. The study makes use of participant observation, the analysis of narrative and conversational exchanges as a means of exploring the mundane world of the shop floor and the role of for-tune telling in terms of the interactional order, practices and values of the women engaged in factory work. The ethnographic account reports on the role of fortune telling in relation to issues surrounding class, gender and 'realistic' fatalism. Clearly, the work draws upon Marxist and feminist ideas but its methods and observations are couched in terms of moral careers, interaction, types and the complex relationship between self-identity, experience and wider social con-siderations.

Other work that has been more explicit in its use of interactionist ideas and concepts in exploring the world of work, the workplace and organizations can be found in the research programme of the Cardiff School of Ethnography. This school refers to a number of interrelated works characterized by a commitment to ethnography and, at the the-oretical level, a particular engagement with symbolic interactionism and various forms of structuralist and post-structuralist thinking. In terms of studies of the workplace where scientific practice is visible, there has also been an epistemological engagement with the sociology of scientific knowledge. Thus while interactionist ideas were prominent in the development of this school they do not represent the sole source of influence. Delamont et al. suggest:

Rather than a pure copying of American interactionist sociology, Cardiff's own 'little tradition' of qualitative research was grounded in, and developed out of, a mix of intellectual traditions. Indeed, it is arguable that insofar as the Cardiff School (if there is one) has any interest beyond the purely parochial, then it lies in the fact that Cardiff is both frontier and microcosm. It is a frontier between various intellectual strands – American, British and European – and a microcosm of how ethnographic methods, interactionist sociology and other intellectual current have intersected. (2002: 16)

Such influences have been unacknowledged. In terms of the Cardiff School's study of work and occupations the interactionist strand remains prominent although a concern with the reproduction of knowledge and other matters are present. The Cardiff papers in qualitative research represent a collection of studies that reflect the important role Cardiff has occupied in the development of qualitative and ethnographic research. The first collection in this series *Occupational Studies and Working Lives* (1994) brings together a number of studies that draw on the ethnographic imagination, although they are not merely interconnected by a methodological tradition. These studies draw on the notion of group, encounters, the management of work identities and moral careers in making sense of occupational groups, interaction and work. For example, Coffey's and Atkinson's research on the early training and assessment experiences of graduate accountants (1994: 23) focuses upon group membership and the interactional dynamics of competing, co-operating and responding to failure. Coffey documents how a group perspective can be understood as a strategic device for coping with early training experiences and making sense of such experiences. For example, the use of informal study groups and the breaking down of work tasks helped deal with the intensity and volume of work experienced by trainee graduate accountants as well as fostering and promoting a sense of togetherness and shared experiences. This interactional resource of a sense of collectivity also enabled the pursuit of collective 'issues'. However, individual failure and repeated failure also generated group distancing from individuals who were in a sustained space of difficulty. While initial failure may have been understood as group failure, repeated failure generated alternate explanations that preserved the notion of the 'group' at the expense of the particularization of the failing 'individual' through various forms of professional and intellectual 'distancing' work.

A further study in this collection complements this approach to understanding places and sites of work. Pithouse's study of social work teams and the practical accomplishment of 'colleagueship'. The study focuses on how the interactional order in social work teams is established and maintained. The construction and management of harmony are understood as a practical bulwark to the uncertainty and dilemmas of working with real lives and client problems. The team also provides a 'safe haven' for a professional group unsure about their public standing. To this extent the 'team' involves a reciprocity of sympathetic perspective and the avoidance of critical scrutiny of each other's practices.

A third study in this collection consists of Robin Bunton's ethnographic enquiry into the reproduction of psychiatric knowledge. This study begins with the observation that 'clinical competence' is a fundamental feature of becoming a psychiatrist. However, such competence is not reached and then dispensed over time, rather, it is being accomplished on a 'no time out' basis. In this study the powerful and path-breaking work of one of the authors on the transmission of clinical knowledge is taken alongside the ethnomethodology of Aaron Cicourel and Harold Garfinkel and the conversation analysis of Hugh Mehan and Don Zimmerman. The examination of psychiatric competence, in this study, is located in a number of visible activities that include the ward round and teamwork. Central to this accomplishment of competence is the production and display of a documentary clinical method. Drawing on the work of Garfinkel, this involves constituting clinical psychiatric conditions through the 'search for underlying patterns'. Breaches of this documentary gloss, within multi-part ward rounds or team situations where clinical trainees or other professionals are present, through the display of explanations that differ from clinical categories or modes of predication, often provoke 'repair work' as a means of preserving clinical documentary reality. This is reinforced through the way in which psychiatric clinicians are routinely seen to exhibit, hold or occupy exclusive speech rights. To this extent this study replicates and draws upon a number of previous studies on clinical practice.

The significance of these studies is the extent to which the occupational sites and experiences of certain professional groups are opened up to ethnographic scrutiny. Within the context of British sociology the lived world of accountants, social workers, lawyers, and so forth, had not been subject to sustained ethnographic research until the 1970s and 1980s. While there are exceptions to this, the ethnographic focus on occupations and its use of interactionist concepts yielded a rich account of occupations and identity, institutional practices and the process of occupational socialization as an on-going process and locally sustained achievement. This work also impacted and connected with the growth in interactional studies of the institutions and the workplace that utilized conversation and discourse analytic approaches. To a certain extent they prefigured the institutional talk programme (Drew and Heritage, 1992) in which the micro-character of institutional dialogue became a focus of study, in the sense that the interactional character of institutional sites was being systematically explored. In some cases, these studies took inspiration from ethnomethodological traditions that focused upon members talk-in-interaction as a means of exploring the reproduction of knowledge within professional or institutional settings (e.g. Robin Bunton's study of psychiatry). To this extent interactionist concerns, the work of Goffman and ethnomethodology were represented in this programme of occupational, professional and institutional research. However, as stated previously, other interpretivist strands, the sociology of knowledge and structuralism also played a part.

In terms of recent ethnographies of work and sociological accounts of careers, that we shall not discuss in detail here, the interplay between Foucauldian concepts of the self, postmodern cultural concepts and interactionist concerns remain potent sources of inspiration. Latimer's (2000) work on nursing represents an example of such modes of enquiry. A concern with practice, discourse and relations provides a powerful theoretical lens through which to peer into the living world of the nursing round, the ward and hierarchies of knowledge within medical settings. While not denying the importance of contemporary ideas, the study of occupational lives and processes remains suffused with 'practices', ways of speaking, presentation of 'self' and relations with both objects and subjects. Such studies, while representing unique work, sustain important interactionist core concepts.

In terms of theoretical commentaries concerning work and occupational practices, a requirement to consider everyday experiences and the mundane logic and experience of the shop floor or organization remain important sources of inspiration for contemporary enquiry. The institutionalization and use of management strategies and styles are also, in some respects, drawing upon interactionist concepts, as a means of managing specific relations and processes of production or forms of organization. Interactionist concepts and observations (as well as sociology in general) have been used to inform such interventions and, among a range of other influences, feed the discourse of management studies itself. At the level of more empirical concerns, studies of teamwork, new management techniques and styles and the social meaning of work within various national and trans-national settings provide a space in which interactionist ideas as well as political economy can be utilized. The social meaning of work and the perception of workers, managers and so forth can be understood in terms of both a flowing milieu of socio-economic factors and interactional relations, processes and practices. Interactionism's relevance to such domains of enquiry remains to be explicitly recognized.

113

CONCLUSION

The prevalence of interactionist themes in studies of medicine, work and education in the United Kingdom has been illustrated in this chapter through reference to some prominent and lesser-known examples of such work. Again, the purpose here is not to provide an exhaustive account but merely to illustrate and explore the intellectual currents of interactionist thought within the UK. In many respects the world of 'work', 'medical practice' and 'education' represent three important institutional and organizational sites in which many human beings in advanced capitalist societies spend much of their time. While the appeal and requirement for increasingly sophisticated quantitative data concerning the constitution and character of such organizational sites are potent, in terms of relevance to wider policy considerations and initiatives, the understanding of experiences and the interactional organization of both work, education and the medical domain have provided empirical insights into the importance of interactionist core themes. It also represents a set of interconnected domains in which institutions, interaction and knowledge figure prominently.

In some respects, the interactionist study of occupational working lives, of learning and becoming represents a tradition that still survives. However, the legacy of interactionism has been obscured by recent developments. This includes a confident reassertion of quantitative methods and forms of research that focus upon pre-defined variables and measurable outcomes, on the one hand, and the deployment of new theoretical concepts, on the other. In one sense, the sociology of institutions has become one that has been superseded by a commitment to substantive domains: food, genetics, the environment, risk, the body, science, consumption, etc. In part, this conceptualization of sociology into substantive domains reflects the decline in theoretical certainties and the uncoupling of research areas from theoretically informed traditions. In one sense, the space opened up by postmodern social commentaries and the disdain for 'dead white males' not only generated exploration into supposedly unexplored topics but also represented a more eclectic mix of ideas and research commitments. However, the themes, ideas and topics that are suggested through the troika of mind, self and society remain sociologically potent. Within the context of British sociology, the concept of career, becoming and the lifeworld represent ways of conceptualizing and understanding the life course. Central to many of these studies are notions of time, temporality and the unfolding process of sociality. If conceptions of time in relation to the workplace and other sites have become a refocused topic of enquiry, then interactionism has had, as we have pointed out, a major part in relating the role of temporal considerations in terms of everyday life in both formal and informal settings. The re-emergence of a concern with life stories and biography contain and include a strong interactionist component, not only in terms of a prominent method of life story analysis (Plummer, 1995) but also in terms of exploring the notion of *process.* As Becker states: 'The life history, more than any other technique except perhaps participant observation, can give meaning to the overworked notion of process. Sociologists like to speak of "ongoing process" and the like but their methods usually prevent them from seeing the processes they talk about so glibly' (1971: 424–5).

The notion of socialization as process, the management of work identities through time as strategic resources and responses to the realities of occupational lives require reconsideration and revaluation in light of the rediscovery of temporal concerns within social enquiry. The process of temporality and its dialectic of the here and now have been a constant and fundamental characteristic of interactionist research, theorizing and thinking. Indeed, the micro-sociology of social time is a well-established sub-field of the interactionist tradition. Further developments within contemporary social theory may well lead for a call to 'temporalize' studies of the workplace and work practices. A retrospective analysis of other forms of sociological enquiry could no doubt, in a state of amnesia, describe previous work as lacking a 'time perspective', the adoption of which will be hailed as a new approach. We claim that any study of encounters and 'practices' and work will inevitably have to reconnect with core interactionist themes such as 'career', 'types' and moral organization. The concept of career in particular reminds us of how time is, has always been, and continues to be central to interactionist thinking both in terms of the work of Mead and beyond. It is of particular significance in terms of the relationship between interaction, co-ordination and social organization; a transposition of Mead's triadic formula.

Furthermore, as stated in other chapters of this book, the action-based perspective to organization remains an important resource for those wishing to remodel or re-engineer institutions. However, a sociology of institutions has, perhaps, passed in to other disciplinary domains where it remains a source of influence. Clearly, the use of ethnography, interactionist principles and ideas remains salient and visible within management science, marketing and human resource management. The migration of interactionist concepts concerning the 'organization' to the variable curricula of such applied disciplines remains a fascinating and poorly understood process in the sociology of the sociology of knowledge.

The interactional concept of learning and socialization as process also finds connections and possible unacknowledged precedents with contemporary fashionable ideas. The notion of the 'learning society' has been taken up as a new and important principle in the design of new educational policies. At its heart is a rejection of education as a fixed moment in the socialization process, rather, education and learning are seen to be processes that occur throughout the life course. While this may often be used to refer to the desire to open up access to educational settings, institutions and the extension of resources to excluded groups, it also represents a conceptual tilt towards the notion of process rather than structure.

The notions of learning, becoming and career are prominent themes in interactionist thinking that find resonance within the conceptual rubric of the social as a process of sustained interaction within a triadic continuum of mind, self and society. The power of these concepts and the sustained relevance of these ideas can be pinpointed in terms of a number of studies and the sustained relevance of such ideas to contemporary sociological understanding of both work and education. The legacy of interactionist thought finds resonance within recent work on time (Adam, 1990) and explorations and debates concerning the lifeworld and lived experience (Gorz, 1999; Habermas, 1979). The return to issues of social philosophy may represent a retreat from a commitment to observation. However, interactionism represents a particular operationalization of a specific social philosophy; it represents a drive from the philosophical into the domain of observational enquiry. Thus questions of being, of becoming, of engaging in the world do not merely remain within a philosophical vacuum. Rather they become sensitized concepts that have driven a whole range of *studies*. To this extent, questions of being and becoming, time, trajectory and the moment are not merely philosophical topics but serious sociological concerns. Interactionism remains an exemplar tradition and method for grounding philosophical issues in a commitment to observing such phenomena in-the-world. Furthermore, while interactionism is not primarily theoretically driven, it is committed to undertaking studies. However, it is clear that the theoretical legacy of interactionism, articulated through observational work, remains to be fully appreciated and understood in terms of the contemporary state of sociological enquiry, in particular, and the human sciences, in general.

five
questions of method

In many ways the impact of interactionist thought has been most pervasive through the promotion of certain kinds of methodology and the conduct of distinctive types of empirical research. As we argue throughout this book, those methodological influences have reflected a practical and eclectic intellectual style rather than a single-mindedly purist pursuit of one theoretical agenda. To that extent, therefore, many of the theoretical underpinnings have been implicit in the style of research and its reporting rather than being encoded in general systems of grand narratives of theoretical propositions.

In some ways it is increasingly difficult to identify the specific role of symbolic interactionism in the promotion and conduct of ethnographic and similar research. There have been methodological inspirations deriving from the second Chicago School authors. Equally, there have been retrospective accounts that link contemporary qualitative research back to the first Chicago School (and we recognize that this may be a mythological charter rather than an accurate representation of research practice at Chicago in the 1920s and 1930s). On the other hand, qualitative research has now become so widespread and so variegated that its inspirations are now diffuse.

Moreover, the interactionist approach to research itself has been transformed. There is now rather little explicit relationship between the methodological precepts and practices of Herbert Blumer (1969), Howard Becker (1971) or Anselm Strauss (1987) and the recent methodological work of Norman Denzin (1997), Patricia Clough (1992) or Laurel Richardson (1994). This disparity exists despite the fact that the latter trio of authors (and many of their contemporaries) continue to write under the auspices of 'interactionism', and to participate in the conferences and publications associated with it (such as the SSSI and the Couch-Stone symposium). In other words, the methodological boundaries and affinities of what passes for interactionism have expanded and become more permeable.

Furthermore, the inspirations for methodological innovation come from many sources. Contemporary interactionism is open to influences from many schools of thought and disciplines in the social sciences and humanities. There are convergences between interactionist sociology, cultural anthropology, literary and cultural studies. The ethnographic imagination is generic across the disciplines, while a renewed interest in language, narrative and textual representations has encouraged new trains of thought in all research domains.

What is undeniable is the extraordinary expansion of ethnographic and other varieties of qualitative research, with a strong influence from Anglo-American interactionist research agendas. That expansion has been global, creating a market for textbooks, journals and conferences concerned with qualitative research. In the United Kingdom a new emphasis on research training and practical research skills at under-graduate and postgraduate levels has created institutional demands and commercial markets. Qualitative, ethnographic research methods have featured with considerable prominence in such courses. Over the past twenty years or so, successive cohorts of students in sociology and other disciplines have been trained in practical and methodological issues reflecting – with different degrees of explicitness – interactionist interests and traditions. A clear exception, by the way, is social anthro-pology, which has largely retained its separate, even exclusive, identity. It has not – in the United Kingdom at any rate – developed research methods training and literature to anything like the same extent as soci-ology or other social sciences. Training for anthropological fieldwork is still treated in many quarters as more of a personal, tacitly acquired set of competences and experiences rather than a suitable topic for explicit methodological reflection (Delamont et al., 2000). Such methodologi-cal literature that exists also tends to ignore developments in other social sciences: that is not a symmetrical relationship.

At the risk of self-indulgence we can offer some illustration of the process through a personal engagement with it. In the late 1970s Paul Atkinson joined forces with Martyn Hammersley of the Open University to write course material for a new Open University degree-level course in Research Methods in Education and the Social Sciences. (The course was later developed at Masters level.) The course team wanted to include different, complementary research strategies, includ-ing ethnography. At that time the range of published sources was extremely limited. They were of two sorts. On the one hand, there was a restricted number of textbooks. They included *Field Research* by Leonard Schatzman and Anselm Strauss (1973) and *Analyzing Social Settings* by John Lofland (1971). Both provided students with clear, concise and practical introductions to the craft of sociological field research. While both came out of California, they had their conceptual origins in the Chicago tradition of interactionist sociology. That West Coast methodological and empirical style was also reflected in the jour-nal *Urban Life and Culture*, later to become the *Journal of*

Contemporary Ethnography. On a more general methodological plane was *The Discovery of Grounded Theory* by Barney Glaser and Anselm Strauss (1967). The latter book outlined a general approach to the generation of sociological theory and middle-range analytic concepts, written from a pragmatist standpoint and stressing the interpretive processes of data collection, analysis and speculation. Although 'grounded theory' was meant to convey general heuristics for any empirical social research, it was widely read, in conjunction with the authors' other publications, as having particular or even exclusive relevance for ethnographic fieldwork. It remains, one suspects, a book that is more cited than read, and 'grounded theory' remains a widely invoked term to justify research strategies that are not especially faithful to the authors' original intentions. (We shall return to this point once more later in the chapter, and the misreading of 'grounded theory' deserves a more extended discussion than is merited in this particular volume.)

The other source of methodological writing was the then smallish corpus of autobiographical accounts and methodological appendices of published monographs. The most famous of those – then as now – was Whyte's (1955) long appendix to his *Street Corner Society*, which ensured the discipline's familiarity with his close relationship with his key sponsor 'Doc' and the personal contingencies of fieldwork in an American urban setting. The collection of personal accounts, edited by Hammond (1964) under the title *Sociologists at Work* was an equally useful source of insights into the everyday realities and personal experiences of researchers 'in the field'.

The main inspirations to be gleaned from the sparse methodological literature and the published research were of three sorts: the practical, the personal and the epistemological. They combined to create an invitation to field research that incorporated a well-established tradition of empirical social research and exploration. By such means were assimilated a set of general perspectives on the relationship between theory and method, and interactionist ideas were included along with them. Having garnered shreds and patches of the available literature in creating the Open University materials, therefore, Hammersley and Atkinson (1983) produced their own book on the principles and practice of ethnography. It was certainly not intended to be a textbook on symbolic interactionism, and although it drew on a broader range of sources than research uniquely in that tradition, it was clearly influenced and inspired by a great deal of work that was. The general approach was informed by a particular set of relationships or elective affinities – between the interactionist model of social life and social actors, on the one hand, and the conduct of social exploration, on the other. This was at least congruent with the interactionist view of knowledge and its creation.

119

Interactionist sociology does not necessarily entail ethnographic research method, and ethnographic research can certainly be conducted under the auspices of different disciplinary and theoretical traditions. Nevertheless, there is a particular congruence between interactionism and ethnography which goes deeper than a mere preference for the 'qualitative'. Notwithstanding the disputed nature of the historical links between interactionism, Chicago sociology and qualitative research methods, there is absolutely no doubt as to the intellectual affinities between interactionist thought and ethnographic research methods (Rock, 1979).

The social actor in interactionist thought has specific characteristics and competences that render her or him distinctively human and social. Such a view of the actor directly reflects the inspiration of George Herbert Mead and subsequent social philosophy inspired by him. Interactionism's social actor has the special capacity to be both subject and object of her or his knowledge and actions. The twin aspects of selfhood are captured in Mead's classic formulation of the I and the Me. The actor can be the initiator of action (I) and the 'other' to whom it is directed (Me). This capacity corresponds to the ability to stimulate other actors in ways that the original actor is not directly stimulated. These two capacities distinguish human action from the behaviour of other species. Human communication escapes the confines of stimulus–response behaviour. The latter – including animal communication – can never transcend the immediate and determinate 'meanings' of specific signals and their evoked responses. The animal that signals 'danger' to fellow members of the herd cannot evoke any response other than the same response to danger on the part of the others. There is no opportunity for the non-human to frighten the others while not experiencing fright itself. The animal cannot, as it were, engage in a discussion about danger and fright; it cannot treat the matter as a practical joke by fooling fellow species-members by signalling danger when none exists; it cannot combine the species's signals into a narrative. (Mead's own views on the unique capacities of human communication, of course, pre-date work on the possibility of genuine linguistic competence among non-human primates. The general point remains valid, however, and still undergirds much interactionist theory.)

The thing that creates this special competence is the evolutionary shift from 'gesture' (shared with non-humans) to the human use of the 'significant symbol'. And language is the main system of significant symbolization. The human capacity for language enables the actor to act towards others and to act towards him- or herself in ways that are decontextualized, not limited to the here-and-now of the stimulus–response gesture. By virtue of language I can discuss things not immediately available to the senses; I can inspire feelings in others that I do not feel myself; I can talk about things in the past, the present and the future; I can talk *about* things rather than just responding to them or vocally pointing to them. The capacities that are conferred by our human mastery of significant symbols mean that we can think of human action in terms of two simultaneous dialogues. I not only engage in a dialogue of symbolic signification with my fellow men and women; I also engage in an inner dialogue between the I and the Me.

The actor of interactionist theory, therefore, is capable of self-consciousness and self-awareness. His or her actions, and his or her potential effects on their perceptions, are thus available for reflective knowledge. Even though many of our actions are – in this context – pre-conscious, in principle the interactionist actor can treat his or her actions in the world and interactions with others as the object of inspection. This activity is social, and the self that emerges out of such dialogic action is equally a social process. This view of the actor is paralleled by the pragmatist view of knowledge that fuels interactionist epistemology and methodology. In this context pragmatism refers to a view of knowledge that stresses its practical achievement. The everyday social actor and the scientist are equally engaged in a practical exploration of the world about them. Scientific knowledge is not warranted by methods that are entirely divorced from those of mundane inquiry. Philosophical understanding, by the same token, is not a matter of pure reflection or speculation. Viewed pragmatically we come to an understanding of the world through repeated transactions with it. To that extent, therefore, our knowledge is necessarily partial and provisional. It is also perspectival, in that our explorations and transactions necessarily reflect our respective positions, our starting points and our interests. This is not an account of knowledge that is based on a solipsistic view of knowledge-construction, or one that equates worldly knowledge with whimsical invention. Knowledge is created through transactions with a world that exists independently of the knower, although it can only be known through human explorations and interpretations of it. The same principles apply whether we consider the natural or the social world. In that sense, therefore, Mead and those he directly inspired did not need to predicate their epistemology on a radical distinction between the natural and the social sciences. Rather than having to argue for a distinctively interpretative domain of the social and cultural disciplines, they rather emphasize the – in that sense – interpretative character of all inquiry. In this respect, therefore, the interactionist tradition could be held to differ from social and philosophical movements that are predicated on such a distinction between the natural and cultural domains. Those include the German historiographical and sociological traditions that stress the difference between *Naturwissenschaft* and *Kulturwissenchaft*. The classical formulations of such differences by Dilthey and Weber, and the articulation of *verstehen* in the social sciences are grounded in a claim for a distinctive domain of the social, and a correspondingly distinctive approach to the social sciences.

Arguably the *verstehen* perspective is right to insist on the interpretative, cultural character of social analysis. But the underlying dichotomy is false. It reflects a view of the natural world and its investigation that is rooted in a positivism that is *passé*. There are at least three possible positions on the unity or otherwise of the sciences and the proper approach to the social sciences. First, one can have the positivist unity of the sciences: this suggests that there is essentially but one scientific method, and that all the disciplines, whatever their subject-matter, should aspire to and converge upon the one ideal. That ideal is predicated on a scientific method modelled on those of the 'hard' sciences. The second, often associated with interpretivist approaches, as we have just seen, divides the natural and the social, implying that the natural world can be understood according to the canons of the natural sciences and the social sciences can obey their own imperatives, recognizing the essential difference between the two. The third – and the one we are associating with interactionist pragmatism – dissolves the dichotomy once again. But it does not do so in order to insist on a unity of the sciences by subsuming them under the model of the physical or laboratory sciences. Rather, it does so in order to insist on the essential similarities between all forms of human inquiry. Whether it be of the natural or social world, our knowledge is based on the same principles of exploration and interpretation. 'Science' is, therefore, to be understood not in terms of abstract philosophical prerequisites, but in terms of human engagement with the world about us. In this sense too the interactionist perspective is far from the idealism that colours interpretivism. Indeed, one could argue more plausibly that in its emphasis on practical work and transactions with the environment (natural and social), interactionism is a materialist as well as a pragmatist view of knowledge.

In its pragmatist and materialist way, therefore, the interactionist view of 'science' helps to dissolve unhelpful and unproductive contrasts between science and non-science. In recent years the longer-standing distinctions between natural sciences and social or cultural sciences have been reaffirmed. In contrast to the positivist desire to assimilate all the disciplines to a single model of science, social scientists have tended to stress the interpretative nature of the social and cultural domains. They stress the inherently meaningful character of social and cultural phenomena. Interpretivism thus insists on the necessary difference between the social and the natural 'sciences'. The pragmatist/interactionist stance suggests a different kind of resolution, however. But it is the polar opposite of the positivist dream. From the interactionist perspective, the natural *and* the social sciences are equally grounded in human agency, socially organized work and acts of interpretation. From this sort of perspective, therefore, there is no radical difference between the natural and social sciences, and the epistemological common ground lies in interpretative work. The human and natural sciences are equally constructed through collective human agency. 'Grounded theory' thus stands, not as a characterization of sociological research and much less of qualitative research alone, but as a description of all scientific or scholarly inquiry.

This pragmatist view of knowledge, gained by successive engagements with the world, is not, however, a recipe for a purely inductive view of scientific or lay knowledge. Our explorations and transactions are not devoid of theories. Pragmatism and interactionism between them do not attempt to celebrate pure 'experience' as the only basis for knowledge acquisition. The true position can be understood – retrospectively to some extent – by a brief consideration of *The Discovery of Grounded Theory* (Glaser and Strauss, 1967). That book served some of its purposes admirably in encouraging a great many students and others to explore the social world in a purposeful and strategic fashion. Inadvertently, however, it helped to create a false impression among many readers. That false impression was probably amplified by wider circles of people who referred to the book but had probably never read it. The misleading impression of 'grounded theory' implies that the generation of ideas emerges mysteriously but inexorably out of the accumulation of data and the close inspection of those data. One collects – systematically, to be sure – a suitable volume of field data (such as interviews or observational records) and then derives analytic categories from methodical readings and re-readings of those materials. In this (mis)representation of grounded theory it is described as an almost purely inductive process of reasoning that leads the analyst from data to theory. Grounded theory can, in this version, be contrasted to the deductive mode of reasoning associated with experimental and other research designs associated with natural scientific models.

Now this caricature is not too far from many representations of grounded theory, and it is one that has – contrary to its originators' own ideas – misrepresented pragmatist and interactionist approaches to research and methodology. But it is a false view which sadly but significantly distorts the true picture and misrepresents the more general approaches that are characteristic of interactionism. The logic of inquiry is by no means based on a crude inductivism. Rather, it is based on the principle of *abductive* logic. This is central to Peirce's pragmatist theory of knowledge, and it illuminates the general thrust of 'grounded theory'. Abduction refers to an interactive process of knowledge, a

123

dialectic between ideas and experience, or between data and theory. For Peirce and for Glaser and Strauss, the generation of ideas – the context of discovery – is just as significant as the testing of them – the context of justification. Inductive reasoning alone cannot generate useful ideas. But purely hypothetico-deductive modes of reasoning are equally limited. They may tell us a good deal about testing ideas, but they have very little to tell us about where plausible and fruitful ideas come from. Even the most ardent of Popperians does not generate and test all possible hypotheses. Plausible hypotheses and lines of inquiry are generated out of the investigator's experience of the field in question, often deriving from preliminary investigations, hunches, chance observations and the like. Peirce's original conception of abduction, therefore, allows a role for experience and observation in the derivation of productive and plausible working hypotheses. In this approach there is a constant interpretive interplay between theorizing and the practical exploration of the social or natural world. One does not rely upon a purely inductive accumulation of data. Far from it, data and experience are always the starting point for the abstraction of ideas. Abduction depends on the tentative formulation of general ideas: the analyst who is confronted by a series of observations must constantly speculate as to what underlying pattern might be derived, what model might be constructed to account for the observed phenomena, and so on. These are 'drawn out' (as the Latin origin of *abduction* implies) from the data, but are used as provisional working ideas in order to re-visit the data with a view to questioning, refining and extending those ideas. The process of deriving an ideal type in sociological reasoning is but one clear example of such abductive reasoning. To return to the specific issue of grounded theorizing, one can thus see that its roots in pragmatist epistemology have to be understood if one is to avoid the popular misconceptions. It is not just a matter of indiscriminate data collection followed by an intense scrutiny of those data in the vague (and often vain) hope that appropriate themes and concepts will somehow 'emerge'. Certainly, new ideas are regarded as emergent phenomena. How could novel ideas be otherwise? But the overall approach insists on the development of ideas, theories, models and working hypotheses.

Viewed from this perspective, then, the ordinary social actor (the man or woman in the street as the phenomenologists might have it) and the social researcher are both 'grounded theorists'. Both are engaged in exploratory transactions with the natural and cultural world around them. They both derive a working knowledge from their experiences and observations. They both generate generalized patterns of expectations, and those are progressively tested against further explorations. There is thus no radical difference between the context of discovery and the context of testing.

Now it is clearly possible to engage in ethnographic social exploration without reference to interactionist traditions or to pragmatist epistemology. There are whole disciplines – like social anthropology – that are rooted in ethnographic research that owe little or nothing to interactionist ideas. The significant contribution of 'community studies', to some extent straddling the anthropological and sociological literatures, owes little directly to interactionism. On the other hand, the affinities between urban sociology, with particular studies of urban communities and local subcultures, and the Chicago School of sociology reflects at least a certain congruence or affinity between the traditions. Nevertheless, the rise of qualitative and ethnographic research in English-language sociology reflects a persistent, if tacit, indebtedness to interactionist perspectives.

Indeed, many of the direct inspirations for the development of qualitative methods on both sides of the Atlantic can be attributed to the work of Chicago School interactionists and those they influenced directly. In addition to the highly influential accounts of grounded theory, there was a series of key methodological papers that clustered in the late 1950s and the 1960s that laid foundations for more widespread methodological advocacy. Those key papers were circulated widely in anthologies of papers that were the staple fare of courses in qualitative research methods in American graduate schools and in the United Kingdom (where in the absence of formal research methods training at that time, the reception of methodological work was more dependent on individual initiative and the interpersonal networks of younger researchers). The two collections of papers edited by McCall and Simmons (1969) and by Filstead (1970) did much to transform a series of journal papers into a canonical set of methodological issues. Many of them were by interactionists. They grew directly out of the authors' own very recent engagement with field research in diverse organizational and other settings.

Those papers, which rapidly became classics in the field, set an agenda of topics for methodological commentary and reflection. They included, for instance, Blanche Geer's (1964) famous formulation of the researcher's intellectual work during her or his 'first days in the field'. The paper reported Geer's own experiences of work among university students, on which she had collaborated with Howard Becker and Everett Hughes, and therefore sprang directly out of the research practices of the second Chicago School. Geer stressed the significance of early days in a new field setting, recognizing that the strangeness of the new setting provided the possibility for significant insights. Becker and Geer together provided a much-cited commentary on the respective strengths of participant observation and interviewing. Their discussion was open to – and received – misinterpretation, for they were not arguing unequivocally for the absolute superiority of participant observation although that is how their argument was often taken. They did argue that there was a particular sense in which participant observation was superior – and that was in the description of events in context. The contrast they drew between events and accounts of events yielded by interviews mirrored another of the classic formulations that was also one of the canonical texts – the often-quoted distinction between 'what people do' and 'what people say they do'. This formulation did not in itself derive explicitly from a symbolic interactionist standpoint, but taken in conjunction with the Chicago School methodological commitments, it helped to provide a powerful rationale for participant observation-based field research in contrast to the sample survey that was readily seen as the dominant mode of sociological research. In a similar vein, the classic papers addressed the vexed question 'How do you know if your informant is telling the truth?' (Dean and Whyte, 1958).

Issues of data analysis were also raised in these classic formulations of methodological problems. Howard Becker (1958) outlined issues of 'inference and proof' in the analysis of field data. He stressed that there were canons of rigour to be employed in the analysis of what would now be called qualitative data. In part this reflected a longer tradition of analysis that was derived from the first Chicago School. Florian Znaniecki outlined what he called 'analytic induction' as a process, through which the researcher could establish a dialectic between data and inferences, inspecting negative or deviant cases in order to modify or refine concepts and derive explanatory frameworks (Znaniecki, 1934). In many ways analytic induction paralleled grounded theory in translating interactionism's pragmatist roots into a practical methodology. Like grounded theory, analytic induction captured a set of heuristic procedures rather than offering a hard-and-fast set of prescriptive formulae. Becker's account of inference and Znaniecki's formulation of analytic induction together helped to define a rationale for rigorous analyses of field data that were faithful to the realities of field experience rather than aping the procedures associated with manipulating statistical data.

The classic papers and the anthologies that incorporated them defined a set of issues and solutions that shaped several generations' understandings of field research, and brought key interactionist ideas into that methodological frame. These perspectives were also enshrined in a relatively small number of methods textbooks that further consolidated the Chicago School influence on research procedures. Among the central figures to contribute to methods writing, Leonard Schatzman and Anselm Strauss co-authored a succinct introduction to field methods that was a *vade-mecum* for many graduate students (Schatzman and Strauss, 1973). This encapsulated basic methodological advice concerning the entire research process. John Lofland (1971) also published an introductory account in *Analyzing Social Settings* – subsequent editions being co-authored with Lyn Lofland (Lofland and Lofland, 1984). These two volumes brought the basics of Chicago-style interactionism to a much wider audience. They were among the very first textbooks (as opposed to readers) to summarize and codify the kinds of procedures that Everett Hughes, Anselm Strauss, Howard Becker, Blanche Geer and their contemporaries had brought to bear in their programmes of empirical sociological research.

More ambitiously, if only in scope and length, Denzin's *The Research Act* (1970) was a major statement of the principles of research in the interactionist tradition. Denzin drew many of the principles that had informed the research of the second Chicago School. He succeeded in bringing together a systematic account of general methodological principles. He stressed, among other things, not only the principles of analytic induction but also the principles of *triangulation*: that is the strategic and purposive deployment of multiple perspectives and bringing them to bear on the same phenomenon. Triangulation could synthesize multiple methods or multiple observers. Like other, similar, formulations, Denzin's treatment of triangulation suggested that rigour could be attained by the use of analytic principles not solely dependent on statistical techniques. His formulation of triangulation reflected a pragmatist appreciation for the perspectival nature of understanding (although it was susceptible to a mechanistic interpretation that implied that one could simply aggregate or synthesize data of different types as if they were simply additive).

Taken together, then, one can see a period in which key methodological texts – papers, elementary textbooks and more ambitious texts – took key authors and ideas from within the interactionist tradition and made them part of a wider codification of qualitative, field-based research approaches. Together they suggested that field research, in organizations or in less formal settings, had its own characteristic set of methodological issues, its own problems and its own solutions. They proposed an array of indigenous justifications and criteria for field research that were not simply derived from other research styles and traditions. They helped researchers escape from the evaluative criteria that had been derived from experimental or survey research designs and the management of data derived from such strategies. American interactionism in the period of the 1960s and 1970s was thus one of the main inspirations for the promotion of field research in sociology, and from which it spread into many other disciplines and empirical fields of inquiry.

127

It was entirely in keeping with the general tenor and spirit of inter-actionist thought that the methodological perspectives derive from engagements with empirical research in key institutional and interpersonal settings. British awareness of ethnographic and other research methods was – as we have suggested – influenced directly by American texts and models. Equally, it derived from the growing corpus of British field research in core areas of social research – the sociological study of deviance, education, medicine, work and the professions among them. The methodological awareness of interactionism in the United Kingdom is a direct reflection of the second Chicago School of work inspired by such leading figures as Everett Hughes, Howard Becker, Blanche Geer and Anselm Strauss. As we suggested in the Introduction, there are close parallels between what one might call the first British School and the second Chicago School in this as in other respects.

In the United Kingdom British sociologists incorporated many of the American methodological writings into a newer wave of methods texts. The growth of methodological literature dates from the late 1970s and early 1980s. Two books – paralleled by collections of papers – embodied the British contributions. In many ways they were very similar. Robert Burgess's *In the Field* (1984) and *Ethnography: Principles in Practice* by Hammersley and Atkinson (1983) both synthesized their authors' own experience of empirical fieldwork and their assimilation of a variety of disciplinary and methodological sources – including the American interactionist literature. They had other similarities too. Burgess and Hammersley had both undertaken fieldwork in educational settings, and were therefore influenced directly by the tradition of school studies that synthesized interactionist and other ideas within that institutional domain.

It is characteristic of the tenor of these books and of the period that Burgess, for instance, should attribute the methodological principles he outlines to symbolic interactionism (1984: 4). It is equally characteristic of the British approach that he also acknowledges other theoretical and methodological commitments, not least those of British social anthropology and Marxism. Burgess and Hammersley and Atkinson succeeded in synthesizing a number of methodological traditions. They brought together the American traditions derived from interactionist urban and institutional field research and other traditions that were shared with British social science. The latter included community studies, which had in turn provided a link between sociological and anthropological studies. The influence of American interactionism was added to a well-established indigenous commitment to field research. The work of community studies and social anthropology in the United Kingdom had not yielded much in the way of methodological literature. There was, therefore, a very clear opportunity for these British authors

128

to establish a distinctive position. The particular time at which these textbooks, and Burgess's companion anthology appeared, was one when there was a burgeoning of qualitative, ethnographic work in the United Kingdom. This was not, of course, a coincidence. There was a simultaneous development of empirical research and methodological interest among British sociologists, in a number of key empirical areas. The research started to flourish at various key sites, among research groupings of doctoral students and their mentors. We have mentioned several of them already. They included the collection of medical sociologists at Aberdeen, the educational research groups at Edinburgh University and Manchester University, and the network of deviance researchers brought together through the National Deviancy Conference. In the late 1960s and 1970s there had developed a growing corpus of published research and doctoral projects that used qualitative research methods, and that was explicitly or implicitly informed by interactionist and related forms of interpretative sociology. By the latter half of the 1970s, therefore, the time was right for methodological interest to take off. The impetus for Hammersley and Atkinson came originally from their collaboration on the Open University research methods course, designed for advanced undergraduate students pursuing distance-learning degree schemes in education and the social sciences. (It was, years later, made into a Master's-level course.) It was characteristic of the time that this course – designed to cover the major areas in a cross-disciplinary course – included systematic treatment of survey research, experiments and ethnographic research. The creation of this course thus provided Hammersley and Atkinson with the opportunity to include ethnographic work within a widely distributed set of teaching materials. (The course units, as the printed materials were called, were sold to the public as well as being part of the supporting materials sent to registered students.) Like many of the earlier Open University course, the research methods course had some degree of influence beyond the OU itself. The inclusion of ethnographic work alongside more traditional methods and statistical analysis gave the former some degree of legitimacy as well.

It is apparent that the methodological literature that appeared in the United Kingdom in the 1980s and later was not exclusively interactionist in inspiration. They drew on a wider and more variegated literature than that. As we have suggested, they incorporated an awareness of anthropological traditions as well. Hammersley and Atkinson did develop a perspective that was readily identified with the interactionist tradition. They proposed a distinctive set of themes that tied together all of the various aspects of ethnographic work, and collected them together under the rubric of 'reflexivity'. This term had been applied already to a variety of phenomena, and would subsequently be applied to even more. The essential point of Hammersley and Atkinson's usage was the insistence that the ethnographer's knowledge is constructed out of her or his transactions with the social world, in which the ethnographer is implicated. The ideal of positive science – especially context-independent measurement and a neutral language of description – is impossible. The ethnographic observer is not a neutral instrument of measurement or recording. He or she co-constructs 'the field' of field research through processes of engagement with a given social world. This principle of reflexivity, they argued, also extends to the ethnographer's means of representation. The ethnographer also re-constructs a social world through the resources of textual conventions and natural language. Atkinson had already written about this specific aspect of ethnographic work (Atkinson, 1983). He had suggested that there was something of a paradox in the development of empirical interactionist work and methodological commentary. He contrasted interactionism's interest in the centrality of language and representation with its practitioner's lack of self-consciousness as to how they used written language to persuade readers of the persuasiveness of their written accounts. Atkinson's argument, which was first published before the appearance of the textbook with Hammersley, was that this was not an inherent fault with interactionism, but rather constituted an extension of its core arguments. The principle of reflexivity suggested that ethnography depended on the homology between the interactionist model of social life and social actors, on the one hand, and the principles of ethnographic research, on the other. Both were predicated on a series of transactions – between the social researcher and her or his hosts, and in the internal dialogue between the participating I and the analytic Me. There is a direct congruence between the interactionist's social actor and the ethnographer as a social explorer. There was, therefore, a profound relationship between interactionist sociology and the ethnographic principles enunciated by Hammersley and Atkinson. Their outline of reflexivity was a re-formulation of some of the pragmatist principles that underpinned the interactionist tradition. The term 'reflexivity' has been applied with different denotations in the context of sociological and anthropological research practices – see Davies (1999) for a valuable review.

Characteristically, therefore, the influential methodological works by British methodologists did two things. They extended and affirmed interactionist principles while simultaneously aligning them with wider sociological and anthropological interests. This is in keeping with the British intellectual context more generally, and can be discerned in other methodological texts. Delamont's methodological account, for instance, is aimed specifically at researchers working in educational settings (Delamont, 1992). It draws on the empirical research conducted by Delamont herself and others in schools and classrooms, much of which owed a major debt to interactionist inspirations, although the explicit debt to interactionism is understated. (These are outlined in Chapter 4, where we discuss the interactionist interest in processes of socialization and personal transformation.) This was also a reflection of the remarkable emphasis on qualitative, ethnographic research that had gripped educational research from the very end of the 1960s. Methodologically, the face of educational research was transformed. The changes took place on both sides of the Atlantic, but British scholars were especially active and prominent. Quasi-experimental research designs for innovations and their evaluation lost their position of dominance, and a multiplicity of strategies flourished, including action-research and case-study methods. The pursuit of ethnographic research at school or classroom level became a major research strategy within educational research more generally. The conduct of educational ethnography was a modest growth industry, spreading from relatively few individuals and research groups to become part of the mainstream. In some quarters among educational researchers at least, the interactionist influence was aligned with ideological commitments. Qualitative research was seen as inherently aligned to ideals of 'democratic' intervention and evaluation. The underlying notions of negotiation between the observer and the observed, the commitment to cultural relativism and to the viewpoint of the 'underdog' were congruent with ideals for educational research embraced by leading scholars such as Stenhouse, who was notable for establishing in the United Kingdom a style of research – especially the evaluation of educational innovations – that celebrated democratic ideals, including the recognition of educators as partners in the research process. This in turn is also related to the development of teacher-research: the conduct of research by practitioners, working in and on their own professional sites. In recent years, the trajectory of the journal *Qualitative Studies in Education* exemplifies some of these tendencies. It started in a fairly conventional ethnographic vein, with a strong emphasis on fairly conventional empirical research and methodology, and has become much more characterized by postmodern, critical, postcolonial discourses, and by a variety of textual genres.

It would be quite wrong, therefore, to attribute the contemporary enthusiasm for qualitative research methods entirely to the influence of interactionism. An inspection of contemporary methodological and empirical writing demonstrates a variety of inspirations and exemplars – among them phenomenology and ethnomethodology, feminist standpoint methods, cultural studies of various persuasions, and ideas derived from post-structuralist analysis. Indeed, the very strength of qualitative research in recent years can be attributed to the variety of

131

theories, standpoints and sympathies with which they can be associated. Even within a narrowly defined symbolic interactionism there is no perfect correlation between the theory and the methods. Indeed, there is a heterodox tradition within symbolic interactionism that is not grounded in ethnographic fieldwork at all. The general relationship between interactionism and qualitative research is a broad family resemblance, based on common principles, rather than a necessary one. Equally, qualitative research can be justified with reference to a variety of perspectives. In the United Kingdom, as we have seen already, inspiration for qualitative research can come from and integrate a variety of sources. For instance Lee Harvey – who had written a monograph on the Chicago School of sociology – advocated a critical ethnography that combined field research with a critical perspective on race, class and gender (Harvey, 1990). This sought to align the ethnographic approach with the larger-scale concerns of social inequality and exclusion. In a very different vein, but with a similar form is the alliance between feminist epistemology and qualitative research. One aspect of this is to be found in the innovative work of Stanley and Wise. In their methodological work *Breaking Out* (though it is far from being just a methods textbook), Liz Stanley and Sue Wise (1983) suggest that there is a close affinity between feminist interests and the sociology of everyday life, drawn from an interpretative perspective. Both approaches seek to make problematic mundane social realities. Feminism is certainly a natural ally with social phenomenology. While not particularly interactionist, Stanley and Wise are part of a general movement that aligns feminist scholarship with varieties of qualitative, interpretative sociology.

Most recently, justifications for qualitative research have included appeals to postmodernism. In itself, postmodernism is an amorphous idea, invoked to legitimize a multitude of different positions. In relation to methods, postmodernism is held to mark a radical break with previous approaches to social research – including more conventional interactionist ethnography. Previous research strategies are, from the postmodern perspective, all denigrated as unduly modernist or positivist. Notwithstanding the attempts of Chicago-School and other field researchers to define research criteria that were appropriate to ethnographic work rather than imposing inappropriate frameworks derived from other paradigms, postmodernists tend to lump them all together and to dismiss them as equally flawed. They are flawed because they retain an implicit commitment to criteria of truth – of validity – that remain unreconstructedly modernist. In contrast, postmodernism embraces a rather different set of rationales for qualitative research. It treats any approximation to conventional notions of validity as inappropriate, instead celebrating a variety of possible criteria. Equally, postmodernist research is held to enshrine perspectival knowledge that is explicitly aimed at giving voice to particular individuals or social groups. It is partisan, and it is critical, but it denies the kind of 'objective' measures of exclusion or inequality that more conventional approaches to social research would employ. In the current climate, therefore, appeals to postmodernism are among the diverse justifications for the use of qualitative research strategies that make few overt claims upon the interactionist tradition. More closely aligned to the long tradition of interactionism is the attempt to document 'lived experience' and to capture the 'voices' of social actors. For the growing influence of postmodernism and its imposition on the base of interactionist ethnography, compare the two editions of the *Handbook of Qualitative Research* (Denzin and Lincoln, 1994, 2000). (We elaborate on this point below.)

Indeed, the United Kingdom has been especially receptive to the promotion of such qualitative methods – more so than the United States – although they undoubtedly flourish worldwide. UK sociology has rarely, if ever, seen the kind of quantitative presence or predominance as has its American counterpart. There has, of course, been a significant tradition of 'political arithmetic' among British social scientists. In particular the British empirical tradition that linked sociology with demography produced some of the most significant and distinctive contributions to the sociology of modern Britain: the successive studies of social mobility established a distinctive collection of research questions, closely related to social-democratic preoccupations of the post-war settlement, the relative permeability of the British class system, patterns of upward and downward social mobility, changing structures of labour markets, the influence of education on occupational class, the reciprocal influence of one's class of origin on educational experience and attainment, the relative mobility of men and women. These and related problems dominated a major strand of British sociology. The quantitative element has been sustained over the same period, with successive cohort and longitudinal studies. The quantitative strengths of British social research have been strengthened by the applications of multidimensional scaling, time-series analysis and other sophisticated techniques of data analysis and modelling. To a considerable extent, however, these have become minority interests. Sophisticated multivariate techniques have certainly not dominated British sociology. Indeed, they have not enjoyed especially high esteem in many quarters, where a somewhat patrician disdain for anything that could be dismissed as mere 'number crunching' has dismissed it as mere artisanal work, devoid of any conceptual significance. (The same kind of disdain has often been levelled at empirical research in a more qualitative vein as well, it must be acknowledged, as some high-status sociology in British proceeds with a lofty disdain for anything that

133

smacks of empirical investigation. It reflects, perhaps, the attitude of the English towards 'trade'.)

The absence of a major quantitative supremacy at any stage in its development does rather distinguish British sociology from its American counterpart. It has perhaps provided a general environment in which qualitative researchers could flourish without having to fight too many unproductive battles for legitimacy. Some sense of the relative position of qualitative, ethnographic research, and the relative under-emphasis on quantitative work can be gained from an inspection of the major British journals. It is noticeable that the field is marked by considerable diversity and eclecticism. There is no obvious pattern of dominance of any one methodological perspective. But the field is certainly not characterized by large numbers of major quantitative projects.

Qualitative research, in a number of major fields of empirical inquiry, has been able to flourish within this intellectual and institutional context. The social as well as academic prominence – albeit in small numbers – of social anthropologists in the United Kingdom, while exerting rather little direct influence, has done no harm to the spread of ethnographic research either. As we have already suggested, the rich tradition of community studies, straddling anthropology and sociology, has for many years provided a niche within which ethnographic field methods have been granted currency. Indeed, the tradition of studies of rural villages, urban working-class neighbourhoods and communities focused on traditional industries such as mining or fishing, while by no means unique to the United Kingdom, does have rather special connotations and resonances in British cultural life. Images of community address an abiding set of mythologies: the mythological narratives of a rural world that is either lost or under threat of extinction (a narrative shared with some romanticized versions of oral history); the imagery of a social environment shaped by intimacy, trust and reciprocal obligation; the world of working-class heroes and heroines inhabiting a culture forged in the struggle for survival and the affirmation of collective worth. We repeat – these are not all interactionist studies, and their American counterparts are not all associated even with the Chicago School of sociological research. We are not attempting to assimilate one tradition into another, and we are not entering exaggerated claims for interactionism's impact on empirical research traditions in the United Kingdom. We do suggest, on the other hand, that various intellectual tendencies in British social science have provided an intellectual environment within which qualitative research could develop and grow. The rise of ethnographic research among British sociologists *is* in part attributable to influences derived more directly from other American sources.

134

The development of qualitative research in the United Kingdom reflects more general trends in sociology and other social-science disciplines. Arguably, it has become the dominant mode of social inquiry. This is perceived as a matter of concern in some quarters. Indeed, there have been repeated moral panics within the higher echelons of social science and higher-education policy. There have been repeated calls for the reinvigoration of quantitative research techniques and their dissemination to graduate students and others. Quantitative methodological innovation has been linked to the unmet needs of British social science on more than one occasion, and even to national needs for the collection, analysis and interpretation of large-scale quantitative data sets (or 'large and complex' data sets as one ESRC research initiative was called). From time to time concern is expressed because very few doctoral students in British sociology are funded to undertake quantitative work: the great majority apply for training grants to the Economic and Social Research Council with plans to undertake qualitative work (if they intend to do empirical work at all). We mention this merely as evidence of the relative significance of qualitative research – ethnographic, biographical, discourse-based – in contemporary British sociology. Similar things could be said about other disciplines too. Educational research shows very similar trends. So too do certain kinds of work in health and nursing research.

The sources of inspiration for these developments are diverse. Indeed, there is no single coherent reason for their influence and popularity. There seem to have converged several different tendencies and preferences, all contributing to a distinctively 'qualitative' approach to social inquiry. The intellectual influences were certainly diverse and cannot be attributed exclusively to an interactionist tradition. In the 1960s and onwards, social phenomenology and ethnomethodology were among the inspirations that led to an emphasis on an approach that could be summarized in terms of interpretative enquiry, and that incorporated particular kinds of ethnographic spirit and fieldwork. Likewise, particular kinds of critical and hermeneutic work led to an ethnographic style. In the United Kingdom, for instance, the work of Birmingham University's Centre for Contemporary Cultural Studies drew together social scientists and literary theorists into a somewhat disparate grouping and a less than perfectly coherent research programme. It did include 'qualitative' research that employed ethnographic fieldwork. The contribution of Paul Willis is a notable case in point. His well-known ethnographic study of working-class young men has become a widely cited text, with particular influence on the sociology of education, youth and deviance studies (Willis, 1977). It seemed to owe rather little to the interactionist tradition directly, and Willis's own account of his intellectual development (Willis, 2001) implies an

135

originality for the CCCS approach that is, perhaps, misplaced. It is clear that there were clear affinities between the ethnographic work of authors like Willis and the tradition of research by Becker and other researchers on deviance.

The phenomenological turn did relatively little directly to inspire the development of qualitative research methods. They suggested a number of analytic concerns, not least an interest in the methods of everyday practical reasoning, such as the construction and use of typifications and recipes of knowledge. The general perspective on the 'social construction of reality' that was promoted by Berger's and Luckmann's exegesis and development of Schutz's social phenomenology was itself part of a general movement towards the ethnographic investigation of everyday life. At the time of their first reception, subsequent divisions between phenomenology, interactionism and ethnomethodology were not apparent. At any rate, they were not adhered to as rigidly as they would be now. For instance, one of the most influential works in the methodological domain was Cicourel's *Method and Measurement in Sociology* (1964). For many years, this was one of the most widely cited books on research methods and one of the most frequently prescribed texts on research methods courses. It applied a critical perspective on 'conventional' research methods of all sorts. Cicourel suggested that what he characterized as conventional method imposed standardized measures and classifications 'by fiat'. In other words, most research practices were not faithful to the phenomena. The examples that all readers and interpreters took from Cicourel's methodological reflections concerned the construction and interpretation of statistical data, from social surveys and from official sources. Indeed, the issue of 'official statistics' became a methodological topic in its own right. Cicourel's general argument rested on the alleged circularity of reasoning that was involved in the production and interpretation of categories. The topic of statistics was a classic case. Data from official sources – such as government statistics – could not, it was argued, be treated at face value as if they transparently reflected the classification and distribution of the phenomena they purported to describe. Enumerations of phenomena like crime and deviance, categorized in accordance with officially prescribed classes of act, do not reflect an independent social reality. First, of course, the classes themselves impose more or less arbitrary boundaries on continuous phenomena. Second, the classification of acts reflects the outcomes of processes of judgement and decision-making on the part of those officially charged with making such decisions. In the case of crime statistics, for instance, the figures reflect the decisions and definitions applied by police officers, prosecutors, courts and others. Changes in the application of conventions and interpretations can readily lead to changes in official rates.

Cicourel's strictures were applied especially to the work of social researchers. The construction of sociological data could be shown to rest on the same processes as data from official sources. Just as crime rates depend on patterns of definition on the part of agencies of social control, so the standard phenomena of sociological research rested on the interpretative work of social researchers. There was thus a circularity in the logic of standard research practices – using unexamined assumptions about meanings and actions in order to make sense of those self-same topics. Cicourel's argument was closely parallel to that of Garfinkel's strictures about conventional sociological reasoning (Garfinkel, 1967). In his classic discussion of coding and inference in the study of a clinical setting, Garfinkel argued that researchers were able to make sense of fragmentary organizational data, such as clinic records, by drawing on their everyday knowledge of how organizations like clinics could be assumed to work. The same circularity of argument seemed to apply.

In the United Kingdom there were various responses to the Cicourel/Garfinkel line of argument. Typically for British sociology, some responses assimilated the phenomenological or ethnomethodological argument to a critical stance. The social construction of official statistics, for instance, was treated as an issue by radical statisticians, who developed the argument to encompass the ideological implications of state data. These were by no means restricted to the phenomenological or interpretative stance, but did represent one characteristic way in which ideas were assimilated to long-standing British interests that included more explicitly political perspectives than those of the American counterparts. British ethnomethodologists also took up the general topic of official categories. Most notably, Maxwell Atkinson undertook a major empirical study of the social organization of suicide verdicts in UK coroners' courts (Atkinson, 1978). This in turn took up the approach developed by Douglas in the United States, who explored from a more phenomenological perspective, the variable and contextual definitions of suicide applied by various agents such as coroners (1970a, 1970b). The topic of suicide was not, of course, accidental. These analyses took up the most classic type-case of Durkheimian sociology and sought to undermine the kind of sociological reasoning that Durkheim had established in that work.

These were not interactionist works. Indeed, their authors were and continue to be highly critical of 'symbolic interactionism'. They were, however, highly influential in a more general intellectual climate. They helped to create a context in which the apparent certainties of 'standard' sociological work were called into question. They provided key reference points in wider debates and contest. Cicourel's book was for a while the most widely cited and most widely set research methods book in UK Departments of Sociology. Even if reference to the general critique was a ritualized rather than a truly transformative one, the presence of the critical stance within general methodological discourse was a notable transformation of the intellectual scene. More generally, however, the weakening of methodological certainty in sociology and other disciplines in the 1960s helped to create the space for more overtly interactionist-inspired ethnographic research methods to gain a certain renewed legitimacy.

A notable example of interactionist influence on methodology was to be found in Plummer's work on life-histories and other 'documents of life'. Some sense of the broadening of methodological influence is detectable by comparing the first and second editions of Plummer's book *Documents of Life* (1983, 2001). Plummer re-traced the signifi-cance of life-documents and the life-history from their central place in Chicago sociology, attributable to the early work of Thomas and Znaniecki. In his discussion of the methods of life-documents, Plummer places Chicago sociology at a critical juncture of their development. He does so by stressing the multiple influences on Chicago sociology and does not over-emphasize 'symbolic interactionism', but he does align his methodological commentary with the interactionist, Chicago tradi-tion. He also stresses that the Chicago influence was by no means unique, and that there were various origins and inspirations for the col-lection and analysis of documents of life. By the second edition of Plummer's book, the overall picture has become more complex. Plummer himself has not in any sense lost his own interest in interac-tionism, but it occupies a less prominent place in the new and enlarged edition. In many ways the newer treatment is a faithful reflection of the state of the field and its changes over the eighteen years between the two versions. The collection and analysis of personal document, testi-mony, life-histories, biographical and autobiographical narratives have all become major themes in the burgeoning development of qualitative research methods generally. Interactionism is still a significant influ-ence, and major figures like Herbert Blumer still feature in the pan-theon of influences. But the inspiration for Plummer's second edition is the major change to have overtaken social research in the 1980s and 1990s. In the first edition of 1983 Plummer was invoking the Chicago tradition in order to make a case for more life-history research, and to enter a plea for sociologists to take documents of life more seriously. By the end of the century, on the other hand, the need to argue the general case has lost its urgency. Now there is a vast amount of empirical liter-ature, and of methodological writing. The influences that have led to this position are various. They include feminism, postcolonialism and postmodernism. Beyond those specific influences, there is also a wider and more amorphous array of influences that contribute to the widespread adoption of qualitative research approaches. These include a commitment to the documentation of 'lives' and the expression of 'voices'. These are felt especially urgently when it comes to the lives and voices of the muted, the marginal and the dispossessed. These aspirations and commitments are not inimical to the traditions of interactionism, but they go beyond them and draw together a much broader set of methodological and ethical priorities.

The methodological streams and convergences are themselves symptomatic of wider affinities. Ideas that have been part of the repertoire of interactionism for many years have become part of the general currency of ideas in the social sciences. We have just seen that the widespread adoption of qualitative research methods is among interactionism's most important legacies, yet qualitative research is often legitimated with reference to other systems of thought. In much the same way, ideas about identity, language, and meanings that are now fashionable in sociology are present in the interactionist tradition. Yet the interactionist influence is often ignored. The very popularity of these ideas, indeed, seems to rest on the appearance of novelty. In all these respects, interactionist sociology seems to be a submerged stream of thought that bubbles up even when its sources are hard to discern.

There are at least two tendencies in contemporary methodology that explicitly acknowledge some debt to the interactionist tradition, and are represented in the interactionist literature. They share common roots, yet they sit uneasily alongside one another. On the one hand, there is 'interactionist' research and methodology that draw on contemporary postmodernism and claim a radical break with past practice. On the other hand, there are authors who re-affirm the methodological precepts established in the past, and affirm continuity rather than discontinuity in the research tradition.

We have touched on the postmodern turn in interactionism already (Chapter 2) and so we do not recapitulate it entirely here. It is worth emphasizing, however, that its greatest impact has been felt in the domain of methodology. This is most evident in the changing rationales proposed for the conduct of qualitative research methods – in the United States and in the United Kingdom – and reflected in the methodological literature. Some sense of the shift can be gained from a comparison of the two editions of the important *Handbook of Qualitative Research* (Denzin and Lincoln, 1994, 2000). Within the space of just six years or so, the editors have come to identify the domain of qualitative research almost exclusively in terms of a series of paradigm shifts away from conventional methodological concerns to produce a heady mix of postmodernist perspectives. This is not a complete break with interactionism, however. One can trace a series of interventions that explicitly link interactionism with postmodern ethnographic practice.

For instance, the series of collections edited by Denzin under the rubric of *Studies in Symbolic Interaction* contains a series of contributions on postmodernism and ethnography (e.g. Austin, 1995; Denzin, 1993; Lincoln, 1995; Richardson, 1993; Rinehart, 1995; White and Kimbell-Amos, 1995).

Equally, however, there are interactionists who are not persuaded by the appeals to postmodernism, and who continue to affirm the continuities with earlier interactionism. For example, Maines and Ulmer (1993) acknowledge the contemporary interest in narrative, but assert that symbolic interactionism is especially well placed to assimilate and develop that work precisely because of its tradition – especially in collective forms of narrative (see also Handel, 1994); Johnson and Altheide (1993) believe that a perspectival view of knowledge is not a recent departure, but a long-standing commitment of symbolic interactionism; Dawson and Prus (1993, 1995) repeatedly argue for the continued vitality of symbolic interactionism's pragmatist epistemology, and against the claims of/for postmodernism; Sanders (1995), while endorsing a critical scrutiny of conventional ethnographic practice, suggests that much of what passes for postmodernist ethnography is stylistically contrived and narcissistic. Best (1995) sums up – sometimes in extreme if engaging ways – some of the more jaundiced responses to postmodernism, which he described as an intellectual fad. Among other things he suggests that the postmodern turn is also a turn away from the serious work of research, leading to the armchair; his view can best be expressed in his own aphorism to the effect that 'Postmodernism is indoor work and requires no heavy lifting' (ibid.: 127).

Contributions from British authors have reflected this tension within contemporary interactionsm, and indeed in the methodological literature in general. Hammersley's methodological work incorporates some of the most important and sustained discussions of methodological problems – engaging directly with the interactionist legacy. Hammersley (1989) uses a commentary on Herbert Blumer's methodological writing to address some of the abiding problems of qualitative research. He describes the fundamental 'dilemma' to be found in Blumer – but this is not just a debate with the past. Hammersley explores recurrent problems that confront qualitative, ethnographic research. There is a commitment to 'naturalism' intended to reflect a fidelity to the phenomena, but it is not clear how any methods can guarantee that one can render their true nature. It is not clear that qualitative research methods can guarantee any more faithful representation of the social world than quantitative methods, for instance. The fundamental problems remain.

Hammersley is quite right to propose that qualitative research does not in itself solve all the recurrent epistemological problems. He is, like other British authors, sceptical about exaggerated claims for qualitative research, notwithstanding his own involvement with them. He does acknowledge that ethnographic research is compatible with interactionism:

> To the extent that naturalistic inquiry is simply a refinement of the methods of inquiry and analysis that we all use in everyday life – talking to people, watching what happens, acting on our interpretations and monitoring the results, reading relevant documents and so forth – naturalistic research has a reflexive relationship to the social world: it is not only attuned to the nature of that world, but in itself exemplifies that world. (1989: 194)

This formulation stresses the *reflexive* character of research methods. It certainly provides an interactionist justification for the ethnographic commitment. It certainly does not suggest that qualitative research provides guaranteed access to the phenomena.

For its critics, however, the claims of postmodernism and cognate perspectives are problematic precisely because their proponents do make claims for the superiority of certain methods, and they include assumptions about the fidelity of their methods. It is, for instance, sometimes argued that postmodern approaches to qualitative research are more faithful to the nature of 'lived experience', because they reflect the voices and experiences of social actors; that they are more faithful to the complexities of social life. But the dilemma that Hammersley derives from Blumer still holds. Many contemporary methodologists seem to want it both ways. They seem to claim simultaneously that knowledge is relativistic and perspectival, and that their approach gives more direct access to the real phenomena of 'lived experience'.

Of course, Hammersley is not the only author to have engaged with some of these problematic claims. As we have seen, Dawson and Prus (1993) have argued for pragmatism – arguing for a reflexive approach to research that continues the interactionist tradition. Charmaz (1995) suggests that distinctions between positivism and postmodernism are ill conceived as the basis for methodological debate. Advocates of postmodernism too readily dismiss previous approaches to qualitative research as 'positivist' in promoting the novelty of their own perspectives. Charmaz, in contrast, emphasizes that an interactionist, interpretative tradition has stood between positivism and postmodernism. She reasserts the interactionist commitment to an interpretative perspective.

This is the message of Hammersley's and Atkinson's version of reflexive ethnography (1983, 1995). They deny the appropriateness of either naturalism or positivism in justifying ethnographic research – or indeed any social research. They suggest that the principle of reflexivity transcends or dissolves the dualism. This is not absolutely tied to interactionist sociology, nor to pragmatist epistemology, but it is entirely congruent with them. Indeed, the pragmatist tradition would not admit of the underlying dualisms in the first place. The pragmatist stance grounds knowledge and intelligence in action. The pragmatist (interactionist) explores the world through acts, through practical transactions with it (which may be everyday activities, scientific experiments or participant observation). She or he makes inferences, creating hypotheses, and thus constructs a practical understanding of the world. Such practical knowledge is the basis for further transaction and is always subject to potential modification. Consequently, that practical understanding is always incomplete, partial and provisional. The understanding that is available at any given time is always grounded in real engagements with an independently real world, and is the product of material acts of exploration and inference. It is socially produced, insofar as practical actors as well as scientific observers use the collective resources of language, common methods of observation, and shared means of representation. To that extent too, therefore, knowledge is socially and culturally relative. From a pragmatist, interactionist perspective, therefore, there need be no dualism between naturalism and positivism, and the supposed contrast between modernism and postmodernism is equally unnecessary.

142

In other words, there is no need to invoke a radical break with the past of interactionism in order to reinvigorate it. There is much to be learned from contemporary perspectives. There can be no quarrel with requirements to take seriously the position of the researcher; there need be no dissent from a self-conscious awareness of the textual and rhetorical conventions used to reconstruct social reality; one need not deny that our understanding is partial and perspectival. But these principles can be derived from the basic tenets of pragmatism, and do not represent radical departures from past scholarship. On the contrary, they align the interactionist tradition with the broader stream of interpretivist social science that long pre-dates postmodernism. Unless one is going to date postmodernism to the early decades of the twentieth century, then one must attribute the contemporary enthusiasm for postmodernist justifications for qualitative research to a mixture of ignorance and amnesia. It is especially ironic when interactionists pay insufficient attention to the interactionist legacy and misrepresent it as an outmoded positivism.

It is, however, the case that qualitative research, ethnography and other such designations have become the most widespread justifications for interactionist research. The explicit theoretical ideas have become increasingly muted, while the methodological principles derived from them have become increasingly visible. In the last two chapters we explored a number of areas where interactionism exerted a direct – if mediated – influence on UK sociological research. One of the most obvious features of those areas – such as the sociology of medical settings and educational institutions – is that explicit interactionism has often been replaced by a designation couched in terms of research methods. In other words, many contemporary researchers and commentators are likely to describe current research in terms of 'the ethnography of educational settings', 'qualitative health research', 'qualitative studies in education' and the like. In other words, *method* seems to have replaced theory in justifying research in many of these domains. We do not endorse this apparent equation of method with theory: we simply note it as a distinct development in recent fields of empirical research. In educational research, for instance, researchers seem much more likely to couch their discussions of field research in terms of 'the ethnography' of education, rather than in terms of an interactionist (or indeed phenomenological) perspective. The pervasive quality of ethnographic and other qualitative research is clearly visible from the published literature. Major works of reference on ethnographic and qualitative research abound (Atkinson et al., 2001; Denzin and Lincoln, 1994, 2000; Gubrium and Holstein, 2002 are just three of the major edited collections). Many of the ideas that inform these methodological developments include those articulated by the interactionists. But they are not always articulated fully, for instance, 'grounded theory' derived from the empirical research of the second Chicago School, but in today's context, many applications of the idea seem to have broken free from their moorings in that tradition; various approximations of grounded theory are used to legitimize a variety of exploratory qualitative research strategies without necessarily being anchored to pragmatist or interactionist theory. The methodological imagination that informs current methodology and research practice contains within it many inspirations derived from the interactionist tradition. They also enshrine other intellectual tendencies as well: much is owed to the insights of feminism, postmodernism, post-structuralism and postcolonialism. As in other contexts, interactionism itself is an understated resource, the influence of which is stronger than overt acknowledgements might seem to imply.

143

six

we are all interactionists now

In this chapter we take up some of the themes we have already addressed. In the same spirit that we began by proposing that 'we were never interactionists' we now want to propose an apparently opposite view – namely that the broad tenets of interactionism have become pervasive in many domains of contemporary social thought. In suggesting that 'we' are now 'interactionists' we are, of course, exaggerating for the purposes of argument. And our argument here is the same as that with which we began. It is not a volte-face on our part, for the contradiction is more apparent than real. We suggested at the outset that British sociologists were rarely interactionists in any pure sense. The intellectual field has been consistently marked by diversity and eclecticism. Ideas have been *used* rather than recycled through theoretical exegesis alone. Influence has sometimes been implicit in the enacted traditions of empirical research. In a similar way, we now suggest that the key ideas and intellectual commitments of interactionist thought are, in many ways, just as urgent and current now as they ever were. But just because interactionist thought has become rather unfashionable, and because European social theory seems more engaging to today's arbiters of taste, and American research less so, the role and relevance of interactionism seem too easily overlooked altogether.

We want to assert that we are all interactionists now in a far from literal sense. Clearly, the majority of British sociologists do not identify themselves as interactionists in any meaningful way. Yet the abiding themes of interactionist sociology are among the contemporary preoccupations of social theory and – *mutatis mutandis* – can directly inform current sociology. Recent sociology has revisited and sometimes reinvented the insights of interactionist inquiry. As we acknowledged in the Introduction, this does not mean that we should thereby privilege interactionist sociology. If George Herbert Mead is a more sociological source for some key ideas than Lacan, or if Erving Goffman is a more sociologically informed author than Baudrillard, or if Everett Hughes has a more secure sense of the social than Michel Foucault, then we do not automatically have to abandon the more fashionable continental theorists. We do not have to resurrect older sociologists only in order to assign them priority. After all we could attribute equally sound and original ideas to Georg Simmel – who also contributed indirectly to the development of interactionist sociology – and who is also being reinterpreted in the light of recent ideas (Frisby, 1992a, 1992b). There is no absolute priority to be claimed or ascribed. Obviously, there are processes of parallel evolution and convergence too.

We are not, therefore, suggesting that all the good ideas can be traced either historically or logically to interactionism. Such reductionist arguments are always pointless and often absurd. No school of social thought can seriously lay claim to a complete and comprehensive theoretical or empirical coverage of the sociological terrain. None can be granted a monopoly of the sociological imagination. On the other hand, W.I. Thomas, Herbert Blumer, Everett Hughes, Anselm Strauss and Erving Goffman (to name but a few obvious examples) did possess a sociological imagination in abundance and we do well to realize that they described the modern – and even the 'postmodern' – condition with considerable aptitude.

We are indeed struck by the extent to which the so-called postmodern condition parallels the descriptions of modernity to be found in the early Chicago School sociologists of the earlier years of the twentieth century. Likewise, the descriptions of identity and identity formation offered by contemporary authors of postmodernity and global culture seem remarkably similar to those offered by classic interactionist sociology. The Chicago sociologists themselves were not entirely novel: the late nineteenth and early twentieth centuries saw many accounts of social selves and identities that pre-figure our own *fin de siècle* preoccupations.

Sociologists and others who reject the 'grand narratives' of history and social change often overlook one basic phenomenon. It may be right to reject a view of history that implies a linear progression and the inexorable revelation of long-term forces. Nevertheless, there are many things that are cyclical or at least recurrent. It is easy to proclaim entirely new states of affairs and the apocalyptic 'end' of all sorts of things (including history itself). It takes more effort to recognize that these are often born of ignorance or disrespect of the past rather than reflecting genuine novelty. Many of the claims for late-modern or post-modern social processes seem to fall into this category. In *The Faultline of Consciousness* David Maines writes:

A few years ago ... I identified twenty points of comparison between postmodernism and pragmatism/interactionism as an invitation to assess their similarities and differences so that we might better understand how to move forward. I pointed out an array of ideas that postmodernists claim as their own but that in fact have long been expressed by pragmatists. These included the following: People are not objective observers of the world, realism is a defunct epistemology. Fiction fuses with fact, representations are based on other representations, knowledge is never final, reality is infinite, symbols and their referents do not always match, pasts and futures are indeterminate, selves are in situations and when we enter situations we sometimes find out that those selves are not really us, identity is often problematic and always information dependent, culture preconfigures discourse, and, in general, things are not what they seem but we have to interpret and deal with them anyway. (2001: 233)

Discontinuity and novelty are fashionable intellectual tropes. The archaeology of knowledge – with its imagery of sharp breaks between discontinuous epochs – is preferred to the processes of historical continuity and transformation. Hence theorists are too eager to proclaim the rapid appearance of new states. The rate of change too seems to accelerate in these treatments. The social world is thus described in terms of a vertiginous onrush of newer and newer phenomena. Fashion-conscious authors can then chase these novelties, for all the world like an immature sports team chasing the ball all over the park.

In commending some attention to the ideas of interaction as a partial corrective to over-heated appeals to the postmodern, the post-structural, and so on, we are not proposing a knee-jerk intellectual conservatism. Our quarrel is not always with the ideas themselves. But many of today's ideas are not all that novel. Some of them are no advance at all on the productive ideas to be found in interactionism. Hence too little heed is paid to its contributions to research. In many respects this conforms to Maines's notions of 'mythic facts' and 'reconstitutive rhetoric' within the human sciences that often characterizes interactionist thought and work in a manner unrecognizable to the actual practitioners of the approach (Maines, 2001). Further, features of the social world that are claimed to be especially recent are also to be found in the sociological accounts of Chicago ethnographers and theorists of a century or so ago.

Far from being merely reactionary, therefore, we see our own inclination more positively. The contentious and argumentative character of the social sciences – and sociology in particular – has placed too high a value on rejecting ideas in order to adopt an exclusive and esoteric 'position' for oneself. Such a position should, it appears, be based on the exclusive and enthusiastic endorsement of one theorist, one school or one grandiose idea. As a consequence we celebrate a narrow selection of ideas and ignore many others. In contrast, we think it more productive to recognize, enjoy and use ideas from wherever they may arise. No one school of thought has all the answers; no one tradition can even pose all the interesting questions. Human intelligence and creativity mercifully transcend narrow specialisms and loyalties. Instead of wholesale neglect, it is more productive to remember them and to use them. The constant, restless search for new theories and theorists drives too many sociologists to chase after ideas (preferably from elsewhere) and to discard others in the pursuit of the radical chic. This is especially apparent when we consider the recent vogue for various 'post' tendencies – post-structuralism and postmodernism in particular. We suggest that recent trends in social thought have been grounded in analytic issues that have always been central to the interactionist tradition: past contributions, including those of interactionism, are all too often overlooked in the pursuit of novelty.

We have already suggested one way of approaching this, in suggesting that 'we are all interactionists now'. As we made clear in the last chapter, we do not mean by that suggestion that all contemporary sociologists explicitly endorse the tenets of symbolic interactionism narrowly defined. That would clearly be absurd. Rather, we meant that many of the commitments of contemporary sociology are at least congruent with those of interactionism, and – the stronger argument – that many are derivable from the interactionist tradition. Not so long ago one could not have made such a claim at all. But interactionism has shifted perceptibly, while the wider context of sociology, the disciplinary matrix, has changed considerably. A few short decades ago the interactionist programme, while undeniably informing some strong agendas for empirical research, was constantly under threat from various directions. There were many among those critics, for instance, who tried to discredit interactionism from an essentially structural perspective, emphasizing macro-level phenomena and asserting interactionism's impotence in the face of such issues.

147

Those criticisms took much the same form irrespective of the specific context or sociological content. Given its emphasis on processes and encounters, analyses of the interaction order, and a view of social order as an emergent, negotiated and impermanent phenomenon, it has always been open to criticism by those who attributed primacy to social 'structures'. Whether those structures were derived from a functionalist, Marxist or other model of society, a commitment to sociology in terms of social structure, structural transformation and the like was thought to be antipathetic to the core commitments of interactionism. Interactionists and other interpretative sociologists could be accused of generating a very restricted version of the discipline – a sociology without society (a phrase derived from the equivalent accusation levelled against ethnomethodology). For those who took for granted the existence of social structures or the primacy of structural phenomena such as social classes, then interactionism seemed an inherently impoverished approach. Admittedly, if grudgingly so, interactionist and Goffmanesque work could be granted a restricted domain of relevance in providing a social psychology of a few processes – such as stigma or status passage – where they were felt to enjoy a limited, conditional legitimacy. That apart, the structural critique of interactionism could – quite erroneously – see it as individualistic, lacking in an appreciation of a distinctively *social* reality. It was noticeable, of course, that the supposed 'failure' of interactionism to address structures was never quite mirrored in general sociological circles by the symmetrical accusation that structural accounts failed to pay attention to action, process and identities: calls for accommodation and compromise always seemed to be asymmetrical. Adherents of structural Marxism, for instance, seemed quite prepared to empty the sociological domain of social actors and intentional social action. Structural functionalists had also assimilated social action to the expression of essentially structurally distributed and determined roles.

In the United Kingdom, while there were relatively few 'pure' structuralists, in theoretical terms, the general climate was for many years antipathetic to a great deal of interactionist work. There was, for instance, a long and resilient tradition of political arithmetic, most notably reflected in successive studies of social class and inter-generational social mobility. For sociologists for whom the survey and the longitudinal study, the measurement of occupational class and income are the height of excitement, interactionism could hold few attractions. Sociologists of that ilk, just like the structural Marxists, have not changed their minds about the proper conduct of sociology. But they are remarkably invisible in the academy at large. The demographers may still be the only British sociologists who can aspire to become Fellows of the British Academy, but their numbers are rather small and their intellectual influence is modest. By contrast, meta-themes of culture, identity and social interaction are of far greater prominence in contemporary British sociology. The same is clearly not true in the United States. There the major journals still carry a quite disproportionate amount of sociological research that is entirely divorced from any interest in interaction, micro-sociology or qualitative method. The continuing marginalization of interactionist and cognate work is by no means absolute. Of course, it flourishes within the confines of its own enclaves, and has its own journals, conferences and centres of excellence. Nevertheless, one needs to recognize that there continue to be some key differences between the national intellectual traditions and contexts.

As we noted in the previous chapters, interactionism's influence in certain areas has been obscured by other fashions and fads, although in recent years there has been a return to a concern with actors, types and the interpretative character of cultural 'consumption' within the domain of cultural studies and other fields of enquiry. The theorization of domains of enquiry that previously consisted of an acknowledgement of interactionist ideas has resulted in a situation where the empirical commitments of interactionists have been glossed over in a fervour of 'theory' or downgraded and ignored by those committed to quantification and variable analysis. Thus, in one sense interactionist ideas have been squeezed within one unit of the matrix of British sociology while developed and embraced within others. However, it is clear that a number of core concepts and themes have remained intact and continue to occupy a central position within sociological analysis.

AMBIGUITIES OF THE SOCIAL SUBJECT

The force of our earlier argument is nowhere more apparent then in the treatment of social actors, selves and identities. Contemporary social theory, under the auspices of various tendencies, including postmodernism but not confined to that alone, treats the production and expression of social selves and identities as a key analytic issue. Likewise, the nature of the social self is portrayed as reflecting contemporary social conditions themselves. Theory reflects the social, and the construction of the self reflects both. In particular, there is a confluence of thought that constructs the social actor in distinctive ways.

149

The recent legacy of structuralist and post-structuralist thought, especially when taken to extremes, expunges the actor altogether or, at least, claims to eliminate a particular kind of social actor. French structuralist and post-structuralist theory in the social, cultural and literary domains denies a 'subjective' view of the human actor. In literary theory, for instance, 'the author' is not treated as an active, creative originator of works of art. The 'death of the author' was thus proclaimed. This view sought to supersede any romantic or humanistic visions of the creative genius, wrestling with his or her inspiration and a recalcitrant medium of expression. It sought to render irrelevant the attempt to understand literary or other cultural products through their creators' biographies. The artist or the author is thus displaced or de-centred in favour of impersonal, or de-personalized, systems of discourse and cultural codes. The actor/author is thus dispersed among the discursive practices of a particular culture or collectivity. The romantic view of creative literary and artistic work is, in the hands of such critical theory, turned on its head. Rather than the author being responsible for the work, the language or the *œuvre*, it is the language of the genre that generates the 'author' as a function of collective discourse. In this scheme of things, therefore, the romantic, unified subject is shattered into a kaleidoscope of discursive practices. The individual actor is no longer privileged or placed at the centre of things. The actor or author is a kind of fiction. The unique biography of the subject is itself a discursive product. It is not an inherent feature of the social or artistic world. It reflects a particular version of it: a romantic and bourgeois fiction that creates the appearance of stable, coherent and consistent actors. Just as the 'characters' of romantic and realist fiction can be de-stabilized and rendered internally contradictory, so too the presence of the author can be decomposed or dematerialized into the flux of language and representation.

Such a perspective is, of course, entirely congruent with the tenets of structuralist or post-structuralist sociology and anthropology. The social actor becomes a mere cipher and social action is under-emphasized in favour of systems of difference and codes of convention. At best the social actor becomes a flimsy affair – an insubstantial wraith left to gibber and wander a sparsely inhabited wilderness. The treatment of the social actor in postmodernism does not mirror the post-structuralist world precisely. But here too the emphasis is on instability. Postmodern social thought constructs the social actor in terms of instability and fragmentation. The postmodern world itself, we are led to believe, generates especially fragmented and unstable social identities. The sites and sources of identity are highly diverse. There is an easy equation to be drawn, in that the 'modern' self is portrayed in terms of relative stability or coherence and the post-modern self in terms of fragmentation and frailty. The parallelism is reflected also in contemporary treatments of the body. The postmodern body is portrayed in terms of its protean qualities, its contingent character and its prosthetic extensions. The postmodern body has permeable and impermanent boundaries. These treatments of the social actor, the social self and the social body all imply, when they do not explicitly state, a contrast. They contrast the contemporary postmodern condition with a 'modern' society and with various modern sociologies – often in inconsistent ways.

Now our response to those contemporary tendencies is at several levels. The general thrust is twofold. First, many of the general ideas about selves, actors and identities are in fact foreshadowed or anticipated in interactionist thought. Second, there is nothing especially new in viewing actors and selves as fragile or fragmented – and consequently nothing inherently postmodern about such a perspective. We should remember that far from endorsing a bourgeois view of modern social actors, interactionism – following the lead of the Chicago School urban sociologists – has consistently promoted a view of modern metropolitan living that engenders fragmented and fragile selves.

It will follow, therefore, that if these general characterizations are accepted, then we need to be clear about what interactionist sociology is and is not. We shall argue that interactionism is not, and never has been, a sociology grounded in individual social actors. By that we mean it has not been premised on stable, consistent human actors. Contrary to many perceptions, interactionism is not an inherently humanist approach to sociology. It has never been dependent on a romantic celebration of the individual or the biographical. It has always had a much more complex and sophisticated view of actors than that. We shall argue, therefore, that symbolic interactionism is often misrepresented as preoccupied with discrete actors, their actions and experiences. On the contrary, we want to reassert that interactionism should be initially in terms of Mead's originating triad. Mind, Self and Society are not three separate entities. Each is an aspect or 'moment' in the flux of process. The social process is never finally resolved into determinate entities, be they mental, personal or social. The circulation of significant symbols, language in particular, does not result in determinate meanings and definitions. Definitions of the situation are always in principle labile, and there is no *a priori* assumption of stability or consensus. If anything has priority in the interactionist world-view it is the dialogic exchange of gestures and symbols. We have already seen Goffman's aphorism 'not men and their moments but moments and their men' asserts the possibility of a radically non-humanist perspective. While Goffman is certainly not representative of symbolic interactionism in itself, in this particular regard he articulates with particular clarity a more general orientation. The fact that Goffman's own sociology is readily misrepresented as a person-centred social psychology lends extra weight to this line of argument. It is important, however, to recognize that the emphasis of symbolic interactionism is precisely what the terms imply – on the *processes* of interaction and exchange, on the negotiation of rules and meanings, and on the use of conventional modes of representation – that furnish the primary analytic level. The outcome of such processes is not a stable social reality, but further processes: negotiation leads to negotiation, not to fixed and immutable outcomes. Order may be achieved, but it is only provisional and contingent. Meanings are emergent phenomena, and are constantly available to change and re-definition. The definition of the situation is not a whimsical act of idiosyncratic or solipsistic will. Situations are not created arbitrarily, irrespective of the socially shared resources that create the possibility of situations at all.

We need therefore to recapitulate the general theory of interactionism and the sociological imagination that informed its birth. The late nineteenth- and early twentieth-century milieu in which a distinctive interactionism developed was definitely *not* marked by social and intellectual stability. The social fabric within which the sociology was born – metropolitan America – was in a state of flux. The birth of Chicago

151

School urban sociology mirrored the extraordinary social and physical transformation of Chicago itself. By the 1920s and 1930s the metropolis was not merely the site of the university and the site of sociological research. It was also the context in which distinctive cultural forms and social types were in process of formation. It was summed up in Wirth's synoptic view of 'urbanism as a way of life', which in turn owed much to Simmel's sense of metropolitan culture and its social types. Not only does the metropolis contain and foster a wide diversity of social actors, it provides a social and physical environment that is restless, nervous and fragmentary. The modern city of the late nineteenth- to early twentieth-century period is thus portrayed as an unstable setting, and its inhabitants as equally unstable. Indeed, what is striking to a contemporary reader of past sociological texts is the remarkable degree of congruence and continuity between views of social actors and their social world in early twentieth-century texts and those at the beginning of the twenty-first century.

Consider, for instance, the classic perspectives of urban sociology to be found in the early Chicago School texts. Wirth's (1938) characterization of 'urbanism as a way of life' is an apt starting-point. Wirth and his Chicago School contemporaries were at pains to describe the city as something more than and different from a merely physical location. They asserted that the modern metropolis created radically new *forms* and new *social types*. Wirth himself suggested that urbanism constituted a new way of life in its own right. The city was characterized not only in terms of its size, but also its complexity and the density of social life within it. The city was physically and socially fragmented. Urban life was described in terms of over-stimulation. The senses were bombarded by diverse stimuli at a rapid rate. The modern urbanite was therefore vulnerable to over-excitement. There was, in this treatment an implicit parallel between the sociological view of modern city dwellers and late nineteenth-century medical anxieties the identified *neurasthenia* as a distinctive malady of civilization.

The neurasthenic personality or social type was by no means restricted to the Chicago School treatment of urban living. It is vividly present in Simmel's treatment of the metropolis and its inhabitants. As Frisby (1985) makes clear, neurasthenic over-stimulation and depletion were explicitly recognized in Simmel's work by his contemporaries. Indeed, the neurasthenic type of metropolitan dweller is to be found in the European images of modernity to be found in Baudelaire, Benjamin and Kracauer, among others. The *modern* metropolis was, therefore, clearly identified with varieties of degeneracy. Equally, it must be remembered, the connotations of neurasthenia were not unrelievedly negative. It reflected a heightened sensibility and sensitivity to external stimuli. Consequently, the urban observer, the aesthete and the social critic could all be thought to exemplify the positive benefits of the neurasthenic state.

Wirth's portrait of modern urban living, therefore, has echoes of neurasthenic civilization. 'Men and women coping with the pace and congestion of the city became irritable, unstable and insecure' (Smith, 1988: 164). Moreover, the metropolis was a city of strangers. Urban dwellers were pictured as rootless and planetary. The metropolis is thus a setting for the anonymous crowd: primary social ties of kinship and mutual obligation were replaced by weaker, secondary links. In the works of early urban ethnography, therefore, the modern metropolis was a site of social dislocation. The social forms and values of traditional societies in the old world (Europe) and the new (including the rural South) were smashed by the demands of the modern urban environment. Collective modes of social solidarity were being replaced by a new individualism and the values of self-interest.

There was, of course, nothing new or specific to the Chicago School sociologists' interest in urban life and social dislocation, nor in their characterization of modern urban living. Their interests coincided with various European traditions of social thought in which the loss of 'community' was contrasted with the rise of individualism, the weakening of mutual obligation compared with the rise of legal contract and commercialized relations. The pessimistic view of the modern city was a widespread one, and was by no means confined to the Chicago commentators. Moreover, as we are well aware, the urban sociology of Chicago was by no means congruent with symbolic interactionism *per se*. Our argument here is not that interactionism *per se* was uniquely interested in the malaise of modern urban living. Self-evidently that is not the case. Rather, we want to develop two things. First, the strand of urban pessimism entered into subsequent sociological analysis that was incorporated into a more explicitly 'interactionist' tradition. Second, there is a direct continuity between the earlier twentieth-century treatment of the issues and that of the latest *fin-de-siècle* preoccupations. There are remarkable parallels and continuities between the sociological and aesthetic treatment of Paris or Berlin and that of Chicago.

Simmel was not a symbolic interactionist, of course, any more than Walter Benjamin was. Again, our intention here is not to assimilate everything potentially interesting into a reconstructed interactionist tradition. Rather, we want to consider the interactionist legacy in its broader intellectual framework. Simmel was extraordinarily influential in the development of Chicago sociology, being the most frequently cited of all sociological theorists in the Chicago School textbook. Further, we have to understand the mixture of ideas that surrounded the development of interactionism in the first half of the twentieth century. It does not have a single source, nor does it have a single,

153

unbroken line of development. The interactionism that we encounter today reflects those various strands and influences. If we are to understand 'interactionism' in the past and in the present, then, we need to take account of those broader intellectual and social matrices.

In a similar vein, therefore, we note the pervasive influence of metaphors of 'the frontier' in early urban sociology at Chicago. The ecological characterization of the city and its growth identified a 'zone of transition' in the inner urban areas. This was the modern metropolitan equivalent of the more conventional 'frontier' of the American West. The immigrant encountered the new realities of the metropolis in this ecological zone. The 'marginal man', as Park described him, was a social type associated with the frontiers and transitions of modern urban life. It was typical of this style of thought that Park should describe the hobo – the seasonal itinerant – as a kind of 'frontiersman'. In that sense, therefore, the rootless urban dweller was not merely a subject for colourful local ethnography: he was a figure iconic of urban conditions.

The frontiersman or the marginal man was akin to Simmel's 'stranger'. A cultural hybrid type, Park's and Simmel's archetypes of modern social life were both detached from the traditional sources of social cohesion. Simmel's stranger has more in common with other European intellectual currents. His planetary urban dweller has affinities with the urban intellectual. The stranger is akin to the urban *flâneur*, enjoying a certain degree of intellectual detachment. Park's marginal man seeks full membership of the social group; Simmel's exploits and relishes the freedom to come and go, and to observe the urban scene (Smith, 1988: 122).

These preoccupations, while by no means 'interactionist' in all their origins, certainly fed into the broader stream of 'interactionist' thought. By the time that American sociology reached the period following the Second World War, the interests of authors like Everett Hughes, Erving Goffman, Howard Becker and Anselm Strauss clearly united, in different ways and to differing degrees, the traditions of urban ethnography and interactionist social psychology. It would clearly be absurd to believe, therefore, that interactionism classically represents a romanticized view of the self or the individual as a stable entity. On the contrary, the interactionist tradition is one among several that has grasped 'modernity' in terms of a fragmented and unstable social self. Erving Goffman's entire output can be read as a troubling vision of the social conditions of modernity and urbanism. The asylum is a microcosm of a terrifying social world – just as surely as is Michel Foucault's panopticist carceral regime. The condition of stigma potentially afflicts all men and women in a modern civilization obsessed with the management of appearances and the control of the body. There is thus an unbroken tradition of sociological work reflecting *fin-de-siècle* anxieties and preoccupations from the beginning of the twentieth century to the beginning of the twenty-first.

A very similar argument can be constructed from other texts too. Arlie Hochschild's monograph *The Managed Heart* (1983) is sometimes cited now as exemplifying something distinctively late modern or postmodern. She conducted empirical research on airline in-flight attendants. She describes the sort of emotion work that attendants perform. This includes the display of inauthentic gratification in response to the demands of clients and employers. Now there is no doubt that Hochschild describes with considerable verve a distinctive form of work. But it is not especially characteristic of late twentieth-century social life, whether one refers to that in terms of late or postmodernity. Of course, the style of research and reportage is different from those of earlier decades, and Goffman's own work is a major influence on the later writer, but Cressey's monograph of the taxi dancer is a classic of the earlier Chicago School urban ethnographies that deals with parallel phenomena. The taxi dance hall is a social milieu in which encounters of intimacy are fleetingly created between strangers. The clients are typically the unattached men of the new metropolis. The taxi dancers are equally characteristic of the new urban setting. Moreover, their contrived displays of intimacy implied that the female dancers exercised control over their clients and over the situation. The rhetoric and the analytic style developed by Cressey differ from Hochschild's, of course. Their sociological treatments necessarily reflect their respect periods. Nevertheless, we can discern the continuities here. The working lives of the taxi dancer and the in-flight attendants share very similar forms. They inhabit recognizably similar social worlds.

The sociologists of the 1920s and 1930s were no more wedded than was Goffman and his successors to a stable social self. The inhabitant of the modern metropolitan scene is individualized, occupies fragmented social worlds and lives in a world of strangers. It is, moreover, a world of appearances. This 'modern' social formation in no way implies a romantic self, therefore. It is not grounded in the bourgeois view of character and identity. It is, rather, modernist in rejecting such a perspective. The Chicago School of urban sociology certainly did not rest on a stable social actor. The flux of the city, the disaggregation of social life and the processes of identity construction are all part of the same restless social process.

There were and are, therefore, continuities between current sociological portrayals of social life and social identities and those of earlier generations of sociologists. There is no sharp divide between the types of identity glimpsed by devotees of postmodernity and those of the early years of the twentieth century. Indeed, the world-weary *flâneur*,

155

or Simmel's *déraciné* stranger seem hardly distinguishable from their counterparts at the end of the twentieth century. Indeed, while not a sociological work, Musil's *The Man without Qualities* (1995) seems a work as perfectly attuned to the exhaustion of the late twentieth century as to the end of Imperial Vienna, in which it is set.

Repeatedly, portrayals of great cities – Paris, Berlin, Vienna, London, Chicago – from the nineteenth century onwards have found the same phenomena: individualism and anonymity, worlds of strangers and fleeting encounters, social fragmentation and fractured identities. They have been reflected in the work not only of sociologists but also of artists, novelists, photographers and film-makers. These versions of metropolitan life are repeatedly poised between a pessimistic and nostalgic yearning for more settled and certain ways of life, and an optimistic and enthusiastic embrace of the exotic social scenes of the *demi-monde*, the cabaret, the street, the criminal.

Having discussed some of the continuities between earlier sociological accounts of social life and the Chicago School and certain 'postmodern' descriptions, we will now seek to explore the influence of pragmaticism and interactionism in terms of futures. Clearly any description of the future is reflexively framed in terms of a past. Therefore the discussion of futures is necessarily linked to certain continuities. In terms of this book we have explored the way in which core interactionist themes and ideas have found both acknowledged and unacknowledged expression in British sociological work. In terms of this section of the book, we will now discuss four principal meta-themes or frames of sociological exploration that we believe represent areas of conceptual continuity but also future frames for interactionism's influence and relevance to be acknowledged, recognized and drawn upon in a way that bypasses the traditional commitment to collective amnesia. This approach to futures recovers a more faithful understanding of interactionism as opposed to the limited, misguided and, sometimes, incorrect frames previously afforded to the approach and tradition. The meta-themes include the cultural turn, identity, language and communication and institutions and interaction. The future of interactionism lies in the durability of its concepts, both in terms of analytical vitality and relevance to current social trends and transformations.

THE CULTURAL TURN

The social sciences – British sociology most prominently – have experienced a 'turn' towards cultural studies. Arguably, indeed, much of the most lively work has been conducted by scholars thinking of themselves as cultural analysts rather than sociologists at all, and many areas of sociological research have been enriched by a renewed emphasis on the production and consumption of culture. There are, as Denzin (1992) has pointed out, many contexts in which interactionist sociology can and should converge with these cultural analyses.

One of the most striking of convergences between interactionism and contemporary theoretical interests concerns the recent rediscovery of 'performance'. From a number of perspectives, and drawing on various conceptual frameworks, a number of contemporary social and cultural commentators have stressed the performative quality of social life and its cultural representations. Tulloch (1999) provides a useful starting point, incorporating his own research in a variety of topics into a conceptual framework that engages with performative work. His analysis ranges over high and low culture, 'expert' and 'everyday' cultural productions. He draws on the literatures of anthropology and theatre studies in order to synthesize a reading of culture that dissolves the categories of genre, in stressing the local and situated performance of lay and expert understandings.

The anthropological preoccupation with performativity is encapsulated in a series of essays edited by Hughes-Freeland (1998) that draw together analyses of 'ritual' – though the term itself is a contested one – theatre, dance, spectacles and everyday encounters. The theoretical inspirations are themselves diverse, including Victor Turner's concept of 'social dramas' and Schechner's work on theatre and ritual. Several of the anthropological authors explicitly acknowledge at least a family resemblance between these recent developments in their own field and those in more sociological traditions. Schieffelin (1998) offers a useful overview. He contrasts two main strands of thought on performance. The first refers to particular kinds of symbolic, aesthetic and expressive activities. He cites Bauman (1986) to exemplify this kind of approach, which stresses the distinctiveness of performances, separating them from other mundane kinds of activity. By contrast, Schieffelin uses the work of Goffman and the symbolic interactionists: 'the focus here is not on a type of event but rather on performativity itself: the expressive processes of strategic impression management and structural improvisation through which human beings normally articulate their purposes, situations and relationships in everyday social life' (1998: 195).

Now Schieffelin and others can undoubtedly be critical of Goffmanesque or interactionist uses of dramaturgy. Viewed from the cross-cultural vantage point of social and cultural anthropology, a narrowly dramaturgical perspective can certainly appear unduly restricted and ethnocentric. They can too readily invoke the taken-for-granted categories of a very specific Western mode of theatrical practice and universalize them to furnish metaphors for human conduct in general.

In that sense, therefore, Goffman's dramaturgy of the everyday and the social encounter is the antithesis of an anthropology of theatricality. Nevertheless, a reading that is more inclined to integrating rather than discriminating between these traditions finds much common ground. Schieffelin's own conclusion is a case in point: 'any ethnography of performance is inherently addressing the issue of the social construction of reality, and ... performativity is not only endemic to human being-in-the-world but fundamental to the process of constructing a human reality' (ibid.: 205).

Undoubtedly, there is need to examine empirically and theoretically the relationships between mundane performance, specific cultural practices and different cultural traditions of the 'theatrical'. Nevertheless, the contemporary invigoration of work on theatricality and performativity draws together significant strands of interactionist inspiration and other traditions of social science.

The convergence of recent writing on performance and performativity with well-established interactionist interests is just one way in which a sometimes submerged stream of thought occasionally rises to the surface and merges with others. The same is clearly true for ideas of 'reflexivity', especially as it has been used in recent accounts of the conduct and representation of social research. It is especially prominent in discussions of ethnographic research and the textual reconstruction of social reality in monographs and other scholarly writing. Reflexivity carries a number of connotations and does not lend itself to simple definition or set of formulae. At root, all its meanings stem from the recognition that there can be no radical separation between the researcher and the researched. As social researchers we are always and inescapably part of what we are trying to understand. There can be no analytic vantage point that is entirely independent or context-free. There is no neutral language of representation. In principle we can never engage with a social world in order to investigate it without some degree of reactivity. In a recent review of the various meanings and dimensions of reflexivity Davies (1999) suggests that they range from the introspection of the researcher who is able to monitor and theorize her or his research transactions through to the obsessive self-absorption of the researcher who is preoccupied with nothing beyond her or his own subjectivity. Most observers, in common with Davies, would wish to stop short of the most extreme forms of reflexivity, that leave room only for solipsistic or narcissistic self-examination or an ethnographic practice that essentially collapses into nothing beyond the autoethnography of the author (Reed-Danahay, 1997). Equally, most would recognize that ethnography, indeed all research, is intrinsically reflexive in the general sense: the reactive presence of the ethnographer is not something to be eliminated or controlled out of existence, but something to be acknowledged and interpreted. Davies's own approach is an interesting one for our purposes. She grounds her own approach to reflexivity in the realism of Bhaskar (e.g. 1989) and in the ideas of George Herbert Mead. Indeed, Davies is unusual – and hence worth mentioning in this context – in recognizing the relevance of Mead in this regard. She does not venture far beyond a summary of the main tenets of Mead's own thought, but it is noteworthy and gratifying that at least one contribution to the contemporary 'reflexivity' tendency recognizes that important and relevant ideas are to be found in the foundational contributions of Mead, and hence within the symbolic interactionist tradition. In particular, Davies uses Mead's view the of social origins and social character of the self as providing a basis for understanding other selves and the ethnographer's self simultaneously. Mead's pragmatism together with Bhaskar's critical realism are offered as a basis for a knowledge of the social that progresses beyond the purely self-referential:

> Mead's conception helps ethnographers to overcome the objection that they cannot possibly have access to the selves of people from other radically different cultural backgrounds. If the self is continually under construction, then ethnographers' experiences when they participate in social interaction in another society clearly alter their own selves in accordance with the cultural expectations of others. Attention to this process of transforming the ethnographer's 'me' can provide genuine knowledge of the nature of others' selves and societies. So the reflexive bent of ... experimental ethnographies seems justified on good realist and pragmatic grounds, so long as they do not lose sight of their responsibility to seek explanatory abstraction and not primarily to report on individual experience. (Davies, 1999: 74)

Leaving aside whether everyone would subscribe so easily to 'explanatory abstraction' as the goal of all ethnographic research, one can applaud this recognition from within anthropology's own often insular discipline that some of its more radical ideas are a little less novel than one might think from their proponents' self-advertisements. It is abundantly clear that while symbolic interactionism has not consistently fostered 'experimental' ethnographic work, its approach to ethnographic understanding has always been grounded in a recognition of the reflexive self. In turn, it has recognized that our knowledge of the social world about us is an emergent process, the outcome of active transactions between the observer and the observed – both sides of which are transformed in the process.

IDENTITY AND INTERACTION

The centrality of matters relating to identity within British sociology cannot be underestimated. In a recent book Williams (2000) notes the

159

various influences and theoretical traditions that studies of identity now draw upon. These include ethnomethodology, post-structuralism, feminism, cultural Marxism and social psychology. However, while there are clear differences and connections in and between the approaches outlined by Williams, the interactionist conceptualization of identity remains not only a core concept but a reservoir, a resource and a foundational keystone to those areas concerned with consumption, identity and everyday life, the social body and other fashionable areas of social research. Within the pragmatist philosophy of James (1890) and Dewey (1925) and the ideas of Herbert Mead, the individual is understood as both an acting subject and object of self and other. Of central relevance here is Mead's formulation of the 'I' and the 'Me' that provides the grounds for exploring the self as a social process. Building on this pioneering tradition, Goffman's work provides a rich resource for exploring the social organization of identity. Goffman builds on the social psychological preoccupation with self (while never losing sight of it) by emphasizing the social processes through which identity is performed and presented. He also explicates the importance of location or place in terms of the moral organization of selves and the patterning of interaction in institutional sites. An important idea here is the relationship between the presentation of self, the interactional accomplishment of identity and its relationship with the 'ritual organization of social encounters' (Goffman, 1967: 45). Goffman's work on identity also explores the realm of 'spoiled identities', stigma and the presentation of selves, lives and biographies. Goffman notes that in the case of institutional identities, spoiled identities, stigma, and so forth, the process of identity is one that is characterized by a degree of layering. Goffman's concept of identity is not one-dimensional. As Williams argues with respect to Goffman's conceptualization of self and identity: 'He seems to imply ... the presence of four identity matters here, each of which is difficult to penetrate: what the individual says, what the individual thinks, what the individual imagines, and what the individual "is"' (2000: 147). This account is especially significant, given that Robin Williams is one of the most consistent of British commentators on interactionism and sociological theory.

This provides a more complex account of self and the social milieu in which the interactional order of sites, rituals and location are loosely coupled with notions of social structure. While many commentators have criticized the manner in which Goffman conceptualizes the interactional order as a 'relatively autonomous entity' (Williams, 2000) he demonstrates the importance of the fine-grained interactional texture of identity in interaction. Goffman notes that how identities become relevant and understood as local expressions or structurally generated phenomena, is complex. However, Goffman argues that such concerns with structure or locality are interactionally generated in the last instance. As Goffman himself puts it:

> The expressions themselves, such as priority in being served, precedence through a door, centrality of seating, access to various public places, preferential interruption rights in talk, selection as addressed recipient, are interactional in substance and in character; at best they are likely to have only loosely coupled relations to anything by way of social structures that might be associated with them. They are sign vehicles fabricated from descriptive materials at hand and what they come to be taken as a reflection of is necessarily an open question. (1983: 14)

As we have previously noted, Goffman's work provides a plenum for a sociology of identity and interaction. It provides a rich seam of concepts through which self, interaction and society can be explored. As indicated in previous chapters, the domain of social identity (and others) has been colonized by theoretical explanations that have, more often than not, emphasized issues and matters surrounding the concept of 'representation', social construction and an under-specified conceptualization of discourse. Within these modes for theorizing identity, the discursive construction and representation of identity gloss over the active character of identity. This approach to theorizing identity as a set of discursive representations has been located primarily within the work of Foucault, although this is not always an accurate assertion. For example, Rabinow (1986) notes that Foucault approaches the thorny issue of identity in three significant ways. First, through the concept of 'dividing practices'. These practices refer to categories and forms of classification that, via discourse, have an effect on the practical processing of individuals. The human sciences have represented one particular species of discourse through which the classification of individuals has had social and spatial effects. Second, the concept of scientific classification. This relates to the first and refers to the constitution of the subject through the operationalization of specific scientific discursive constructions e.g. the rational actor in economics, the speaking subject of linguistics, the consumer of marketing science, and so forth. Third, Foucault invokes the notion of 'subjectification'; this refers to internal psychological introspection and social interaction. In some cases, the process of subjectification can be informed by various discourses e.g. religion, psychology, psychoanalysis, therapy, and so on. In terms of the Foucault's three approaches to understanding identity, it is the first two that have been used by analysts in charting various representational signatures of such modes through the operationalization of semiology and other structuralist-oriented methods. Foucault's concern with the realm of interaction has not been so prominent. Thus, the colonization of identity by theorists who accentuate the representational character of identity can only be partially connected to Foucault. Rather, it is the

161

methodology of French semiology and semiotics that marshals the trajectory of such studies.

In terms of futures, any claims are bound to be refuted by events. However, one possible scenario may well be that the concerns of interactionism, of lived practices, types and careers will return to view within the domain of identity studies and concerns. Recent work in ethnomethodology and discursive psychology has emphasized, in interconnected but also distinct ways, the import of examining identity as an interactional accomplishment. To this extent at least one constituent concern of interactionism within the area of the sociology of identity is making a significant return driven by forms of sociological enquiry that, while not clear descendants of interactionist sociology, have clear and recognizable links with some of its core concepts. A second concept that continues to have resonance across Goffmanesque, ethnomethodological and discursive explorations of identity in interaction is the concept of types, 'categories' and other interconnected, mutually referential, post-Schutzian concepts. Less prominent has been the concept of career. In some respects, the concept of career has become so taken for granted that, with respect to debates concerning identity, it forms a central concept in identity trajectories and the temporal investigation/examination of concretized forms of identity and patterns of behaviour (e.g. criminal, learner, yuppie). In some respects recent quantitative studies of criminal behaviour, learning identities and lifestyles have, at their heart, a concept of career largely derived from the often unacknowledged tradition of interactionist enquiry.

In addition to this, new activities, technology and forms of communication have opened new sites of enquiry where the relationship between self, identity and interaction raise new questions and issues. The development and extension of ethnographic work into the domain of electronic networks, the Internet and virtual worlds have provided an avenue for the application of ideas associated with the interactionist tradition. A further dimension of the reconsideration of identity matters must also be understood in terms of the rise and rise of identity politics. From feminism, to post-colonial theory, disability rights to new social movements, identity has become both a site of struggle and a resource for resistance. The realm of identity and interaction, experience and the lifeworld have become sites upon which much sociological attention has been focused. Increasingly the character of interaction, of careers, discourse and experience have been invoked as a means of understanding 'identity matters'. It is clear that the interactionist conceptualization of identity is of extreme import to this project. However, while not always acknowledged, it is interesting to note how the contemporary sociology of identity, drawing on a range of theoretical sources including Foucauldian theory, feminism and the postmodern, is exhibiting increasingly interactionist credentials in terms of its preoccupations and concerns (Maines, 2001).

In recent years a plethora of studies have examined the conceptual issues and processes, popularized by the work of Goffman, of language and interaction. In terms of its development, interactionism as a distinct approach to the study of discourse has not always figured prominently *per se*. Four principal approaches do, however, namely, conversation analysis, categorization analysis, narrative analysis and discursive psychology. The first two owe much of their development to the work of Harvey Sacks and Harold Garfinkel. The third draws more explicitly on interactionist ideas but also locates itself within the field of discourse studies in which an increasing cross-fertilization and exchange of ideas are taking place, while the fourth has drawn on the post-structuralist thought of Michel Foucault (1973), the discourse theory of Laclau and Mouffe (2001) and ethnomethodology. However, these trends can be located within a moment in the history of ideas within the human sciences, namely, the so-called 'linguistic' turn.

The notion of the linguistic turn within the human sciences is one that has been identified and discussed by a number of commentators. However, it seems strange and incongruous that despite the centrality of language and symbolic action to the concerns of interactionism the linguistic turn is often seen to approximate to theoretical antecedents that stand outside the empirical work and observations of interactionist influenced work. Indeed, the whole notion of language, interaction, meaning and communication has been central to much interactionist work. In terms of symbolic interactionism Rock suggests that:

> The forms of language mediate the workings of consciousness, the self and social interchange. In turn, those forms provide symbolic interactionism with its own logic of explanation. Society is held to emerge from discourse and symbolisation. The metaphors which phrase that vision borrow heavily from an imagery of everyday speech. Interactionism portrays social life as an ongoing series of conversational encounters. (1979: 116)

More recently, this conceptualization of the linguistic turn has been questioned by contemporary ethnomethodologists who point to the much earlier work of Harvey Sacks and his concern with according talk-in-interaction a central place within his framework of sociological analysis (Hester and Francis, 2000). To this assertion we may confidently add the work of Erving Goffman who had began to develop a concern with the role of language in developing sociological accounts of everyday life and interaction. To this extent, it has been stated that the linguistic turn can be understood in terms of two principal manifestations. First, as with the phenomenological turn, between empirical (ethnomethodology, symbolic interactionism) and theoretical narratives (structuralism, post-structuralism, deconstructionism) and, second, through Anglo-American and European approaches to sociological enquiry. While we recognize the shortcoming of these dichotomies, they aid an understanding of the character and genealogy of the different influences that these approaches to language and the social involve. It is to a more detailed description of these two precedents that we now turn, if only in order to help trace and provide a 'remembering' of the source and character of these ideas as a means of grounding our claim to the persistence and relevance of core interactionist themes to the future of sociological enquiry.

The story of the theoretical rediscovery of the importance of language to understanding the social begins with the work of the Swiss linguist Ferdinand de Saussure. De Saussure has been often cited as the founder of modern formal linguistics. He was also influenced by the work of the great sociologist Emile Durkheim. De Saussure's main observation was that language could be understood as a type of system. Furthermore, language was conceived of as a functional entity that was the means through which 'meaning' was communicated. Signs are inherently arbitrary, and are only potentially meaningful insofar as there are systematic relations of difference and similarity between them.

In the cultural and social disciplines writers such as Roland Barthes and the French school of structuralism reinvigorated de Saussure's work. They were interested in the way in which language could be said to consist of a number of different systems that circulated throughout the social body. Utilizing the tools of semiology a new school of cultural analysis began not only to analyse meaning in terms of different language systems but also in terms of myths, narratives and (eventually) discourses that were seen to be present within various cultural representations and practices. In particular, the emergence of new popular forms of culture provided fertile ground and material for this development in semiotic/structuralist analysis. The meaning of certain words could be viewed to be subject to particular paradigmatic and syntagmatic arrangements. Furthermore, the historical and cultural effect on a language system (e.g. imperialism, the subjugation of women) could be decoded and fleshed out through careful semiotic analysis. These developments were therefore building on de Saussure's basic ideas as a means of analysing the social and ideological code of texts and language. Clearly, a view of the sign as ideological, rather than arbitrary – as proposed by Voloshinov, albeit within a different site of theoretical elaboration and development – provided a starting point for a view of narratives and myths as distortions of a clearly identifiable reality. The task of the semiotician was to decode these messages and meta-myths in terms of their ideological construction, character and content. Thus the task of the structuralist semiotician was to de-code systems of signification (e.g. texts, narratives, novels, newspapers, and so forth) and show how ideological factors were embedded in the linguistic constructions of various cultural products. For influential English-language accounts of these perspectives, see Hawkes (1977), Culler (1975, 1988) and Lodge (1981).

The identification of the 'linguistic turn', within sociology, can be viewed in terms of the growth of interest in cultural phenomena and powerful theoretical developments which have generated important debates within the human sciences. The radicalization of Ferdinand de Saussure's semiology and the explosion of interest in post-structuralism, deconstruction and various species of semiotics have placed language at the centre of sociological debate. The realization that language is central to the process of examining the 'social' (and *being* social) has led to a focus upon a range of phenomena which are tangible, observable and available. The 'linguistic turn' within the human sciences has been associated with the postmodernist, post-structuralist and post-sociological arguments advanced during the late 1970s and 1980s within which the universal claims of the Enlightenment, exemplified by the rational subject and Cartesian epistemology, were seen to be de-centred through a re-reading of Saussurian linguistics, Althusserian structuralism (1970), Freudian psychoanalysis, feminism and the emergence of post-colonial narrative (Said, 1978). Furthermore, the failure of Marxist praxis at the barricades in 1968 had opened up the opaque character of language and undermined faith in the grand narrative of world socialism. The Heideggerian connection between 'language and being' became a central concern for Marxist intellectuals, present at the barricades in 1968, as the multiple readings of Marxist discourse were used to justify and promote a variety of practices which were perceived as reactionary. Within the context of British sociology this resulted in an array of studies and theoretical treatises upon the status and character of discourse within social relations, institutions, and so forth. However, this often meant the analysis of discursive representations rather than interactions. However, it was only at a later stage that such theoretical concerns could imprint themselves upon empirical and observational work.

The alternative manifestation of the linguistic turn within the human sciences has received little attention in the literature that purports to present accounts of the linguistic turn within the human sciences. This is perhaps because a *sociological* concern with language has a more established history within the United States than within established

European schools of thought until recently. Consequently, the discovery of 'language' was not news to more North American forms of sociological practice. Alongside and indeed, before, the so-called 'linguistic turn' the work of Harold Garfinkel, Harvey Sacks and Erving Goffman had made great strides in investigating the relationship between language and the sociological. Furthermore, this 'linguistic turn' was one that was empirical rather than theoretical in orientation.

In many respects the sociologists identified above are not strictly interactionist. Clearly, Garfinkel (1967) and Sacks (1992a, 1992b) were both heavily involved with the establishment of a radically local sociological form of analysis, while, on the other hand, Goffman has never been understood to be representative of 'orthodox' symbolic interactionism. However, all three sociologists worked in close proximity and were working towards conclusions that, from a certain perspective, have much in common. Within the context of the United Kingdom it is more difficult to suggest that the influence of these thinkers and analysts was felt in a distinct and discrete fashion. However, ethnomethodology and its programme of analysing 'talk-in-interaction' have made a significant impact upon sociology within Britain as has Goffman's conceptual foundations and ideas concerning the orders of interaction. In both cases the significance of language and language use *within interaction* have been areas that have preoccupied both ethnomethodology and the interactionism of Goffman.

From the standpoint of contemporary histories of social science, the influence of interactionism may not be evident. But we are advancing the argument that the success of the analysis of language and interaction owes much to the analytic space partly opened up by interactionist work, particularly by the work of Goffman. The fact that the research programmes of conversation analysis and discourse analysis draw on ethnomethodology and not symbolic interactionism or the interactionist perspective of Goffman is due, in part, to the historical location of their development. On the one hand, the development of Sacks's work (though influenced in part by the work of Goffman) has been located within the domain of ethnomethodology whose popularity reached a climax in the 1970s and 1980s, a time when the coherence of symbolic interactionism as a distinct research perspective was very much on the wane. Discourse analysis draws on the Anglo-American 'linguistic turn' but also from its theoretically driven continental alter ego that, within the UK, reached prominence during the 1980s. However, in terms of futures, the core interactionist concept of language and interaction remains intact. It is clearly problematic to assume that the research programme of conversation analysis and discourse analysis can be subsumed or described within an interactionist lineage of ideas. However, it is clear that they have (sometimes critically)

connected with earlier interactionist literature and developed an attention to the detailed machinery of social life that has clear resonance
with the tradition and its core concerns. That is to say, in part, with
respect to conversation analysis (and therefore discursive psychology
due to its explicit reliance on ethnomethodology and the work of
Sacks) interactionist concerns intersected with the development of these
approaches. In Schegloff's summary:

> At a very general level, of course, Goffman's analytic enterprise had
> undertaken to establish the study of face to face interaction as a domain
> of inquiry in its own right, and his work was very likely central in
> recruiting Sacks' attention to face to face interaction as a focus for the
> concern with practical theorizing and commonsense reasoning which
> animated the ethnomethodological enterprise. (1992: xxiii)

As we have seen, attention to the role of language use in a number of
diverse settings has meant that talk and interaction are now understood
to be an important social process in their own right. This may be within
the context of understanding institutional practices, the mobilization of
weak ties by new social movements and anti-capitalist protestors or the
accomplishment of various forms of identity. In large part, this is a
space opened up by Goffman's development and promotion of interactionist concerns and the face-to-face interaction as a legitimate and
important domain of enquiry.

167

INSTITUTIONS AND INTERACTION

A further site of enquiry in which the core concepts of interactionism
remain intact is within the study of institutions and organizations. The
work of Goffman, Bittner and others has helped to define the area of
institutions and organizations as one where interactionism has made a
significant sociological contribution. Within conversation analysis the
interactionist space of the institution has, in recent years, been explored
under the auspices of the Institutional Talk Programme. Within ethnography the concerns of Goffman have been synthesized with
Foucauldian ideas concerning power/knowledge, discourse and institutional practices. Thus, in one sense a concern with institutions and
interaction has made some return to the central concerns of sociological enquiry. However, this work has often been conducted in business
schools, management settings and other departmental sites other than
schools of sociology. However, in recent years, with the development of
a 'new synthesis in sociological enquiry', the interactionist approach to
institutions may well return to favour in the market place of ideas.
The reason for this assertion lies in a contemporary concern with the
re-engineering of institutions (Hammer and Champey, 1993). This

concern with re-engineering or re-shaping institutions and interaction is driven, in part, from two principal sources. First, a move from middle range theorizing towards a concern with institutional practices drawing on the continued relevance of the 'action model of organizations' as proposed by Silverman (1970) and others within certain management approaches influenced by a cross-fertilization with ideas and practices (e.g. qualitative methods, ethnography, discourse analysis) generated in other disciplinary environments. This move, allied with concerns with the reflective practitioner and organizations, promotes (via research) forms of continued, reflective and sustained micro-intervention as a form of practice that should be an institutional goal in itself. Second, from the risk society thesis of Ulrich Beck (1992) and other related theorists who, in terms of late modernity, argue that a new enlightenment is necessary in order to respond to new risks and demands generated by the success of the modern project. In the sense that the modernization of society has led to a situation within which the new risks and hazards facing humanity are generated from the social system itself (as opposed to external, 'natural' causes). Beck argues that one of the crucial sites for this process can be found in the institutional sphere. Beck, in line with the trajectory of his argument, takes a particular interest in the relationship between science, legal structures and democratic institutions. The new risks generated by new forms of *technology* (not the science) (e.g. genetic engineering and other applications as opposed to genetics *per se*) should be mediated through democratically accountable institutions. Thus initial solutions refer to the need to 'democratize science' and an establishment of a science court that would adjudicate upon issues of scientific knowledge and its social application through the development of various types of technologies. However, it is clear that, though Beck and other theorists do not explicitly refer to it, the re-engineering of institutions along normative principles and reasoned objectives will demand some consideration of how institutions work and how they are changed. Questions related to decision-making, accountability, knowledge and expertise become central to any such proposed enterprise, especially if one was using the example of a science court, or citizen forum for matters concerning local technological interventions (e.g. the establishment of power stations, cell phone masts etc.). In particular, the role of expertise and knowledge in relation to the need not only to develop but revolutionize institutions has become a prominent dimension of this debate. It remains to be seen whether the detailed interactionist-oriented ethnography of Atkinson, Silverman and others within the domain of knowledge and expertise will figure prominently within the emerging research programmes for institutional renewal and the place of knowledge and expertise within these decision-making/knowledge settings and sites. However, it would seem a crucial inclusion if the normative, theoretically driven, goals of institutional renewal are to 'work' in the sense that it has been a crucial observation of interactionist studies of such matters that the formal accounts of institutional organization seldom reflect the informal realities of the 'living world' of the institution. The re-engineering of institutional sites and establishment of new forms and institutional practices will have to deal with the interactional dimensions of knowledge, expertise, the distinction between professional and lay spheres and communicative practices.

An interesting example of the application of the action model of organization and Goffmanesque concepts and ideas can be found in studies that have explored the organization of new social movements. In one sense new social movements represent a form of 'non-organization', although it is interesting to note how such civil organizations develop into more formal types of institution (as with Greenpeace during the 1970s). Snow et al. (1986) pioneered the use of Goffman's frame analysis in order to chart and explore the way in which individual interpretive schema are translated into collective ones in the form of new social movement or social movement organizations. Of particular concern is how specific frame alignments relate to what Goffman (1974) calls 'strips of activity'. Goffman, building on the work of Bateson describes frames as essentially a resource for providing 'definitions of the situation'. In terms of less organized movements Welsh and Chesters (2001) have noted how networks and 'weak ties' (Granovetter, 1973) are central to understanding how the diffusion of information is dependent upon word of mouth and other face-to-face processes during the task of mobilizing interested parties, agents and citizens. It is argued that many less formally organized social movements are aware of the power of 'weak ties' in communicating information and popularizing resistance to particular issues in the media and contemporary events. Welsh and Chesters (2001) note that this informal, interactive work of certain social movements presents problems for those political leaders and organizations who wish to manage popular opinion via official forms of media output and the traditional apparatus of press briefings, announcements and news releases. However, what is interesting about these studies is that they make use of key interactionist ideas in understanding social movements as organizations and in documenting the way in which social movements reflexively make use of such interactional understandings in developing tactics and strategies oriented to specific goals.

In this section of the chapter we have explored four thematic areas in which the future use and trajectory of interactionist core concepts and ideas can be appreciated. Consequently, we view the endurance of interactionist thought not just within a narrow perspectivalism but in terms of the durability, applicability and relevance of a rich tradition. In terms of theoretical concerns interactionism has not produced a grand theoretical narrative *a priori*. However, as Maines (2001) notes, it would be disingenuous to suggest that interactionism and pragmatic sociology are 'atheoretical'. Within the United Kingdom representations of interactionism have often placed interactionist 'theory' on one side of a number of classificatory apparatus. One of the most notable of these classificatory fictions is the (false) suggestion that interactionism is committed to one particular form of methodological perspective, although perhaps the one that has been used to limit and consign interactionism to marginality is the invocation of the structure vs action dualism. In many respects interactionism's location within an 'action perspective' classification represents one of the more interesting and dubious mythic facts surrounding interactionist sociology. Furthermore, the recent drive towards synthesis, through which dualisms such as macro vs micro, agency vs structure and objectivity vs subjectivity will be overcome has, often through secondary commentary, placed interactionism as representative of a form of sociology (among others) that deals in the stock and trade of such dualisms. Such 'mythic facts' do great intellectual violence to the character and general history of interactionist sociology. It is to this 'collective amnesia' and the use of a misreading of interactionist thinking at the level of general theoretical commentary that we now turn.

170

STRUCTURE AND ACTION: INTERACTIONISM AND SYNTHESIS?

Some commentators have suggested that the future of sociological enquiry lies in the analysis of large data sets and a recommitment to political arithmetic. Other analysts have pointed to the analysis of non-linear dynamics within complex systems as the future of social science. It is clear that in a data-rich society sophisticated quantitative analysis of financial markets, population dynamics, consumer behaviour will take a greater role in social description and prediction. However, the future of the interactional milieux and its analysis will remain a central concern of social enquiry. These concerns are reflected in much contemporary social theory, for example Habermas's concern with the colonization of the lifeworld by the 'system' is indicative of the importance that the interactionist perspective potentially occupies. Furthermore the drive towards synthesis by Habermas (1979), Mouzelis (1990), Bourdieu (1992) and Giddens (1976, 1984) within sociological theory has reaffirmed the continued importance of action, agency and interaction. This synthesis has often involved the invocation of a set of pre-constituted dualisms in some cases by the authors of new 'synthetic' ideas and commentators upon contemporary social theory. For example, Jeffrey Alexander (1998) utilizes notions of macro vs micro and action vs structure to characterize different traditions. In the accounts provided by these theorists and commentators 'mythic facts' and reconstitutive rhetorics once again make an appearance. In Mouzelis's account the portrayal of interactionist sociologies centres on an accusation that they have failed to take account of wider social processes: an incorrect assertion. Mouzelis's position is near to a form of neo-functionalism in which discourses and forms of life are organized in terms of a state of relative autonomy within a hierarchical system of social organization. In terms of Giddens's contribution to the new synthesis in social theory his starting point began with a critique of functionalism. While Giddens rejects Parsonian functionalism, he accepts the general thrust of the approach in terms of its attempt to build a general theory of social explanation. In order to do this, Giddens uses ideas and concepts drawn from across the sociological tradition. Giddens's theory of structuration asserts that traditional social theory has been characterized by a clear set of inter-related distinctions. These distinctions include action versus structure, objectivity versus subjectivity and macro versus micro. This framework serves as a suitable set of 'mythic facts' through which various traditions e.g. functionalism, Marxism or interactionism can be assigned. In terms of Giddens's drive towards synthesis, the 'mythic fact' that is utilized is the oppositional distinction between structure and action.

171

Some sociological theories, it is asserted, focus on the importance of individual actions, interactions and interpretations in understanding social processes. Actors are conceived as applying meaning to their actions and being able to plan and reflect on their conduct. Consequently 'action' theories take a bottom-up approach to understanding how social organization is achieved. 'Structural' theories take a top-down view that perceives society as exhibiting patterns and processes over and above individual actions. Furthermore, social structure is understood to constrain and constitute individual action and agency. Giddens argues that both these (reconstructed) positions are relevant. Social organization does seem to stand over and above individual actions (providing we choose to ignore the myriad of actions that make up such an entity). However, social structures can be understood to be accomplished, sustained and recreated through action. In one sense society can be understood to be characterized by both dimensions. Giddens calls this the 'duality of structure' i.e. action and structure. The duality of structure is realized through the process of structuration. Actions inform and create structures and structures inform action in a reflexive and circular manner. According to Giddens, traditional structural-oriented theories have viewed structure as constraining, constituting and determining the precise configuration of social action. However, Giddens notes how structure can also be understood to enable action. Structures provide frameworks of rules through which action can be articulated, displayed and recognized. The theory of structuration can be summarized through three main meta-concepts.

The first concept refers to the notion of action and agency as behaviour that is 'rule-following'. Drawing on the 'linguistic turn' within the social sciences Giddens translates de Saussure's distinction between speech (*parole*) and language (*langue*) into a distinction between action and practices. Practices can be understood as forms of action which are governed through rules. Practices mediate between structure and action through a rule-governing framework. Giddens draws on the Wittgensteinian concept of language games in articulating this concept.

The second concept of resources refers to any resources that actors within institutions, organizations or other forms of social system use in order to realize their goals. These may be material, symbolic, cultural, cognitive or discursive. Finally, Giddens refers to the concept of structures that can be understood as phenomena that are characterized by an organized patterns of rules and uses of different resources. It is through rules and practices and the use of resources that actors continually reproduce and sustain social structures. Giddens notes that rules as practices and resources are not confined to a particular location. He argues that such features of structuration transcend temporal and spatial configurations. He suggests that the relationship between social organization and time and space has been neglected by social theory.

These meta-concepts are bolstered by Giddens's theory concerning the modality of structure. The relationship between actions and structures (and the reproduction of structures) can be understood in terms of the following ideas. Language and communication are central to understanding the relationship between rules, resources, action and structure. Structuration necessarily involves a conceptualization of rules and (some) resources as being largely semiological (i.e. expressed in terms of codes and meanings). Giddens notes that hierarchical frameworks exist. The relationship of human beings to each other is mediated by structures and practices of domination. Giddens's concept of legitimation refers to the moral organization of the social, the sets of norms and values shared by a given society. He argues that normative assessments are realized through this moral order although not all members of society share the same outlook.

What is striking about Giddens's development of the concept of structuration is the lack of recognition or reference to interactionist thought. Continental interpretivist traditions, the phenomenology of Schutz, the ethnomethodology of Garfinkel, the functionalism of

Parsons, the works of Marx, Durkheim and Weber are all present. Yet, the category of action theory has been subsequently used by sociological commentators to include interactionist work and ideas. However, as Maines has already pointed out such a reconstituted characterization of interactionism fails to fully appreciate its full complexity and awareness of phenomena that Giddens describes as the duality of structure. Indeed, Maines (2001) refers to W.I. Thomas's work *Primitive Behaviour* (1937) in which he writes and refers to the 'structuralization of cultures' as well as the definition of the situation. To be fair to Giddens, it is perhaps the way in which readings of 'structuration theory' have been used and the constructed positions within this conceptual framework that can cause difficulties. Indeed, we can also appreciate that in terms of Giddens's structuration theory, although not always accepting the restrictive definition of action theories as applied to interactionism, its success and reception during the 1990s testify to the continued relevance of core interactionist themes through which social organization and structures and interaction are both seen as sides of the same coin.

Similarly, the work of Bourdieu has provided a rich conceptual framework through which the notion of habitus, practices, fields and cultural capital have been used as a means of straddling the divide between 'action and structure', 'macro and micro', 'objectivity and subjectivity'. Bourdieu's influences, like Giddens's, derive from sources and traditions that do not include the Chicago School or its descendants. The primary influence here is continental phenomenology, although a certain Weberian strand can also be discerned. Bourdieu's concepts have had great influence in providing a space through which sociologists working in various fields of enquiry can attempt to describe interaction and relate it to wider social processes and ideas. In some cases certain commentators have held up Bourdieu and Giddens as representative of a new synthesis within sociological enquiry (Alexander, 1998). However, in both cases the attempts at synthesis implicitly, and sometime explicitly, assume that interactionism (as a supposed example of an action type approach) is symptomatic with purely 'micro' concerns, subjective states and action as opposed to structure. In fact, it can confidently be argued that interactionism, along with ethnomethodology, does not even recognize these distinctions never mind acknowledge their framing within such dualisms. Thus, while celebrating the spaces of enquiry that make use of such ideas, such a drive to 'synthesis' needs also to acknowledge living traditions that have already combined many of the concerns highlighted by such approaches. Indeed, it should be emphasized that there is great inadequacy in consigning the interactionist tradition to the confines of one side of a structure vs action dualism. Such dualisms are not the stock and trade of interactionist and pragmatic sociology. The beating heart of interactionism testifies,

173

draws upon and displays an understanding of social structure and order as a manifestation of process. The division between structure and action is therefore one not recognized by interactionist studies, concepts and understandings of the social.

Despite these conceptual difficulties, reconstituted rhetorics and the imprecise, distorted and sometimes incorrect framing of interactionism within various historical matrices and banal conceptual reductionism, the core interactionist concepts presented in this book as applied to the study of culture, identity, communication and institutions will remain of import whether they are acknowledged or not. The requirement to understand the meaningful character and dimensions of social organization is one that quantification or theoretical abstraction does not explore, capture or address. It is precisely through this requirement in understanding the new spaces opened up by larger-scale transformations in terms of the meaningful and strategic character of action that interactionism can and will make a contribution toward. As suggested earlier, perhaps not as a clear perspective or unified research programme, but through the relevance and application of its ideas and core concepts.

Furthermore, while in recent years social representations have become an increasingly important area of enquiry, the interactional processes through which representations are built up, exchanged and received remain central to any coherent sociological enterprise. Indeed, the concern with social organization as an emergent property of a myriad of interactions that are required not only in order to build social organization but also to sustain it is one of sociology's most important insights. It may well be that this insight is radicalized through the introduction and synthesis of interactionist ideas with complexity theory and principles of non-linear dynamics as a means of exploring emergent phenomena in a statistically rigorous non-Newtonian manner. On the other hand, the coupled principles of 'interaction and emergence' together with a profound vision of everyday social ontology and values as necessary preconditions for social life exhibited and affirmed through interactionist studies necessitate an openness to a variety of methods within the interactionist frame. That being so, interactionism can and should not be subject to the simplistic dualism of quantitative versus qualitative. Such a reading can prove useful, but it may also confound the important set of observations and empirically generated ideas that interactionism continues to provide often as a hidden and unacknowledged source.

As we have stated throughout this book we do not seek to advocate or call for a return to perspectival purity or the policing of boundaries or arguments concerning the genesis of ideas. We do contest 'mythic facts' and imprecise characterizations of general theoretical properties.

We do, however, assert that what we have called willed amnesia and Sorokin (1956) and Maines (2001) have called collective amnesia has operated with respect to interactionism. We agree with Maines that the interactionist tradition has all too often been subject to certain mythic facts and 'reconstitutive legitimacies'. In part, this book represents a British account of the story of interactionism, and we have sought to rescue interactionism from certain forms of conceptual stereotyping and demonstrate how its core ideas continue to have direct and central thematic relevance to mainstream sociology. Indeed, viewed this way, interactionism is not only alive and well but is one of the primary sociological fields of enquiry and well of conceptual resources. Acknowledgement of this would open up a range of important studies that could inform first hand, as opposed to the filters of commentary, contemporary work. In terms of the future of sociology and the society in which we live, interactionism's concerns are becoming increasingly important. To that extent, we are all interactionists now.

seven
epilogue

In this book we have explored a range of concepts and ideas that have sought to show how the legacy of interactionism, while overlooked and sometimes unrecognized, continues to have a direct connection and primary relevance to the concerns of contemporary sociological enquiry. For much of the book, therefore, we have focused on the reception of interactionist ideas in British sociology in the late 1960s and the 1970s. We have stressed that interactionism, derived from American sociology, had a significant impact on the conduct and content of key areas of empirical research in the United Kingdom. It had a major influence on the development and expansion of the sociologies of health, education, deviance and work. Over the subsequent years it has exerted a major significance on the promotion and development of methodological work. These impacts were not uniform. The reception and use of the ideas were most vivid in the field of deviance studies, where account of exotic subcultures and processes of deviance amplification reached a very wide audience beyond the confines of the speciality of deviance studies or criminology. Equally, however, the flowering was rather brief. The new criminology – often practised by the same people who had embraced integrationist ideas – was widely perceived to have superseded the perspectives derived from labelling theory and interactionist ethnography. Criminology supplanted deviance studies in many contexts.

In the sociology of health and illness, and the sociology of education, the influence of interactionism has been more sustained and more visible. There has been a strong British tradition of empirical research in clinical and other settings of medical work, and on social encounters between health professionals and their clients. These have been nurtured by repeated inputs from American interactionists, such as Anselm Strauss and Virginia Olesen, who have continued to make distinguished contributions to the sociology of health and illness. It has also been sustained by the huge growth in social research on health and illness. The ideas themselves proved accessible, relevant and fruitful to the emergent cadres of social researchers in the health professions. While the ideas continue to have importance, they have not resulted in a purely interactionist sociology. They have fed into a wider stream of ideas. The latter have included various versions of constructivist sociology of scientific and medical knowledge. Feminist research interests have also fed off interactionist ideas, supplemented them and transformed them in the process.

In slightly different ways, the sociology of educational settings has also been a major site and source for interactionist work. Analyses of schools and classrooms as social systems, and as settings for social encounters have been a major strand in the discipline for several decades. Interestingly, this happened despite the relative neglect of American interactionist studies of schools and classrooms themselves. The Chicago School provided exemplars derived from studies of higher education and occupational socialization. In the United Kingdom the interactionist perspectives were translated into a more mainstream educational sociology, in which social processes were located within institutional and structural contexts. Moreover, the influence was felt through teacher training, where – in the 1970s and 1980s at least – sociology was one of the foundational disciplines. The ideas derived from interactionism were thus disseminated widely through the academy and the teaching profession. In recent years, the same ideas have continued to be of relevance. They are less likely, however, to be attributed directly to the interactionist influence. As in other fields, they are more likely to be assimilated to methodological or broad epistemological commitments (qualitative or ethnographic studies of social settings or subsumed under a more general interpretivist framework). Equally, there has been a more explicit turn towards policy – such as the analysis of marketization in schools.

As we have argued, the powerful but diffuse influence of interactionism can be identified in the development of research methods. Again, this is an impure line of development. Ethnographic and other qualitative research has become pervasive in the social and cultural disciplines. In the United Kingdom especially, this has been accompanied by a professional, recurrent moral panic concerning the weakness of quantitative methods. More positively, it has become a distinctive strength of British social science. The United Kingdom is an acknowledged source of international excellence. In part, as we have suggested, this can be traced to the impact of interactionist work in the substantive fields. It can also be attributed to the reception of interactionist authors like Becker, Geer, Glaser and Strauss, the Loflands, and so on. Over the past three decades, however, the justification for qualitative or ethnographic research has become more diffuse. In many quarters – not always for the better – the methods have taken on the appearance of being a self-justifying paradigm. Researchers seem as likely to describe themselves as 'ethnographers' as 'interactionists'. Moreover, the repertoire of research perspectives has become increasingly diverse. Recent textbooks and edited collections of qualitative research – and they abound – are testimony to the diversity of approaches, as well as to the vigour of their reception in the academy. Consequently, the justifications for qualitative research – the contexts of justification for their use – have become diverse. Researchers are likely to appeal to various ideological or standpoint justifications (e.g. feminism, critical race theory) and to various meta-analytic perspectives such as postmodernism and post-structuralism. As a consequence, the ideas of interactionism that informed earlier work in methodology have been supplemented and hybridized with other intellectual strands. Their influence has been at its widest when it has been least visible.

We have also stressed that this reception did not result in the development of a 'pure' interactionist sociology. Characteristic of British sociology – and British intellectual life more generally – there was a more pragmatic and eclectic approach. The influence of European social philosophy was perhaps more common than in American Departments of Sociology, and a more generic 'interpretative' or 'hermeneutic' perspective embraced interactionist ideas, while interactionism did not present itself as an indigenous alternative to a mainstream (as was generally the case in the United States). Contributing to more general sociological movements, therefore, interactionism has been even more understated in British sociology than in its American homeland.

On the other hand, the ideas that informed interactionism, the empirical topics that inspired its research programmes, and its general epistemology are all especially current in contemporary sociology. While its direct impact has been diffused, there is a strong sense in which the time has come for interactionism's key ideas. A central argument that has emerged within this book is an identification of a momentum and drive towards forms of sociological enquiry that are amenable to dialogue with the rich tradition of interactionism. Central to this argument is the emerging conceptualization of the social in terms of process, flux and movement. Many of these ideas have been located in postmodern thinking. It is interesting to note that many of the ideas concerning the social as process, the flux and flow of identity and the character of communicative practice within postmodern theory have been connected with neo-pragmatism. However, in terms of the arguments presented in this book, contemporary social thought may well benefit from a reconsideration and engagement with the development of the pragmatist tradition in and through interactionist ideas and studies. Indeed, the recent rehabilitation of thinkers such as Simmel, Benjamin and Kracauer testifies to the continued relevance of submerged traditions after the postmodern moment. To these observers of early twentieth-century metropolitan life should be added the ethnographers of Chicago.

In many respects the 'Newtonian model' of a clockwork social universe is only now being dismantled many years after interactionism's analysis of social relations, social organization and social selves as social processes. Correspondingly, a conceptualization of social forms and structures as emergent properties of a myriad of interactions provides a space in which the complexity of social forms can be appreciated. While this also provides for the utilization of complex mathematics and an appreciation of non-linear dynamics to understanding social events, it also provides for the reflexive and interpretative appreciation and understanding of the various new levels of complexity attributed to the social. Furthermore, the importance of interaction to understanding the social as *process* is rapidly becoming a fundamental core idea within sociology and related disciplines. The future of interactionism is, we believe, not one that is merely confined to a recognized and aware 'core set' of practitioners, it is to be felt in its future impact upon practical studies and reflections of social life during this time of rapid social transformation. It is to be found in the changing cultural character of urban life, the re-recognition of multiple social identities, the development of new media and communications, inter-personal technologies, the re-engineering of institutions, the changing character of the workplace, new forms of medical practice and delivery of healthcare. Furthermore, this impact will, we believe, benefit from a consideration of interactionist core concepts alongside the more contemporary grounding and application of grand theoretical ideas. We believe that this represents a fruitful, powerful and unique opportunity for carrying forward the eclectic mix of sociological concepts and ideas in understanding contemporary transformation. However, if this book is to have relevance, then such a move should also acknowledge previous sources and dialogues as a means of recording such intellectual contact and cross-fertilization in order to secure (or at least promote) the efficacy of developments, innovations and sociological knowledge for the future. A commitment to some form of record of past ideas and developments, that may well be contested, negotiated and discussed, is the surest way of mapping the future directions of sociological enquiry.

Interactionism represents a case that displays the effects of collective amnesia. It may well be noted by sociologists that the culture of amnesia is being exported into the offspring of the sociological tradition. Contemporary cultural studies, contemporary criminology and management studies often pay little respect to their sociological origins, often developing reconstitutive legitimacies, while utilizing the broad sweep of sociological concepts, ideas and methods. The answer here is one that begins at home. Sociology needs to maintain some preoccupation with

179

a history of sociological ideas. However, the synchronic obsession with substantive domains within some theoretical commentary renders such a narrative invisible. The first attempt at prompts aimed at the recovery of memory can often be painful and, in some cases, provoke anger, disorientation and denial. Such prompts and their reactions are necessary if the reconstitutive legitimacies and 'mythic facts' pertaining to interactionism are to be placed in the intellectual dustbin. We believe that the humble but extremely important themes and concepts of interactionism deserve recognition in terms of their continued relevance and source of inspiration for current empirical work and resource for mapping out future contours of enquiry during times of great change and new social horizons. To this extent, this book represents a small but significant step in the direction of legitimate rehabilitation and recognition. Arguably, sociological amnesia is not confined to the treatment of interactionism. Indeed, it seems to be a recurrent phenomenon. Too often claims for theoretical novelty turn out to be the products of ignorance and oversight rather than being grounded in genuinely new ideas and insights. Sociology has an ambivalent attitude towards its own past. In some contexts, the so-called classic texts are returned to over and over again. The nineteenth-century founding fathers and (rarely) mothers are revered. But it is equally possible to find major authors of the more recent past completely overlooked, and key ideas being recapitulated. Ideas are often translated into fashionable terminologies, and fashionable rhetoric can be used to dress up older – even rather stale – ideas. The pursuit of novelty does not always result in genuinely new theory, as opposed to new glosses on old perspectives. The recent fashion for late modernism and postmodernism is a case in point, where older insights can get recycled and refurbished. The fate of interactionist ideas in British sociology is but one case of a more general process in the reception, use, neglect and appropriation of ideas in the social sciences.

references

Abbott, A. (1999) *Department and Discipline: Chicago Sociology at One Hundred.* Chicago: University of Chicago Press.

Adam, B. (1990) *Time and Social Theory.* Oxford: Polity Press.

Adler, P.A., Adler, P. and Fontana, A. (1987) 'Everyday life in sociology', *Annual Review of Sociology*, 13: 217–35.

Alexander, J.C. (1998) *Neofunctionalism and After.* Oxford: Blackwell.

Altheide, D.L. and Johnson, J.M. (1993) 'Reflections on voice in ethnography', in N.K. Denzin (ed.), *Studies in Symbolic Interaction*, vol. 15. Greenwich, CT: JAI Press, pp. 71-82.

Anderson, P. (1969) 'Components of the national culture', in R. Blackburn and A. Cockburn (eds), *Student Power.* Harmondsworth: Penguin, pp. 214–84.

Atkinson, J.M. (1978) *Discovering Suicide: Studies in the Social Organization of Sudden Death.* London: Macmillan.

Atkinson, P.A. (1981) *The Clinical Experience: The Construction and Reconstruction of Medical Reality.* Aldershot: Gower.

Atkinson, P.A. (1983) 'Writing ethnography', in H.J. Helle (ed.), *Kultur und Institution.* Berlin: Duncker und Humblot, pp. 77–105.

Atkinson, P.A. (1985) *Language, Structure and Reproduction: An Introduction to the Sociology of Basil Bernstein.* London: Methuen.

Atkinson, P.A. (1989) 'Goffman's poetics', *Human Studies*, 12: 59–76.

Atkinson, P.A. (1990) *The Ethnographic Imagination: Textual Constructions of Reality.* London: Routledge.

Atkinson, P.A. (1996) *Sociological Readings and Re-Readings.* Aldershot: Ashgate.

Atkinson, P.A., Coffey, A.J. and Delamont, S. (1999) 'Ethnography, post, past and present', *Journal of Contemporary Ethnography*, 28: 460-71.

Atkinson, P.A., Coffey, A.J., Delamont, S., Lofland, J. and Lofland, L. (eds) (2001) *Handbook of Ethnography.* London: Sage.

Atkinson, P.A. and Delamont, S. (1976) 'Mock-ups and cock-ups: the stage-management of guided discovery instruction', in M. Hammersley and P. Woods (eds), *The Process of Schooling.* London: Routledge and Kegan Paul, pp. 133–42.

Atkinson, P.A. and Delamont, S. (forthcoming, 2003) 'Qualitative research and the postmodern turn', in A. Bryman and M. Hardy (eds), *Handbook of Data Analysis.* London: Sage.

Austin, D.A. (1995) 'An African-American success story: one man's narrative journey', in N.K. Denzin (ed.), *Studies in Symbolic Interaction*, vol. 19. Greenwich, CT: JAI Press, pp. 89-108.

Bacon-Smith, C. (1992) *Enterprising Women: Television Fandom and the Creation of the Popular Myth.* Philadelphia, PA: University of Pennsylvania Press.

Ball, S.J. (1981) *Beachside Comprehensive: A Case-Study of Secondary Schooling.* Cambridge: Cambridge University Press.

Banton, M. (1964) *Roles: An Introduction to the Study of Social Relations.* London:

Tavistock.

Baszanger, I. (1998) *Inventing Pain Medicine*. New Brunswick, NJ: Rutgers University Press.

Bauman, R. (1986) *Story, Performance, and Event*. Cambridge: Cambridge University Press.

Bauman, Z. (1978) *Hermeneutics and Social Science: Approaches to Understanding*. London: Hutchinson.

Bauman, Z. (1992) *Intimations of Postmodernity*. London: Routledge.

Beck, U. (1992) *Risk Society: Towards a New Modernity*. London: Sage.

Becker, H.S. (1953a) 'Becoming a marijuana user', *American Journal of Sociology*, 59: 235–42.

Becker, H.S. (1953b) 'The teacher in the authority system of the public school', *Journal of Educational Sociology*, 27: 128–41.

Becker, H.S. (1958) 'Problems of inference and proof in participant observation', *American Sociological Review*, 23: 652–60.

Becker, H.S. (1963) *Outsiders*. New York: Collier-Macmillan.

Becker, H.S. (ed.) (1964) *The Other Side*. New York: Collier-Macmillan.

Becker, H.S. (1971) *Sociological Work*. London: Allen Lane.

Becker, H.S. and Carper, J.W. (1956) 'Elements of identification with an occupation', *American Sociological Review*, 21: 341–8.

Becker, H.S., Geer, B. and Hughes, E.C. (1968a) *Making the Grade*. Chicago: University of Chicago Press.

Becker, H.S., Geer, B., Hughes, E.C. and Strauss, A.L. (1961) *Boys in White: Student Culture in Medical School*. Chicago: University of Chicago Press.

Becker, H.S., Geer, B., Riesman, D. and Weiss, R. (eds) (1968b) *Institutions and the Person*. Chicago: Aldine.

Berger, P.L. (1971) 'Identity as a problem in the sociology of knowledge', in Cosin, B.R., Dale, I.R., Esland, G.M. and Swift, D.F. (eds), *School and Society: A Sociological Reader*. London: Routledge and Kegan Paul, pp. 107–12.

Berger, P.L. and Luckmann, T. (1967) *The Social Construction of Reality*. New York: Doubleday.

Bernstein, B. (1990) *The Structuring of Pedagogic Discourse*. London: Routledge.

Best, J. (1995) 'Lost in the ozone again: the postmodernist fad and interactionist foibles', in N.K. Denzin (ed.), *Studies in Symbolic Interaction*. vol. 17, Greenwich, CT: JAI Press, pp. 125–30.

Beynon, H. (1975) *Working for Ford*. Wakefield: E.P. Publishing.

Bhabba, H.K. (1994) *The Location of Culture*. London: Routledge.

Bhaskar, R. (1989) *Reclaiming Reality: A Critical Introduction to Contemporary Philosophy*. London: Verso.

Billig, M. (1984) *Banal Nationalism*. London: Sage.

Binswanger, L. (1963) *Being-in-the-World*. New York: Basic Books.

Bloor, M. (1997) *Selected Writings in Medical Sociological Research*. Aldershot: Ashgate.

Bloor, M. (2001) 'The ethnography of health and medicine', in P.A. Atkinson, A.J. Coffey, S. Delamont, J. Lofland and L. Lofland (eds), *Handbook of Ethnography*. London: Sage, pp. 177–87.

Bloor, M. and McKeganey, N. (1986) 'Conceptions of therapeutic communities', *International Journal of Sociology and Social Policy*, 6: 68–79.

Bloor, M. and McIntosh, J. (1989) 'Power, surveillance and resistance', in S. Cunningham Burley and N. McKeganey (eds), *Readings in Medical Sociology*. London: Tavistock, pp. 159–81.

Bloor, M., McKeganey, N. and Fonkert, D. (1988) *One Foot in Eden: A Sociological Study of the Range of Therapeutic Community Practice*. London: Routledge.

182

Blumer, H. (1962) 'Society as symbolic interaction', in A. Rose (ed.), *Human Behavior and Social Processes*. Boston: Houghton-Mifflin, pp. 179–92.

Blumer, H. (1969) *Symbolic Interactionism: Perspective and Method*. Englewood Cliffs, NJ: Prentice-Hall.

Bourdieu, P. (1992) *Language and Symbolic Power*. Cambridge: Polity Press.

Bourdieu, P. (1996) *The State Nobility: Elite Schools in the Field of Power*. Oxford: Polity Press.

Bourdieu, P. and Passeron, J.-C. (1977) *Reproduction in Education and Society*. London: Sage.

Brittan, A. (1973) *Meanings and Situations*. London: Routledge and Kegan Paul.

Brittan, A. (1977) *The Privatised World*. London: Routledge and Kegan Paul.

Bulmer, M. (1984) *The Chicago School of Sociology: Institutionalization, Diversity, and the Rise of Sociological Research*. Chicago: University of Chicago Press.

Burgess, R.G. (1983) *Experiencing Comprehensive Education*. London: Methuen.

Burgess, R.G. (1984) *In the Field: An Introduction to Field Research*. London: George Allen and Unwin.

Cappetti, P. (1993) *Writing Chicago*. New York: Columbia University Press.

Carey, J.T. (1975) *Sociology and Public Affairs: The Chicago School*. Beverly Hills, CA: Sage.

Charmaz, K. (1995) 'Between positivism and postmodernism: implications for methods', in N.K. Denzin (ed.), *Studies in Symbolic Interaction*, vol. 17. Greenwich, CT: JAI Press, pp. 43–72.

Cicourel, A. (1964) *Method and Measurement in Sociology*. New York: Free Press.

Cicourel, A. and Kitsuse, J. (1963) *The Educational Decision Makers*. Indianapolis: Bobbs-Merrill.

Clifford, J. and Marcus, G.E. (eds) (1986) *Writing Culture: The Poetics and Politics of Ethnography*. Berkeley, CA: University of California Press.

Clough, P.T. (1992) *The End(s) of Ethnography: From Realism to Social Criticism*. Newbury Park, CA: Sage.

Coffey, A. and Atkinson, P. (eds) (1994) *Occupational Socialization and Working Lives*. Aldershot: Ashgate.

Cohen, P. (1980) 'Subcultural conflict and working-class community', in S. Hall, D. Hobson, A. Lowe and P. Willis (eds), *Culture, Media, Language: Working Papers in Cultural Studies*, 1972-79. London: Hutchinson, pp. 78–87.

Cohen, S. (ed.) (1971) *Images of Deviance*. Harmondsworth: Penguin.

Cohen, S. (1973) *Folk Devils and Moral Panics: The Creation of the Mods and Rockers*. St Albans: Paladin.

Collins, R. (1981) 'On the microfoundations of macrosociology', *American Journal of Sociology*, 86: 984–1014.

Cooley, C.H. (1902) *Human Nature and the Social Order*. New York: Charles Scribner's Sons.

Cooper, D. (1968) *Psychiatry and Anti-Psychiatry*. London: Tavistock.

Cooper, D. (1971) *The Death of the Family*. New York: Pantheon.

Cosin, B.R., Dale, I.R., Esland, G.M. and Swift, D.F. (eds) (1971) *School and Society: A Sociological Reader*. London: Routledge and Kegan Paul.

Cressey, P. (1932) *The Taxi-Dance Hall*. Chicago: University of Chicago Press.

Cuff, E.C., Sharrock, W.W. and Francis, D.W. (1998) *Perspectives in Sociology*. London: Routledge.

Culler, J. (1975) *Structuralist Poetics: Structuralism, Linguistics and the Study of Literature*. London: Routledge and Kegan Paul.

Culler, J. (1988) *Framing the Sign*. Oxford: Basil Blackwell.

Davies, C.A. (1999) *Reflexive Ethnography: A Guide to Researching Selves and Others*. London: Routledge.

Davis, A.G. (ed.) (1978) *Relationships between Doctors and Patients*. Farnborough: Saxon House.

Davis, A.G. (1982) *Children in Clinics: A Sociological Analysis of Medical Work with Children*. London: Tavistock.

Davis, A.G. and Strong, P.M. (1976) 'Aren't children wonderful? A study of the allocation of identity in development assessment', in M. Stacey (ed.), *The Sociology of the Health Service* (Sociological Review Monograph No. 22). Keele: Sociological Review, pp. 156–75.

Dawe, A. (1967) 'The two sociologies', *British Journal of Sociology,* 21: 207–18.

Dawson, L.L. and Prus, R.C. (1993) 'Interactionist ethnography and postmodernist discourse: affinities and disjunctures in approaching human lived experiences', in N.K. Denzin (ed.), *Studies in Symbolic Interaction*, vol. 15. Greenwich, CT: JAI Press, pp. 147–77.

Dawson, L.L. and Prus, R.C. (1995) 'Postmodernism and linguistic reality versus symbolic interactionism and obdurate reality', in N.K. Denzin (ed.), *Studies in Symbolic Interaction*, vol. 17. Greenwich, CT: JAI Press, pp. 105–24.

Dean, J.P. and Whyte, W.F. (1958) 'How do you know if the informant is telling the truth?', Human Organization, 17: 34–8.

Deegan, M.J. (1988) *Jane Addams and the Men of the Chicago School, 1892–1920*. New Brunswick, NJ: Transaction Books.

Deegan, M.J. (1995) 'The second sex and the women of the Chicago School, women's accounts, knowledge and work, 1945-1960', in G.A. Fine (ed.), *A Second Chicago School?* . Chicago: University of Chicago Press, pp. 322–64.

Deegan, M.J. (2001) 'The Chicago school of ethnography', in P.A. Atkinson, A.J. Coffey, S. Delamont, J. Lofland and L. Lofland (eds), *Handbook of Ethnography*. London: Sage, pp. 11–25.

Deegan, M.J. and Hill, M.R. (eds) (1987) *Women and Symbolic Interaction*. Boston: Allen and Unwin.

Delamont, S. (1976) *Interaction in the Classroom*. London: Methuen.

Delamont, S. (1984a) 'The old girl network: reflections on the fieldwork at St Luke's', in R.G. Burgess (ed.), *The Research Process in Educational Settings*. Lewes: Falmer, pp. 15–38.

Delamont, S. (1984b) 'Debs, dollies, swots and weeds: classroom styles at St Luke's', in G. Walford (ed.), *British Public Schools: Policy and Practice*. London: Falmer, pp. 65–86.

Delamont, S. (1989) *Knowledgeable Women*. London: Routledge.

Delamont, S. (1992) *Fieldwork in Educational Settings: Methods, Pitfalls and Perspectives*. London: Falmer.

Delamont, S. (2000) 'The anomalous beasts: hooligans and the sociology of education', *Sociology*, 34: 95–112.

Delamont, S. and Atkinson, P. (1995) *Fighting Familiarity: Essays on Education and Ethnography*. Cresskill, NJ: Hampton Press.

Delamont, S., Atkinson, P.A., Coffey, A. and Burgess, R. (2002) An Open Exploratory Spirit? Ethnography at Cardiff 1974-2001 (*Working Paper 20*). Cardiff: Cardiff School of Social Sciences.

Delamont, S., Atkinson, P.A. and Parry, O. (2000) *The Doctoral Experience: Success and Failure in Graduate School*. London: Falmer.

Denzin, N.K. (1970) *The Research Act*. Chicago: Aldine.

Denzin, N.K. (1989a) *Interpretive Biography*. Newbury Park, CA: Sage.

Denzin, N.K. (1989b) *Interpretive Interactionism*. Newbury Park, CA: Sage.

Denzin, N.K. (1991) *Hollywood Shot by Shot: Alcoholism in American Cinema*. New York: Aldine de Gruyter.

Denzin, N.K. (1992) *Symbolic Interactionism and Cultural Studies: The Politics of*

Interpretation. Oxford: Blackwell.

Denzin, N.K. (1993) 'The postmodern sensibility', in N.K. Denzin (ed.), *Studies in Symbolic Interaction*, vol. 15. Greenwich, CT: JAI Press, pp. 177–88.

Denzin, N.K. (1995) *The Cinematic Society: The Voyeur's Gaze.* London: Sage.

Denzin, N.K. (1997) *Interpretive Ethnography: Ethnographic Practices for the 21st Century.* London: Sage.

Denzin, N.K. and Lincoln, Y.S. (eds) (1994) *Handbook of Qualitative Research.* Thousand Oaks, CA: Sage.

Denzin, N.K. and Lincoln, Y.S. (eds) (2000) *Handbook of Qualitative Research*, 2nd edn. Thousand Oaks, CA: Sage.

Detman, L.A. (1993) 'Negotiating the woman of broadcast news', in N.K. Denzin (ed.), *Studies in Symbolic Interaction*, vol. 15. Greenwich, CT: JAI Press, pp. 3–14.

Dewey, J. (1925) *Experience and Nature.* Chicago: Open Court.

Ditton, J. (1977) *Part-Time Crime: An Ethnography of Fiddling and Pilferage.* London: Macmillan.

Douglas, J.D. (1970a) *The Social Meanings of Suicide.* Princeton, NJ: Princeton University Press.

Douglas, J.D. (ed.) (1970b) *Deviance and Respectability: The Social Construction of Moral Meanings.* New York: Basic Books.

Douglas, M. (1966) *Purity and Danger.* London: Routledge and Kegan Paul.

Drew, P. and Heritage, J. (1992) *Talk at Work: Interaction in Institutional Settings.* Cambridge: Cambridge University Press.

Ellis, C. (1995) *Final Negotiations.* Philadelphia, PA: Temple University Press.

Erikson, K. (1962) 'Notes on the sociology of deviance', *Social Problems*, 9: 307–14.

Faris, R.E.L. (1967) *Chicago Sociology 1920-1932.* Chicago: University of Chicago Press.

Featherstone, M. (1990) 'The body in consumer culture', in M. Featherstone, M. Hepworth and B.S. Turner (eds), *The Body: Social Process and Cultural Theory.* London: Sage, pp. 170–96.

Filmer, P., Phillipson, M., Silverman, D. and Walsh, D. (1972) *New Directions in Sociology.* London: Collier-Macmillan.

Filstead, W.J. (ed.) (1970) *Qualitative Methodology: Firsthand Involvement with the Social World.* Chicago: Markham.

Fine, G.A. (ed.) (1995) *A Second Chicago School? The Development of a Postwar American Sociology.* Chicago: University of Chicago Press.

Fine, G.A. (2000) 'Review of G. Tomasi (ed.), The Tradition of the Chicago School of Sociology', *Contemporary Sociology*, 29 (4): 674–5.

Fine, G.A. and Kleinman, S. (1979) 'Rethinking subculture: an interactionist analysis', *American Journal of Sociology*, 85: 1–20.

Fisher, B.M. and Strauss, A.L. (1978a) 'Interactionism', in T. Bottomore and R. Nisbet (eds), *A History of Sociological Analysis.* London: Heinemann, pp. 457–98.

Fisher, B.M. and Strauss, A.L. (1978b) 'The Chicago tradition and social change: Thomas, Park and their successors', *Symbolic Interaction*, 1: 5–23.

Fisher, B.M. and Strauss, A.L. (1979) 'George Herbert Mead and the Chicago tradition of sociology', *Symbolic Interaction*, 2: 9–25.

Fontana, A. and Tillett, S. (1993) 'Deconstructing the self: new metaphors for a postmodern self', in N.K. Denzin (ed.), *Studies in Symbolic Interaction*, vol. 14. Greenwich, CT: JAI Press, pp. 35–42.

Foucault, M. (1973) *The Birth of the Clinic.* London: Tavistock.

Freidson, E. (1970) *Profession of Medicine.* New York: Dodd Mead.

Frisby, D. (1985) *Fragments of Modernity: Theories of Modernity in the Work of Simmel, Kracauer and Benjamin.* London: Routledge.

Frisby, D. (1992a) *Simmel and Since.* London: Routledge.

Frisby, D. (1992b) *Sociological Impressionism: A Reassessment of Georg Simmel's Social Theory*, 2nd edn. London: Routledge.

Garfinkel, H. (1956) 'Conditions of successful degradation ceremonies', *American Journal of Sociology*, 61: 240–4.

Garfinkel, H. (1967) *Studies in Ethnomethodology*. Englewood Cliffs, NJ: Prentice-Hall.

Geer, B. (1964) 'First days in the field', in P.E. Hammond (ed.), *Sociologists at Work: Essays on the Craft of Social Research*. New York: Basic Books, pp 322–44.

Geer. B. (1971) 'Teaching', in Cosin, B.R., Dale, I.R., Esland, G.M. and Swift, D.F. (eds), *School and Society: A Sociological Reader*. London: Routledge and Kegan Paul, pp. 3–8.

Gerhardt, U. (1989) *Ideas about Illness: An Intellectual and Political History of Medical Sociology*. New York: New York University Press.

Giddens, A. (1976) *New Rules of Sociological Method: A Positive Critique of Interpretivist Sociologies*. London: Hutchinson.

Giddens, A. (1984) *The Constitution of Society: Outline of the Theory of Structuration*. Cambridge: Polity Press.

Giddens, A. (1991) *Modernity and Self-Identity: Self and Society in the Late Modern Age*. Cambridge: Polity Press.

Glaser, B. and Strauss, A.L. (1967) *The Discovery of Grounded Theory*. Chicago: Aldine.

Goff, T.W. (1980) *Marx and Mead: Contributions to a Sociology of Knowledge*. London: Routledge and Kegan Paul.

Goffman, E. (1953) 'Rules regarding social interaction in a rural community', PhD dissertation, Department of Sociology, University of Chicago.

Goffman, E. (1959) *The Presentation of Self in Everyday Life*. Garden City, NY: Anchor.

Goffman, E. (1961) *Asylums*. New York: Anchor.

Goffman, E. (1963) *Stigma: Notes on the Management of Spoiled Identity*. Englewood Cliffs, NJ: Prentice-Hall.

Goffman, E. (1967) *Interaction Ritual: Essays on Face-to-Face Behavior*. New York: Pantheon Books.

Goffman, E. (1972) 'On face work: an analysis of ritual elements in social interaction. communication', in J. Lever (ed.), *Face to Face Interaction*, pp. 319–46.

Goffman, E. (1974) *Frame Analysis: An Essay on the Organisation of Experience*. New York: Northeastern University Press.

Goffman, E. (1983) 'The interaction order', *American Sociological Review*, 48: 1–17.

Gorz, A. (1999) *Reclaiming Work: Beyond the Wage-Based Society*. Oxford: Blackwell Science.

Gouldner, A. (1968) 'The sociologist as partisan: sociology and the welfare state', *American Sociologist*, 3: 103–16.

Gouldner, A. (1970) *The Coming Crisis of Western Sociology*. New York: Basic Books.

Granovetter, M.S. (1973) 'The strength of weak ties', *American Journal of Sociology*, 78: 1360–80.

Gubrium, J.F. and Holstein, J.A. (eds) (2002) *Handbook of Interview Research: Contexts and Methods*. Thousand Oaks, CA: Sage.

Habermas, J. (1979) *Communication and the Evolution of Society*. Oxford: Polity Press.

Hall, S. (1977) 'Culture, the media and the "ideological effect"', in J. Curran et al., *Mass Communication and Society*. London: Arnold, pp. 315–48.

Hammer, M. and Champney, J. (1993) *Re-engineering the Corporation: A Manifesto for Business Revolution*. London: Business Books.

Hammersley, M. (ed.) (1983) *The Ethnography of Schooling*. Driffield: Nafferton Books.

Hammersley, M. (1989) *The Dilemma of Qualitative Method: Herbert Blumer and the Chicago Tradition*. London: Routledge.

Hammersley, M. (1991) *Reading Ethnographic Research: A Critical Guide*. London: Longmans.

Hammersley, M. (1992) *What's Wrong with Ethnography?* London: Routledge.

Hammersley, M. and Atkinson, P.A. (1983) *Ethnography: Principles in Practice*. London: Tavistock.

Hammersley, M. and Atkinson, P.A. (1995) *Ethnography: Principles in Practice*, 2nd edn. London: Routledge.

Hammersley, M. and Woods, P. (eds) (1976) *The Process of Schooling: A Sociological Reader*. London: Routledge and Kegan Paul.

Hammersley, M. and Woods, P. (eds) (1984) *Life in School: The Sociology of Pupil Culture*. Milton Keynes: Open University Press.

Hammond, P. (ed.) (1964) *Sociologists at Work*. New York: Basic Books.

Handel, G. (1994) 'Life course as reflexive object: some constituent elements in the life histories of working-class men', in N.K. Denzin (ed.), *Studies in Symbolic Interaction*, vol. 16. Greenwich, CT: JAI Press, pp. 295–306.

Hargreaves, D.H. (1967) *Social Relations in a Secondary School*. London: Routledge and Kegan Paul.

Hargreaves, D.H. (1972) *Interpersonal Relations and Education*. London: Routledge and Kegan Paul.

Hargreaves, D.H. (1976) 'Reactions to labelling', in M. Hammersley and P. Woods (eds), *The Process of Schooling*. London: Routledge and Kegan Paul, pp. 201–7.

Hargreaves, D.H. (1977) 'The process of typification in the classroom: models and methods', *British Journal of Educational Psychology*, 47: 274–84.

Hargreaves, D.H. (1978) 'Whatever happened to symbolic interactionism?', in L. Barton and R. Meighan (eds), *Sociological Interpretations of Schooling and Classrooms*. Driffield: Nafferton Books, pp. 7–22.

Hargreaves, D.H., Hester, S.K. and Mellor, F.J. (1975) *Deviance in Classrooms*. London: Routledge and Kegan Paul.

Harvey, L. (1987) *Myths of the Chicago School*. Aldershot: Gower.

Harvey, L. (1990) *Critical Social Research*. London: Allen and Unwin.

Hawkes, T. (1977) *Structuralism and Semiotics*. London: Methuen.

Hebdige, D. (1979) *Subculture: The Meaning of Style*. New York, Routledge.

Helle, H.J. and Eisenstadt, S.N. (eds) (1985) *Perspectives on Sociological Theory*, vol. 2: *Micro-Sociological Theory*. London: Sage.

Hester, S. and Francis, D. (2000) *Local Educational Order: Ethnomethodological Studies of Knowledge in Action*. Amsterdam: John Benjamins.

Hester, S. and Housley, W. (eds) (2002) *Language, Interaction and National Identity*. Aldershot: Ashgate.

Hobbs, D. (2001) 'Ethnography and the study of deviance', in P.A. Atkinson, A. Coffey, S. Delamont, J. Lofland and L. Lofland (eds), *Handbook of Ethnography*. London: Sage, pp, 204–19.

Hochschild, A.R. (1979) 'Emotion work, feeling rules and social structure', *American Journal of Sociology*, 85: 551–75.

Hochschild, A.R. (1983) *The Managed Heart: Commercialization of Human Feeling*. Berkeley, CA: University of California Press.

Hughes-Freeland, F. (ed.) (1998) *Ritual, Performance, Media*. London: Routledge.

Husting, V. (1993) 'Up by her garter straps: reading Working Girl', in N.K. Denzin (ed.), *Studies in Symbolic Interaction*, vol. 15. Greenwich, CT: JAI Press, pp. 15–26.

James, W. (1890) *Principles in Psychology*. New York: Henry Holt.

Jeffery, R. (1979) 'Normal rubbish: deviant patients in casualty departments', *Sociology of Health and Illness*, 1: 40–68.

Jenkins, R. (1992) *Textual Poachers: Television Fans and Participatory Culture*. New York: Routledge.

Jenson, J. (1992) 'Fandom as pathology: the consequences of characterisation', in L. Lewis (ed.), *The Adoring Audience: Fan Culture and Popular Media*. London: Routledge, pp. 9–29.

Joas, H. (1985) *G.H. Mead: A Contemporary Re-Examination of his Thought*. Cambridge: Polity Press.

Johnson, J.M. and Altheide, D.L. (1993) 'The ethnographic ethic', in N.K. Denzin (ed.), *Studies in Symbolic Interaction*, vol. 14. Greenwich, CT: JAI Press, pp. 95–107.

Junker, B. (1960) *Field Work*. Chicago: University of Chicago Press.

Kaiser, S.B., Freeman, C.M. and Chandler, J.L. (1993) 'Favorite clothes and gendered subjectivities: multiple readings', in N.K. Denzin (ed.), *Studies in Symbolic Interaction*, vol. 15. Greenwich, CT: JAI Press, pp. 27–50.

Karabel, J. and Halsey, A.H. (eds) (1977) *Power and Ideology in Education*. New York: Oxford University Press.

Kassabian, A. (1993) 'A women scored: feminist theory and the study of popular music', in N.K. Denzin (ed.), *Studies in Symbolic Interaction*, vol. 15. Greenwich, CT: JAI Press, pp. 51–68.

Kitsuse, J.I. (1962) 'Societal reaction to deviant behaviour: problems of theory and methods', *Social Problems*, 9: 247–56.

Lacey, C. (1970) *Hightown Grammar: The School as a Social System*. Manchester: Manchester University Press.

Laclau, E. and Mouffe, C. (2001) *Hegemony and Socialist Strategy: Towards a Radical Democratic Politics*. London: Verso.

Lambart, A. (1976) 'The sisterhood', in M. Hammersley and P. Woods (eds), *The Process of Schooling*. London: Routledge and Kegan Paul.

Lasch, C. (1980) *The Culture of Narcissism*. London: Abacus.

Latimer, J. (2000) *The Conduct of Care*. London: Blackwell.

Lemert, E.M. (1967) *Human Deviance, Social Problems and Social Control*. Englewood Cliffs, NJ: Prentice-Hall.

Lengermann, P. and Niebrugge-Brantley, J. (1998) *The Women Founders of the Social Sciences*. New York: McGraw-Hill.

Lewis, D.J. and Smith, R.L. (1980) *American Sociology and Pragmatism: Mead, Chicago Sociology and Symbolic Interactionism*. Chicago: University of Chicago Press.

Lincoln, Y.S. (1995) 'The sixth moment: emerging problems in qualitative research', in N.K. Denzin (ed.), *Studies in Symbolic Interaction*, vol. 19. Greenwich, CT: JAI Press, pp. 37–55.

Lincoln, Y.S. and Denzin, N.K. (1994) 'The fifth moment', in N.K. Denzin and Y.S. Lincoln (eds), *Handbook of Qualitative Research*. Thousand Oaks, CA: Sage, pp. 575–86.

Lodge, D. (1981) *Working with Structuralism*. London: Routledge and Kegan Paul.

Lofland, J. (1971) *Analyzing Social Settings: A Guide to Qualitative Observation and Analysis*. Belmont, CA: Wadsworth.

Lofland, J. (1974) 'Styles of reporting qualitative field research', *American Anthropologist*, 9 (August): 101–11.

Lofland, J. and Lofland, L.H. (1984) *Analyzing Social Settings*, 2nd edn. Belmont, CA: Wadsworth.

Lofland, L.H. (1985) 'The social shaping of emotion: the case of grief', *Symbolic Interaction*, 8: 171–90.

Lyman, S.M. and Scott, M.B. (1970) *A Sociology of the Absurd*. New York: Appleton-Century-Crofts.

Macintyre, S. (1976) 'Who wants babies? The social construction of instinct', in D. Barker and S. Allen (eds), *Sexual Divisions and Society: Process and Change*. London: Tavistock, pp. 150–73.

Macintyre, S. (1977) *Single and Pregnant*. London: Croom Helm.

Maffesoli, M. (1996) *Time of the Tribes: The Decline of Individualism in Mass Society*. London: Sage.

Maines, D.R. (2001) *The Faultline of Consciousness: A View of Interactionism in Sociology*. New York: Aldine de Gruyter.

Maines, D.R. and Ulmer, J.T. (1993) 'The relevance of narrative for interactionist thought', in N.K. Denzin (ed.), *Studies in Symbolic Interaction*, vol. 14. Greenwich, CT: JAI Press, pp. 109–24.

Manis, J.G. and Meltzer, B.N. (eds) (1967) *Symbolic Interaction*. Boston: Allyn and Bacon.

Manning, P.K. (1973) 'Existential sociology', *Sociological Quarterly*, 14: 200–25.

Maso, I. (2001) 'Phenomenology and ethnography', in P.A. Atkinson, A.J. Coffey, S. Delamont, J. Lofland and L. Lofland (eds), *Handbook of Ethnography*. London: Sage, pp. 136–44.

Matthews, F. (1977) *Quest for an American Sociology: Robert E. Park and the Chicago School*. Montreal: McGill-Queen's University Press.

Matza, D. (1964) *Delinquency and Drift*. New York: Wiley.

Matza, D. (1969) *Becoming Deviant*. Englewood Cliffs, NJ: Prentice-Hall.

Mays, J. (1954) *Growing Up in the City: A Study of Juvenile Delinquency in an Urban Neighbourhood*. Liverpool: University of Liverpool Press.

McCall, G.J. and Simmons, J.L. (eds) (1969) *Issues in Participant Observation*. Reading, MA: Addison-Wesley.

McGregor, G. (1995) 'Gender advertisements then and now: Goffman, symbolic inter-actionism, and the problem of history', in N.K. Denzin (ed.), *Studies in Symbolic Interaction*, vol. 17. Greenwich, CT: JAI Press, pp. 3–42.

Mead, G.H. (1932) *The Philosophy of the Present*. Chicago: University of Chicago Press.

Mead, G.H. (1934) *Mind, Self and Society*. Chicago: University of Chicago Press.

Mead, G.H. (1938) *The Philosophy of the Act*. Chicago: University of Chicago Press.

Meltzer, B.N., Petras, J.W. and Reynolds, L.T. (1975) *Symbolic Interactionism: Genesis, Varieties and Criticism*. London: Routledge and Kegan Paul.

Melucci, A. (1996) *The Playing Self: Person and Meaning in the Planetary Society*. Cambridge: Cambridge University Press.

Merleau-Ponty, M. (1962) *Phenomenology of Perception*. London: Routledge and Kegan Paul.

Mouzelis, N.P. (1990) *Back to Sociological Theory*. London: Macmillan.

Muggleton, D. (1997) 'The post-subculturalist', in S. Redhead with D. Wynne and J. O'Connor (eds), *The Clubcultures Reader: Readings in Popular Cultural Studies*. Oxford: Blackwell, pp. 185-203.

Mullins, N.C. (1973) *Theories and Theory Groups in Contemporary American Sociology*. New York: Harper and Row.

Musil, R. (1995) *The Man without Qualities* (translated S. Wilkins and B. Pike). New York: Knopf.

Noblit, G.W. and Hare, R.D. (1988) *Meta-Ethnography: Synthesizing Qualitative Studies*. Newbury Park, CA: Sage.

Oleson, V. and Whittaker, E. (1968) *The Silent Dialogue*, San Francisco: Jossey-Bass.

Park, R.E. and Burgess, E. (1921) *Introduction to the Science of Society*. Chicago: University of Chicago Press.

Parker, H. (1974) *View from the Boys: A Sociology of Down Town Adolescents*. Newton Abbott: David and Charles.

Parsons, D.L. (2000) *Streetwalking the Metropolis: Women, the City and Modernity*. Oxford: Oxford University Press.

Platt, J. (1983) 'The development of "participant observation" method in sociology: origin, myth and history', *Journal of the History of the Behavioral Sciences*, 19: 379-93.

Platt, J. (1996) *A History of Sociological Research Methods in America, 1920-1960*. Cambridge: Cambridge University Press.

Plummer, K. (1975) *Sexual Stigma: An Interactionist Account*. London: Routledge and Kegan Paul.

Plummer, K. (1979) 'Misunderstanding labelling perspectives', in D. Downes and P. Rock (eds), *Deviant Interpretations*. Oxford: Oxford University Press, pp. 85–121.

Plummer, K. (1983) *Documents of Life: An Introduction to the Problems and Literature of a Humanistic Method*. London: George Allen and Unwin.

Plummer, K. (ed.) (1991) *Symbolic Interactionism*, 2 vols. Aldershot: Edward Elgar.

Plummer, K. (1995) *Telling Sexual Stories: Power, Change, and Social Worlds*. London: Routledge.

Plummer, K. (ed.) (1997a) *The Chicago School: Critical Assessments*, 4 vols. London: Routledge.

Plummer, K. (1997b) 'Introducing Chicago sociology: the foundations and contributions of a major sociological tradition', in K. Plummer (ed.), *The Chicago School: Critical Assessments*, vol. 1. London: Routledge, pp. 3-40.

Plummer, K. (2001) *Documents of Life 2: An Invitation to a Critical Humanism*. London: Sage.

Pollard, A. (1985) *The Social World of the Primary School*. London: Holt, Rinehart and Winston.

Psathas, G. (ed.) (1973) *Phenomenological Sociology*. New York: Wiley.

Purcell, K. (1988) *More in Hope than Anticipation: Fatalism and Fortune Telling amongst Women Factory Workers*. Manchester: Manchester University Press.

Rabinow, P. (ed.) (1986) *The Foucault Reader*. Harmondsworth: Penguin.

Reed-Danahay, D.E. (ed.) (1997) *Auto/Ethnography: Rewriting the Self and the Social*. Oxford: Berg.

Richardson, L. (1993) 'Interpreting discursive spaces: consequences for the sociological self', in N.K. Denzin (ed.), *Studies in Symbolic Interaction*, vol. 14. Greenwich, CT: JAI Press, pp. 77–83.

Richardson, L. (1994) 'Writing: a method of inquiry', in N.K. Denzin and Y.S. Lincoln (eds), *Handbook of Qualitative Research*. Thousand Oaks, CA: Sage, pp. 516–29.

Richman, J. (1983) *Traffic Wardens*. Manchester: Manchester University Press.

Rinehart, R. (1995) 'Pentecostal aquatics: sacrifice, redemption and secrecy at camp', in N.K. Denzin (ed.), *Studies in Symbolic Interaction*, vol. 19. Greenwich, CT: JAI Press, pp. 109–21.

Roche, M. (1973) *Phenomenology, Language and the Social Sciences*. London: Routledge and Kegan Paul.

Rock, P. (1973) *Making People Pay*. London: Routledge and Kegan Paul.

Rock, P. (1979) *The Making of Symbolic Interactionism*. London: Macmillan.

Rock, P. (1991) 'Symbolic interactionism and labelling theory', in K. Plummer (ed.), *Symbolic Interactionism, vol. 1: Foundations and History*. Aldershot: Edward Elgar.

Rock, P. (2001) 'Symbolic interactionism and ethnography', in P.A. Atkinson, A.J. Coffey, S. Delamont, J. Lofland and L. Lofland (eds), *Handbook of Ethnography*. London: Sage, pp. 26–38.

Rose, A.M. (ed.) (1962) *Human Behavior and Social Processes*. Boston: Houghton-Mifflin.

Rosenthal, R. and Jacobson, L.F. (1968) *Pygmalion in the Classroom*. London: Holt, Rinehart and Winston.

Roth, J. (1963) *Timetables*. Indianapolis: Bobbs-Merrill.

Rubington, E. and Weinberg, M.A. (eds) (1968) *Deviance: The Interactionist Perspective*. New York: Collier-Macmillan.

Sacks, H. (1992a) *Lectures on Conversation*, vol. 1. Oxford: Blackwell.

Sacks, H. (1992b) Lectures on Conversation, vol. 2. Oxford: Blackwell.

Said, E. (1978) *Orientalism*. New York: Pantheon.

Salaman, G. (1974) *Community and Occupation: An Exploration of Work/Leisure Relationships*. Cambridge: Cambridge University Press.

Sanders, C.L. (1995) 'Stranger than fiction: insights and pitfalls in post-modern ethnography', in N.K. Denzin (ed.), *Studies in Symbolic Interaction*, vol. 17. Greenwich, CT: JAI Press, pp. 89–104.

Schatzman, L. and Strauss, A.L. (1973) *Field Research: Strategies for a Natural Sociology*. Englewood Cliffs, NJ: Prentice-Hall.

Scheff, T.J. (1966) *Being Mentally Ill: A Sociological Theory*. London: Weidenfeld and Nicolson.

Schegloff, M. (1992) 'Introduction' to H. Sacks, *Lectures on Conversation*, vol. 1. Oxford: Blackwell.

Schieffelin, E.L. (1998) 'Problematizing performance', in F. Hughes-Freeland (ed.), *Ritual, Performance, Media*. London: Routledge, pp. 194–207.

Schmitt, R.L. (1993) 'Cornerville as obdurate reality: retooling the research act through postmodernism', in N.K. Denzin (ed.), *Studies in Symbolic Interaction*, vol. 15. Greenwich, CT: JAI Press, pp. 121–45.

Schutz, A. (1967) *The Phenomenology of the Social World*. Evanston, IL: Northwestern University Press.

Shalin, D.N. (1988) 'G.H. Mead, socialism and the progressive agenda', *American Journal of Sociology*, 93: 913–51.

Silverman, D. (1970) *The Theory of Organisations: A Sociological Framework*. London: Heinemann.

Silverman, D. and Torode, B. (1980) *The Material Word: Some Theories of Language and its Limits*. London: Routledge and Kegan Paul.

Smith, D. (1988) *The Chicago School: A Liberal Critique of Capitalism*. London: Macmillan.

Snow, D.A. et al. (1986) 'Frame alignment processes, micromobilization and movement participation', *American Sociological Review*, 51: 464–81.

Sorokin, P. (1956) *Fads and Foibles in Modern Sociology and Related Sciences*. Chicago: Henry Regnery.

Stanley, L. and Wise, S. (1983) *Breaking Out: Feminist Consciousness and Feminist Research*. London: Routledge and Kegan Paul.

Strauss, A.L. (1959) *Mirrors and Masks*. Glencoe, IL: Free Press.

Strauss, A.L. (1978) *Negotiations: Varieties, Contexts, Processes and Social Order*. San Francisco: Jossey-Bass.

Strauss, A.L. (1987) *Qualitative Analysis for Social Scientists*. Cambridge: Cambridge University Press.

Strauss, A.L. (1993) *Continual Permutations for Action*. New York: Aldine de Gruyter.

Strauss, A.L. (1994) 'From whence to whither: Chicago-style interactionism', in N.K. Denzin (ed.), *Studies in Symbolic Interaction*, vol. 16. Greenwich, CT: JAI Press, pp. 3–8.

Strauss, A.L., Schatzman, L., Bucher, R., Ehrlich, D. and Sabshin, M. (1964) *Psychiatric Ideologies and Institutions*. New York: Free Press.

Strong, P.M. (1979) *The Ceremonial Order of the Clinic: Parents, Doctors and Medical Bureaucracies*. London: Routledge and Kegan Paul. (2nd edn, edited Robert Dingwall, 2001, Aldershot: Ashgate.)

Strong, P.M. and Davis, A.G. (1978) 'Who's who in paediatric encounters: morality, expertise and the generation of identity and action in medical settings', in A.G. Davis (ed.), *Relations between Doctors and Patients*. Farnborough: Saxon House, pp. 48–75.

Stryker, S. (1987) 'The vitalization of symbolic interactionism', *Social Psychology Quarterly*, 50: 83–94.

Sudnow, D. (1965) 'Normal crimes', *Social Problems*, 12: 255–76.

Sudnow, D. (1967) *Passing On*. Englewood Cliffs, NJ: Prentice–Hall.

Sumner, C. (1994) *The Sociology of Deviance: An Obituary*. Buckingham: Open University Press.

Szasz, T.S. (1962) *The Myth of Mental Illness: Foundations of a Theory of Personal Conduct*. London: Secker and Warburg.

Szasz, T.S. (1971) *The Manufacture of Madness*. London: Routledge and Kegan Paul.

Taylor, I.R. (1971) 'Soccer consciousness and soccer hooliganism', in S. Cohen (ed.), *Images of Deviance*. Harmondsworth: Penguin, pp. 134–64.

Taylor, L. and Walton, P. (1971) 'Industrial sabotage: motives and meanings', in S. Cohen (ed.), *Images of Deviance*. Harmondsworth: Penguin, pp. 219–45.

Tester, K. (ed.) (1994) *The Flâneur*. London: Routledge.

Thomas, W.I. (1923) *The Unadjusted Girl*. Boston: Little, Brown.

Thomas, W.I. (1937) *Primitive Behaviour*. New York: McGraw-Hill.

Thomas, W.I., Park, R.E. and Miller, H.A. (1921) *Old World Traits Transplanted*. New York: Harper and Brothers.

Thomas, W.I. and Znaniecki, F. (1918–20) *The Polish Peasant in Europe and America*, 5 vols. Boston: Richard G. Badger.

Thrasher, F. (1927) *The Gang*. Chicago: University of Chicago Press.

Timmermans, S. (1994) 'Sociological poetics', in N.K. Denzin (ed.), *Studies in Symbolic Interaction*, vol. 16. Greenwich, CT: JAI Press, pp. 3–8.

Titscher, S., Meyer, M., Wodak, R. and Vetter, E. (2000) *Methods of Text and Discourse Analysis*. London: Sage.

Tomasi, G. (ed.) (1998) *The Tradition of the Chicago School of Sociology*. Aldershot: Ashgate.

Travisano, R.V. (1993) 'Meaning without symbols: toward revising symbolic interaction', in N.K. Denzin (ed.), *Studies in Symbolic Interaction*, vol. 14. Greenwich, CT: JAI Press, pp. 3–28.

Tulloch, J. (1999) *Performing Culture*. London: Sage.

van Maanen, J. (1988) *Tales of the Field: On Writing Ethnography*. Chicago: University of Chicago Press.

Voysey, M. (1975) *A Constant Burden*. London: Routledge and Kegan Paul.

Wacker, R.F. (1995) 'The sociology of race and ethnicity in the second Chicago school', in G.A. Fine (ed.), *A Second Chicago School? The Development of a Postwar American Sociology*. Chicago: University of Chicago Press, pp. 136–63.

Waller, W.W. (1932) *The Sociology of Teaching*. New York: John Wiley and Sons.

Waller, W.W. (1970) *On the Family, Education, and War* (selected writings, edited W.J. Goode, F.F. Funsterberg, Jr and L.R. Mitchell). Chicago: University of Chicago Press.

Welsh, I. and Chesters, G. (2001) Re-Framing Social Movements. Margins, Meanings and Governance (*Working Paper 19*). Cardiff: Cardiff School of Social Sciences.

White, C.J. and Kimbell-Amos, B. (1995) 'Validity, truth, and method in postmodern university classrooms: mystory writing and the incurably informed', in N.K. Denzin (ed.), *Studies in Symbolic Interaction*, vol. 19. Greenwich, CT: JAI Press, pp. 69–88.

Whyte, W.F. (1955) *Street Corner Society: The Social Structure of an Italian Slum*, 2nd edn. Chicago: University of Chicago Press.

Widdicombe, S. and Woofit, R. (1995) *The Language of Youth Subcultures: Social Identity in Action*. Hemel Hempstead: Harvester Wheatsheaf.

Williams, R. (1976) 'Symbolic interactionism: the fusion of theory and method?', in D.C. Thomas (ed.), *New Directions in Sociology*. Newton Abbott: David and Charles, pp. 115–38.

Williams, R. (1981) 'Learning to do field research: intimacy and inquiry in social life', *Sociology*, 15: 557–64.

Williams, R. (2000) *Making Identity Matter: Identity, Society and Social Interaction*. Durham: sociologypress.

Willis, P. (1977) *Learning to Labour: How Working Class Kids Get Working Class Jobs*. Farnborough: Saxon House.

Willis, P. (2001) *The Ethnographic Imagination*. Cambridge: Polity Press.

Wilson, E. (2001) *The Contradictions of Culture: Cities, Culture, Women*. London: Sage.

Wirth, L. (1938) 'Urbanism as a way of life', *American Journal of Sociology*, 44: 1–24.

Woods, P. (1976) 'Having a laugh: an antidote to schooling', in M. Hammersley and P. Woods (eds), *The Process of Schooling*. London: Routledge and Kegan Paul, pp. 178–87.

Woods, P. (1979) *The Divided School*. London: Routledge and Kegan Paul.

Woods, P. (ed.) (1980) *Teacher Strategies*. London: Croom Helm.

Woods, P. (1986) *Inside Schools: Ethnography in Educational Research*. London: Routledge and Kegan Paul.

Worsley, P. (ed.) (1970) *Introducing Sociology*. Harmondsworth: Penguin.

Young, M.F.D. (ed.) (1971) *Knowledge and Control*. London: Collier-Macmillan.

Znaniecki, F. (1934) *The Method of Sociology*. New York: Farrar and Rinehart.

Zorbaugh, H. (1929) *The Gold Coast and the Slum*. Chicago: University of Chicago Press.

193

index

195

196